Penguin Books
Men Who Play God

Norman Moss is a British journalist who grew up
and was educated mostly in the United States. He
has worked for Reuter, the Associated Press of
America and the *Sunday Times,* and is now the
Chief European Correspondent of an American
radio network. He has also contributed to some
leading magazines. Moss has pursued for some
years a horrified interest in the H-bomb and its
problems. He completed the researches for this
book with several months of interviewing and
study in America. He lives in London, and is married with two small children.

Norman Moss

Men Who Play God

The Story of the Hydrogen Bomb

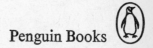
Penguin Books

Penguin Books Ltd, Harmondsworth,
Middlesex, England
Penguin Books Australia Ltd, Ringwood,
Victoria, Australia

First published by Victor Gollancz 1968
Published in Penguin Books 1970
Copyright © Norman Moss, 1968

Made and printed in Great Britain by
Hazell Watson & Viney Ltd,
Aylesbury, Bucks
Set in Linotype Times

Contents

There is an immense gulf between the atomic and hydrogen bombs. The atomic bomb, with all its terrors, did not carry us outside the scope of human control or manageable events, in thought or action, in peace or war. But when Mr Sterling Cole, the Chairman of the United States Congressional Committee, gave out, a year ago, the first comprehensive review of the hydrogen bomb, the entire foundation of human affairs was revolutionized, and mankind placed in a situation both measureless and laden with doom.

Sir Winston Churchill

'Sometimes, events get too big for people.'
'But we've got to act as if they are not.'

from *The New Men* by C. P. Snow

Introduction

A few years ago, I paid a visit as a reporter to the United States Sixth Fleet in the Mediterranean. I had no special interest in military affairs, but it was damp and grey in London, so when the invitation came, I accepted it, and sailed for a week on an aircraft carrier and a cruiser, in and out of Naples and Palermo.

A Navy information officer on a carrier explained to me one day the system of ever-ready planes, with two planes always ready on deck to take off at a few moments' notice and go on their nuclear war missions. The next afternoon, I sat in an armchair on the bridge, and found myself facing, a few yards away, a fighter-bomber standing on deck with a guard armed with a rifle standing in front of it. Though no one mentioned it, I decided this was the ready plane.

Attached to the bottom of its fuselage was a thin object about twelve feet long, roughly the size and shape of a torpedo, wrapped loosely in brown sacking. This, I realized, must be a hydrogen bomb. It was the first time I had ever seen one.

The sun beamed down amiably and glittered on the steel deck, a balmy breeze wafted an occasional cloud across the sky to break the blue monotony, ripples on the sea stroked the sides of the huge ship. There was little activity on the flight deck, and the few sailors there seemed to be going about their work in a leisurely fashion. It was a relaxing scene.

I sat back in my chair, and for much of that afternoon, I stared at that long, slim, thinly concealed object, and tried to relate it to the life around me, the smart young sailor on his two-hour guard duty, the friendly, agreeable officers with whom I ate my meals, the city I lived in, crammed full of vulnerable flesh and blood, the international politics I talked about with my friends, and, most of all, the men who had created the bomb and those who might wield it, so much smaller in stature, whoever they were, than the consequences they could wreak. I had thought about the bomb before, of course. When I worked for the London bureau of the Associated Press, I covered the first Aldermaston March, and reported other, more desperate anti-bomb protests; I had some friends who took part, and heard the arguments. I had some idea of the new kind of power inherent in the hydrogen bomb, so much greater than that of the earlier atomic bomb. But looking now at that bomb, and knowing some of the pilots who flew with it, seemed to anchor the thinking more firmly in reality, to put flesh on the skeleton of ideas.

The researches that led ultimately to this book had their origins in that afternoon, for I tried to bridge with knowledge the gulf in imagination between individual actions, isolated or in series, and this one effect, so gigantic in its potential. The book is an attempt to show how the hydrogen bomb got here, how and why it was created, the way people learned to use it and not to use it, and how a place was found for it in the world.

Though it is in some ways a history, it is not in strict narrative form, with the possible exception of the first chapter. It examines different aspects of the bomb's development, and most sections link up with the present-day scene.

I have tried to see the hydrogen bomb always in relation to people, approaching it from one or another direction, fitting it into their different perspectives and roles. To this end, I give pictures of three different kinds of individuals and their involvement with the hydrogen bomb: a scientist who played a key role in building it, a conscientious objector to the bomb's presence, and a strategist concerned with employing it intelligently.

A note on sources: most of this information was obtained by talking to the people involved in the events described. In many cases, the source of a story is not the person most directly involved. Naturally, I am indebted to many people for giving me their time and co-operation. I am not listing them because, without a breakdown showing who contributed what, it would be mere name-dropping; such a breakdown cannot be complete in the nature of things, since impressions and general observations contribute to a picture as well as specific items of information, and furthermore, in many cases, giving the source of a particular fact or episode would be a breach of confidence. Some parts of the book, such as a visit to a missile site or a scientific laboratory, or an account of a flight in a nuclear bomber, are obviously the results of my own observation.

Where anyone is quoted as saying something without any statement of where and to whom he said it, it can be taken that this was said to me. The one exception to this is the first chapter, where several remarks quoted were made at the hearings into the suspension of Dr Oppenheimer. The transcript of these was published by the U.S. Atomic Energy Commission under the title *In the Matter of J. Robert Oppenheimer*.

No acknowledgement is given where something quoted is a matter of public record, or else has been told in print by several people who participated, such as statesmen in their memoirs Otherwise, where anything is taken from previously published material, the source is given.

1. Should Man Play God?

On the weekend of 29 October 1949 eight men met in Washington D.C. to consider a question more momentous than most that have ever been given to men to answer. The question was whether the United States Government should try to acquire the power to destroy whole cities, whole nations even, at a single blow.

These eight men, with a ninth who could not be present, made up the General Advisory Committee of the Atomic Energy Commission. The A.E.C. is the agency established in 1946 to regulate and control America's atomic power and its products. Because the members of the commission are mostly laymen, a panel of part-time advisers was set up to give counsel on scientific matters; this is the General Advisory Committee. The members all hold high positions in the academic world or in industry, and they meet several times a year, whenever the A.E.C. calls on them for advice. The Chairman of the Committee then was J. Robert Oppenheimer, the wartime administrator of the laboratory at Los Alamos, New Mexico, where the atom bomb was constructed, at this time the Director of the Institute for Advanced Study and the most prestigious figure in American science.

They were summoned to Washington to consider a question that only a few people in the world knew could even be asked: should the United States go full speed ahead to try to produce a thermonuclear fusion bomb, that could be hundreds of times as powerful as the fission bombs then in existence?

It was a grey, cloudy weekend, when Washington was not at its best for the visitors, with mild-to-warm weather but intermittent drizzle. Most Washingtonians stayed at home that weekend, watched football on television – a new pastime – and read their fat Sunday newspapers.

The newspapers on Sunday carried a report of a speech in New York by the President of the United Nations General Assembly, Brigadier-General Carlos Romulo of the Philippines. He forecast an international agreement on the control of atomic energy, in these terms: 'We must reach agreement in order to survive. An agreement will be found because it must be found.' This was a *non sequitur*, but one that was to be heard again and again, as men confronted the dilemmas of the atomic bomb, and tried to believe that the worst could not happen.

The newspapers carried no mention of the G.A.C. meeting, called to discuss a new possibility that could make the worst much worse than even a man in General Romulo's position dreamed.

The G.A.C. members, as men of science, were in a position to understand some of the features of this projected new explosive: its almost inconceivable destructive power, its open-endedness – unlike the fission bomb, there would be no limit to the size of a fusion bomb – and its powerful and uncertain effects. They knew that if it came into existence, it would bring new dangers and new fears to the people who were staying at home with their children and papers and television sets while they conferred.

There was no doubt that if the United States succeeded in building a fusion bomb, Russia would do so sooner or later, and perhaps other countries as well. The world would be in a new era, in which men would have the power to alter the human environment and damage the human species, and perhaps to end its life on earth.

One scientist who was not on the G.A.C., but who took part in discussions of the fusion bomb during this period, said he saw the question as 'Should Man play God?'

The G.A.C. had been asked to give an opinion in response to a new situation: the ending of America's nuclear monopoly the month before by the explosion of a Soviet atom bomb, nicknamed Joe One after Joseph Stalin. This came much sooner than the American Government had expected.

Ever since the early days of the atom bomb project, some nuclear physicists had thought about a completely different kind of nuclear explosive, one that would dwarf an atom bomb* in its power as the atom bomb dwarfed high explosives. In their conversations, they called it simply 'the super'. A super might not work, but it might. It would release explosive power, not through the fission of heavy atoms but through the fusion of very lightweight atoms. A fission bomb would be used as a sort of trigger, to provide the necessary heat. With the awesome power of the atom bomb behind them, most scientists spoke of this, figuratively, in whispers. Accounts of work in this field were buried in the periodic and secret reports drawn up by A.E.C. scientists.

One man who followed these accounts closely was Lewis L. Strauss, a member of the A.E.C. Apart from Henry Smyth, who was a physicist, he was the only one of the five commissioners to have had many years' contact with the field of atomic science. This was circumstantial. Strauss rose from a humble start to a successful career in banking and public service. Both his parents died of cancer, and Strauss, a wealthy man by this time, set up a trust dedicated to seeking a cure for the disease. A method that seemed promising involved the use of radioactive materials. Strauss borrowed a laboratory at the California Institute of Technology to create these materials, in 1938. Several nuclear physicists who were later to become famous did some work there including Leo Szilard and Edward Teller. After the war, Teller kept Strauss informed of research on the super, and Strauss came to have a high regard for him.

Strauss is a small, dapper man, whose views are usually mild in expression and conservative in content. He was very worried

* A distinction has grown up in common terminology. Illogically, the phrase 'atom bomb' or 'atomic bomb' has come to mean only a fission bomb, a fusion bomb is called a 'hydrogen bomb', and the term 'nuclear bomb' covers both kinds. The terms are employed in this way here to conform to general use.

by Joe One. He had a private theory that the Russians were even further ahead than anyone knew, that the explosion that was detected was not the first. As an A.E.C. member, he knew that the American radiation detection patrols that found evidence in the stratosphere of the Russian test were fairly casual – they did not fly in bad weather, for instance. He thought they might well have missed an earlier Soviet atomic bomb test.

On 5 October he sat down and wrote a formal letter to his four fellow commissioners. He began by warning of the dangers of Soviet aggression backed by atomic bombs, and of the very limited security provided by having more atomic bombs. 'It seems to me', he continued, 'that the time has now come for a quantum jump in our planning (to borrow a metaphor from our scientist friends) – this is to say, that we should now make an intensive effort to get ahead with the super. . . . I recommend that we immediately consult the General Advisory Committee to ascertain their views on how we can proceed with expedition.'

The Chairman of the A.E.C., David E. Lilienthal, agreed to convene the G.A.C. But he did not ask them to consider, in Strauss's words, *how* to proceed with expedition. He was not sure that proceeding with expedition was the right thing. He asked them to consider *whether* to do so, whether, in the light of Joe One, to push ahead with an all-out programme to develop the super.

He contacted Oppenheimer, and the meeting was set for Saturday, 29 October. Weekends were best for these men, because they all had other responsibilities.

Oppenheimer had not so far committed himself on the super question. A tall, frail-looking, highly cultivated scholar, who studied French medieval poetry and Sanskrit as hobbies, he represented in many people's eyes the anguished but worldly conscience of American science. Five years later, he was to seem to symbolize the conscience of America's liberal intellectuals, when his security clearance was suspended and his loyalty impugned. But his was not a bold or outspoken conscience in the 1940s. He had more influence in Government circles than any other scientist, and was a member of many committees, but he rarely spoke out on Government policies, and took no part in most of the atomic scientists' campaigns, such as the one against military control of atomic energy.

When he did speak, even in private, he was listened to by his colleagues. Oppenheimer made a number of contributions to physics as a young man, but his principal achievement was as a scientist-administrator. During the years 1943-5, as director of the Los Alamos laboratory, he created there an extraordinary spirit of dedication and unity. Oppenheimer emerged with the respect of his peers, and he retained it. No one who has moved in the circles of the atomic scientists since 1945 can fail to be struck by the high regard and admiration in which he was held by some of the most intelligent men in the world.

In the day before the G.A.C. meeting, some of the members discussed the super question among themselves. Most of them had worked on the wartime atom bomb programme, and were among the small number of people who already knew about the possibility of a super.

Dr James Conant, a G.A.C. member and the President of Harvard University, a pillar of the American Establishment, set out his views in a letter to Oppenheimer. They were strong and simple. Four years earlier, as one of the inner council of the atomic bomb project, he sat on the Interim Committee that reported that they could see no alternative to the military use of the bomb against Japan. Now he wrote about nuclear bombs with repugnance. He said he had gone along with the A.E.C. decision to build more atomic bombs for as long as he could, but this talk of a super was altogether too much. He was absolutely against it.

Oppenheimer wrote a reply on 21 October, eight days before the date of the meeting, which was more moderate. He referred to the new agitation for a super in some circles, then said it might be impossible to build and unusable as a weapon. But this was not what was worrying him. 'What does worry me',

15

he wrote, 'is that this thing appears to have caught the imagination both of the congressional and the military people as *the* answer to the problem posed by the Russian advance.'

Isidor Rabi in New York was certainly alarmed by Joe One, but he did not see the super as the answer. In a talk with Oppenheimer in his Riverside Drive apartment, he suggested another response. The United States should say to Russia: 'Now you have an atomic bomb, and we have a lot of them. The atomic arms race is over. We'll both give up our weapons to international control. If you don't agree to this plan, we'll force it on you.' Oppenheimer seemed for the moment to go a long way with the idea. Today, this sounds like the most extreme belligerency, but its aim was peaceful and internationalist. In the climate of the time, it was a drastic plan for ending immediately a situation that was new and uniquely perilous, the atomic arms race.

The eight G.A.C. members* assembled on Saturday morning, 29 October, in what was then the A.E.C. building, at 1401 Constitution Avenue. They met first with Lilienthal, the Chairman of the A.E.C., some military liaison officers, and General Omar Bradley, the Chairman of the Joint Chiefs of Staff.

Lilienthal gives an account of this morning meeting in the second volume of his journals, *The Atomic Energy Years*. First, they discussed the military uses of a super. General Bradley surprised the others by saying that the chief value would be psychological.

Oliver Buckley, President of the American Telephone and Telegraph Company, said there was no moral issue involved, that, after the atom bomb, a super would be only a quantitative change. Conant disagreed – Lilienthal, in a poignant phrase, describes him as 'looking almost translucent, so grey'. He said there were different grades of morality. He felt that

---

* In addition to Oppenheimer, the G.A.C. members present were; James B. Conant; Lee DuBridge; Enrico Fermi; I. I. Rabi; Hartley Rowe; Oliver Buckley, President of the American Telephone and Telegraph Company; and Professor Cyril S. Smith of the University of Chicago.

the moral issue was vital, and that whether the super was built would depend on how the country viewed this.

Rabi said gloomily that the decision to go ahead would be taken anyway, that the only question was who was willing to go along with it. Lilienthal denied that there was anything inevitable about it. Rabi may have been thinking of the wartime atom bomb project, when the scientists became the servants of the country's war machine. Others certainly were. Hartley Rowe said: 'We built one Frankenstein'. And at another point, Conant interjected: 'This whole discussion makes me feel I'm seeing the same film, and a punk one, for the second time.'

In the afternoon, Lilienthal and the others left and the G.A.C. members met alone. Oppenheimer, at the head of the table, asked each person in turn to give his views. Each spoke for between five and ten minutes. Everyone, to one degree or another, spoke against the super.

Conant argued passionately, doggedly, that it would be immoral. Dr Lee DuBridge,* the President of the California Institute of Technology, said it would be a gesture of great moral leadership if the President of the United States were to tell the world that America would not build this terrible thing. Rabi, the stubby, shrewd, brilliant New Yorker, son of an immigrant tailor from Austria, Nobel Prize winner, expressed strong doubts about whether the device could ever be built. If it were built, he said, it would be too cumbersome to be dropped as a bomb, and too powerful to be used for anything but genocide. The consequences would be a new and even more terrible arms race.

There was a strong technical case against a crash programme on the super, and this was aired. A super might prove impossible to build; it was even more likely that if one ever were built, it would be too large to be an effective weapon. Yet to set about building one would require the production of tritium, employing uranium piles that could otherwise be used to make the material for fission bombs. This was at a time when the

*In 1969 Dr DuBridge became President Nixon's Science Adviser.

atomic weapons laboratories, which had already made fission bombs more powerful, were learning how to make them more cheaply, smaller and with a variety of uses, including tactical, or battlefield use. It seemed to be a choice between bigger weapons and smaller ones, a choice that opened up a rift that was to continue down through the years.

After everyone around the G.A.C. table had spoken Oppenheimer said, 'I certainly agree', and then went on to give his views in some detail.

The meeting was left with the impression that the G.A.C. members were unanimous in their sentiments. Actually, this was not so. The ninth member, Dr Glen Seaborg, was abroad, on a visit to Sweden. Earlier in the month, knowing that he was going to miss the meeting, he had written to Oppenheimer from California, setting out his views on the super. 'Although I deplore the prospect of our country putting a tremendous effort into this,' he wrote, 'I must confess that I have been unable to come to the conclusion that we should not.' Oppenheimer did not tell any of the other G.A.C. members that one of them had come out reluctantly in favour of a super programme, nor did he tell the A.E.C. when he presented their report.

All day Sunday, 30 October, the members of the G.A.C. drafted their report to the A.E.C.

Before dealing with the super, they made recommendations on the number and kinds of fission bombs that should be produced, taking advantage of the new possibilities of diversification. These were not nuclear disarmers. Then their report gave an account of what a super might be like: unwieldy, expensive in money and materials, and, unlike atomic fission, devoid of any peaceful application. It suggested its military shortcomings: it could be used only to raze cities. It said a super programme could have an adverse effect upon America's standing in the world.

When the Committee turned to the prospects of success, they did not allow their objections to bias their scientific judgement on the side of pessimism. They said: 'An imaginative and concerted attack on the problem has a better than even chance of producing the weapon within five years.'

Then they gave political and moral reasons why they thought their country should refrain from making this concerted attack just then. America's role in the world, and the arms race, were factors. They went on to recommend that the A.E.C. should not embark on an all-out super programme.

The recommendation was for a single act of abstention, not a policy. It did not answer the painful question of what to do if Russia went ahead to build the super. It did not say what should be done about the limited research on thermonuclear fusion that was then going on. But the sense of the report was clear.

The text of the G.A.C. report has never been made public. But brief majority and minority supplementary statements have been declassified.

The minority report was signed by Rabi and Fermi, the brilliant Italian who won a Nobel Prize for Physics when he was still in his thirties. It was generally assumed when it was first written to be the more radical of the two, because of its moral tone. The authors intended it to be the more cautious, however, to say only that the United States should not be the first to build a super, but should reserve the right to do so if another power did. They also wanted the President to announce the decision.

Their statement reads:

The fact that no limit exists to the destructiveness of this weapon makes its very existence and the knowledge of its construction a danger to humanity as a whole. For these reasons, we believe it important for the President of the United States to tell the American people and the world that we think it wrong on fundamental ethical principles to initiate the development of such a weapon.

Those who read in this an unqualified rejection of the super saw the key words as 'fundamental ethical principles'. To Fermi and Rabi, the key word was 'initiate'.

The majority statement, signed by the other six, expressed a somewhat similar feeling, and showed in the last sentence the scope of the Committee's concern:

We all hope that by one means or another the development of these weapons can be avoided. We are all reluctant to see the United States take the initiative in precipitating this development. We are all agreed that it would be wrong at the present moment to commit ourselves to an all-out effort towards its development.

In determining not to proceed to develop the super bomb, we see a unique opportunity of providing by example some limitations on the totality of war, and thus eliminating the fear and rousing the hopes of mankind.

It seemed for a time that what was going on in Washington in the last three months of 1949 was a process rare in history. A decision was being reached of historic importance, and at least some of the people taking part knew what they were deciding and just how important it was.

Usually, decisions that shape an era are taken for short-term, sometimes even trivial reasons, so that only historians looking back can discern the fork in the road. This time, there was a pause for reflection at the fork, and the direction signs could be read. Knowledge of the implications of the super question was not lacking. On the contrary, there has rarely been a major national decision of which the consequences were so clearly foreseen. What was lacking was any means by which this knowledge could be applied.

Prophets of the atomic age were saying already that the human race must unite or perish, that it must do this or that. But the human race, though it can be considered as a biological or an ethnic entity, is not yet a political one. It cannot choose, or decide, anything. Decisions in the fields of human affairs are taken by governments or by other groups of individuals, always representing only one section of the human race, usually a very small one.

Those people in Washington that winter who participated in this decision were not there to represent the human race, nor was there anyone in Moscow with that brief. They were put there by the American nation, or a section of it, to represent a special interest. They were deciding an issue that would alter the conditions under which men live on this planet. Yet the only framework within which they could decide this was a narrow, parochial one; their only points of reference were the old ones created for lesser issues: Congress, the Russians, the American national security. These will all be forgotten in a few millennia, when history has flowed on around a few more turnings, but the potential of the super will still be there, carried along with the flow.

Many of those involved in the discussion of the super had worked in the wartime atomic bomb programme, or the Manhattan Project, to use the code name by which it was known. They saw how, in the adrenalin, single-purpose atmosphere of wartime, the decision to drop the bomb was motivated by short-term factors, with little consideration of the new era that would be opened up.

Several high-level committees considered then what to do with the atom bomb. In the context of the time, they recommended dropping the bomb on Japan. The aim was to avoid the slaughter that would follow an American invasion of the Japanese home islands.

President Truman, who gave the order, did not know of the bomb's existence six months earlier. He was told about it for the first time by Henry L. Stimson, his Secretary of War, after his first cabinet meeting as President, on the day that President Roosevelt died. By that time, four years and two billion dollars had been spent on it. As Major-General Leslie Groves, the military chief of the atom bomb project, said later, President Truman was 'a little like a boy on a toboggan. He never had an opportunity to say "We will drop the bomb". All he could say was "No".' He added that Truman would have been 'crucified' if he had refrained from dropping the bomb and American lives were lost in an invasion of Japan.*

It soon became clear that the atom bomb raids on Hiro-

* This is quoted in *No High Ground* by Fletcher Knebel and Charles W. Bailey II.

shima and Nagasaki were not just the surprise twist to the last act of the Second World War, but the beginning of a new era of history. After five years of aerial bombardment, the existence of a single bomb that could obliterate a town seemed to many to make war impossible.

Modern Man is Obsolete was the title of one pamphlet widely read in America at the time, written by Norman Cousins. Another, by a group of prominent Americans, proclaimed in its title: *One World or None*. But the choice was to be evaded for a long time more, and in the face of far more terrible weapons than these writers conceived of.

The leaders of the American Government were well aware of the unique perils of the atomic age. Late in 1945, Henry Stimson canvassed selected scientists and industrialists for opinions on how long it would take Russia to build an atomic bomb. Information on Soviet resources was scanty, and the consensus was a wide estimate: between five and twenty years. Later, the Central Intelligence Agency assured the Administration that the earliest date was well into the 1950s.

Everyone was saying that new approaches were needed to meet the new situation in the world. The U.S. Government tried a new kind of disarmament proposal in the United Nations. It came to be called the Baruch Plan after Bernard Baruch, who was chosen to present it. If it was pursued in good faith, it would have meant the surrender of America's atomic power to international control, an act without precedent. There were rumblings in Congress, and some people in Washington said the Senate would never ratify it.

It did not come to this, for the Russians rejected it. They were suspicious of the way in which it would be carried out, and they were opposed implacably to the inspection of Soviet territory that would be involved. Nor were they alone in their suspicions; the British Government was also cool to the plan. Still smarting at the abrupt ending of the wartime partnership with the United States in atomic power development, the British wanted the freest possible hand to develop the potentialities of atomic power for industry.

Andrei Gromyko put forward an alternative disarmament plan, calling for the outlawing of nuclear weapons and the abolition of stockpiles before inspection and control. This was clearly unacceptable to the United States, and the two rival plans remained on the table.

Among those who were most vociferously concerned with nuclear disarmament were the atomic scientists. The scientists who made the atomic bomb felt a moral responsibility, with varying degrees of anguish. As Oppenheimer wrote in an article in 1948, in a much-quoted phrase, 'The physicists have known sin'.

In the first few weeks after the war, most of these atomic scientists found they shared this feeling of responsibility for what they had built and a concern that its implications should be understood. They formed associations at the main centres where work on the bomb was carried out, and these coalesced into the Federation of Atomic Scientists (this later became the Federation of American Scientists). The general current of opinion among them was liberal and internationalist.

They set out to educate the public on the facts of the new age. This was not difficult in these first post-Hiroshima months, because people were willing and anxious to listen to anything an atomic scientist had to say. In the public mind, these men had something of the aura of magicians; they seemed to possess power, of a kind that no mere politician could match.

In Chicago, the Federation started the monthly *Bulletin of the Atomic Scientists*. It was devoted very broadly to science and world affairs, and is still one of the most informative magazines in America. The *Bulletin*'s cover was different every month, but one motif remained the same: a small clock with the hands indicating eight minutes to midnight. This signified that in the age of the atomic bomb, time was running out for humanity. In late 1949, the minute hand was moved, so that the clock read three minutes to midnight. There was even less time left. This was the *Bulletin* editors' reaction to Joe One.

It matched the mood of the moment. When cabinet officers were told on 19 September that high-flying detection aircraft

23

had found traces of a Soviet atomic explosion, they were stunned. The five members of the A.E.C. were summoned to a meeting the same day. All five urged President Truman to make public the discovery, and beat the Russians to the announcement.

Truman himself still had some doubts. He kept asking, 'Are you *sure*?', and someone would explain again about the fogged plates in the aeroplane, and the radioactive ash in the stratosphere. No one had actually seen a Soviet atomic explosion, and though in his mind Truman took the word of the scientists, he could not in his heart bring himself to accept so shattering an event on such recondite evidence. The lurking disbelief surfaced three years later, when he had left behind the responsibilities of office and could allow his inner feelings free rein. As ex-President Truman, he told a group of reporters, to their surprise: 'I'm not convinced that Russia has the bomb. I'm not convinced that the Russians have achieved the know-how to put the complicated mechanism together to make an A-bomb work.'

But now he let himself be convinced by the evidence, and on 22 September, the White House announced that Russia had exploded an atomic bomb.

In the wake of this shock, others besides Lewis Strauss turned their thoughts towards the super, as a way of retaining the accustomed American superiority. A few of them were atomic scientists. At the University of California, three of these talked about the super at the faculty club at Berkeley a few days after the White House announcement, in fact, on the same day that Strauss was writing his letter. They were Ernest O. Lawrence, Wendell Latimer, the chemist, and Luis Alvarez. All three agreed that if Soviet scientists had built an atom bomb, they might be working on a super, and that it was essential that the United States get there first. They were all going to a scientific conference in Washington in a few days' time.

Lawrence and Alvarez decided to stop off at Los Alamos on the way, to discuss the prospects of a super with anyone they could find there. Both had worked on the atom bomb during the war and had done consultancy work for the A.E.C. since then, so they had security clearance to discuss these things. They flew to Albuquerque, and then took the four-seater air taxi out over the canyons to Los Alamos. In the laboratories, they talked about the prospects for a super with several scientists, George Gamow, Stanislaw Ulam, and also Edward Teller, who was spending a year at Los Alamos on leave from the University of Chicago.

Dr Teller, a brilliant, effervescent Hungarian-born physicist, had wanted to go all-out for a super as soon as the fission bomb was finished, and he had felt frustrated ever since. He was also a particularly fervent anti-Communist. The day after Joe One was announced, he telephoned Oppenheimer long-distance to demand, 'What do we do now?'

'Keep your shirt on,' Oppenheimer advised him. He probably gave this anodyne answer to dampen the fire of Teller's reaction. A.E.C. members who met with Oppenheimer when Joe One was first detected found him very alarmed.

In Los Alamos, Teller was so excited to receive two visitors who shared his feelings that he flew back with them in the air taxi to Albuquerque, and talked about the super with them in their hotel right through the evening. Teller also decided that after returning to Chicago, he would go to Washington himself, to make his views known. Like the trio from California, like all the important atomic scientists, in fact, Teller had given briefings to groups of congressmen and military men in the past four years, and had made some contacts among them.

Alvarez did not share the qualms about moral responsibility that preoccupied so many atomic scientists during these years. As an experimental physicist at Los Alamos, he had devised the implosion method by which the Nagasaki atomic bomb was triggered. He went out to Tinian Island where the atom bomb squadron was based, and flew in an observation plane on the Hiroshima raid. When he returned to the United States, he expected to find among his fellow scientists the same feeling of elation and victory that he saw among the fliers on Tinian. The brooding sense of guilt surprised and dismayed him. He felt that this did not represent the feelings of the millions of Americans who had sons or husbands serving in the Pacific.

The super issue was a simple one to him. If Russia had it and the United States did not, Russia would dominate the United States. He had not worked this out in detail, but if you had to ask the details on this, he said, then you just did not understand the situation.

After his hopeful meeting at Los Alamos, Alvarez went on to Washington. There, he lunched with Oppenheimer and another of the old Los Alamos crowd, Robert Serber. Both men said they did not think America should build the super. Alvarez was astonished. Oppenheimer explained his reasoning: the Soviet atomic bomb programme seemed to be imitative. If the United States went ahead and built a super, Russia would certainly follow suit. If America did not, Russia would not.

At about this time, Teller went to see Senator Brian McMahon, the Chairman of the Joint Congressional Committee on Atomic Energy. Senator McMahon, a Democrat from Connecticut, was a liberal in many respects, very much in favour of the Baruch Plan, but until the day of international control of atomic power came, he was determined to guard America's superiority zealously, and, as the McMahon Bill showed, to guard its secrets. He was very receptive to Teller's message about the super, and he arranged for him to address the members of his committee over lunch in his office.

While the senators and congressmen munched through steak and salad, Teller gave an account of the prospect and the need for a super. His foreign accent seemed to mark him as a man of intellectual distinction, his excited gestures showed his sincerity, and his anti-Communism struck the right patriotic note. The members decided that the super question merited urgent study. They set up a subcommittee of four senators and representatives to investigate and report, headed by Representative Chet Holifield of California. These four saw people in Washington, and then set out on a ten-day tour of scientific centres to sample the opinion of leading atomic scientists. They were still on their tour when the General Advisory Committee met.

Meanwhile, Teller and Lawrence were talking up the super to the Air Force. Lawrence was a particularly impressive figure; a Nobel Prize winner (in 1938, for the invention of the cyclotron), he was a tall, powerfully-built, dynamic man with the drive of a high-powered business executive. Along with Norris Bradbury, the Director of the Los Alamos laboratory, he addressed the Armed Forces Special Weapons Project, while Teller talked to another group of high-ranking officers.

At first, the military were not very interested in a super. They were put off by the thought that it would mean less uranium for atom bombs. But the pro-super scientists changed some minds on this, and they reached General Hoyt Vandenberg, the Air Force Chief of Staff. He sold the Joint Chiefs of Staff on the idea. The ball was rolling now.

On 17 October the Joint Chiefs sent a memorandum to the A.E.C. asking for more information on a fusion explosive, and expressing concern that the A.E.C. had not asked for funds to develop one.

The pro-super men were not having the same success everywhere. Sometimes, they encountered a resistance that seemed instinctive rather than reasoned. A.E.C commissioner Gordon Dean recalled later a 'visceral reaction' among scientists against the idea of a fusion bomb.

There seems to have been something of this in Lilienthal's first response. He was a long-time and dedicated New Dealer who headed the Tennessee Valley Authority, that archetypal New Deal public power project that transformed an area of the backward South. As A.E.C. Chairman, he was keen on the prospects of peacetime exploitation of atomic power, and regarded the production of bombs as a grim but regrettably necessary task. When Alvarez and Lawrence went to see him in his office in early October, and told him their ideas about the new and immensely bigger nuclear bomb, Lilienthal turned his back on them and looked out of the window in silence. 'We got the idea', Alvarez said later, 'that he did not even want to discuss it.'

27

When the A.E.C. met on the subject, Strauss was surprised to find at first that he was alone in wanting a crash programme for a super. But he was soon joined by Gordon Dean, a new appointee to the Commission, an able and intelligent lawyer, whose chief qualification for this place, nevertheless, was a friendship and law partnership with Senator McMahon. Of the other commissioners, Sumner Pike, a New Dealer from Wall Street, and Henry de Wolfe Smyth, the scientist member and a Professor of Physics at Princeton University, could not support Strauss's attitude.

Lilienthal said he was alarmed already at the extent to which America was dependent on atomic bombs to fight a war. He felt that building a vastly more powerful nuclear bomb would not help, that to try to solve problems this way was dangerous 'gadget-mindedness'. (The others did not know it, but Lilienthal was due to resign. He had told Truman, but had agreed to stay on until the issue of the super was settled.)

After nineteen years in public life, Lilienthal was skilled at managing committees and working out compromises. But this time, he made no attempt to patch up the differences among the five A.E.C. members and reach a consensus. The question of the thermonuclear bomb did not seem to him suitable material on which to practise the political arts. It seemed a profound one and a complex one, that should be answered within the individual human mind and heart. In his journal, he told himself: 'You are participating in a great and tragic issue.'

They decided to submit to the President, not a consensual A.E.C. position, but five individual positions, prefaced by a joint statement.

The statement they drew up recognized, at least on the political level, the significance of the issue. It said this was not a technical matter to be decided by the A.E.C., but was of great national importance, and a decision should be made only by the President. It said the question brought many other questions along in its train, and listed for the President's attention three:

Could the decision on the super be used to break the stale-mate in the United Nations on international control of nuclear weapons?

How would such a decision affect America's relations with her allies and with the rest of the world?

Would a greatly accelerated effort to achieve a super really strengthen the U.S. position?

In their individual statements, Strauss and Dean both said, in effect: let's build the super quickly, and see if this can't bring the Russians around to accepting international control. Smyth and Pike were both reluctant to take the fateful step; both wanted to see first whether the whole question could not be used to make another effort to reach agreement with the Soviet Union. Lilienthal was firmly against.

Meanwhile the four-man congressional subcommittee had returned from its travels and was preparing its report. They came out for rapid development of the super. Naturally, the congressmen were too busy to write the report on their findings themselves, and they assigned this to the Executive Director of the Committee staff who had accompanied them on their travels, William Borden. If his views crept into the report he wrote, they would have the effect of stiffening and strengthening its tone. Borden and his views were to have a considerable influence in the lives of several people involved in the super story.

A former Second World War bomber pilot who retained many links with the Air Force, and the author of a briefly noted book extolling the power of the atom bomb, Borden was horrified at the G.A.C. recommendation against a super pro-gramme when he learned of it. Two years later, he smelled mischief when this same Oppenheimer helped to write a report on defence policy called Project Vista that wanted to de-emphasize nuclear bombing, particularly of cities. When Bor-den left the Committee's employ to become an executive in the Westinghouse Corporation's Atomic Power Division, having seen by then Oppenheimer's security file, he wrote to J. Edgar Hoover of the F.B.I. that Oppenheimer was 'more probably than not an agent of the Soviet Union'. This set off the suspension of Oppenheimer's security clearance.

McMahon and Holifield took the 5,000-word report as written by Borden to Truman, and spent forty-five minutes with him discussing it. The President promised to consider the report carefully.

Holifield is a professional politician. Recalling these events today, he remembers who served on what committee more clearly than the sequence of decision about the bomb. But he is sensitive to the horrors of nuclear weapons. When, later on, he became Chairman of a subcommittee of the Joint Committee on Atomic Energy, he sponsored a detailed public study of a nuclear attack on the United States, to show how terrible this would be. He played a major part in disseminating knowledge of fallout, against the wishes of some who wanted to play down the dangers.

However, there was no question in his mind but that if this new weapon was to be so powerful and so terrible, America must have it. Over the stone fireplace in his house in Montebello, California, he keeps a long-barrelled rifle with which his great-grandfather fought Indians. He no more questioned that in this world of conflict America needed the most powerful weapons there were, than he would question that in the pioneering days of the West his great-grandfather needed that rifle. From the time he left Truman's office without a positive assurance of the President's decision, he was on tenterhooks.

A pro-super lobby was forming. Whatever the fears for humanity that motivated the men of the General Advisory Committee when they called for renunciation, they were lost on Senator McMahon. 'I read this report and it just makes me sick,' he told Teller.

He called on the President and argued the super case, but Truman would not commit himself. However, McMahon extracted from him a promise: if he decided that America should not push ahead to the super, as the G.A.C. recommended, he would let the Senator know. McMahon wanted one last chance to try to change the decision. In the next few weeks, Mc-

Mahon wrote five letters to the President on the super. In one of these, he put the threat as he saw it at its simplest and starkest. Sole possession of the bomb was 'total power'; Russia was 'total evil'.

Strauss had similar anxieties. He went to the Secretary of Defense, Louis Johnson, and urged him to throw the weight of his department behind the super. Johnson agreed, and the Defense Department sent a memorandum to the A.E.C. saying America must have the fusion bomb.

Most of the lobbying was on one side only. As one G.A.C. member, Dr Rabi, said later, 'We just wrote our report and then went home, and left the field to others. That was a mistake. If we hadn't done that, history might have been different.'

The arguments, too, were mostly on one side. It could hardly be otherwise in the political capital of a great sovereign nation, which was created and lives to preserve and enhance that nation's well-being and sovereignty. Even if one considered the wider interests of humanity, there was the telling argument that to renounce such a weapon might mean giving the power to the most unscrupulous. It was easy to feel in Washington that America should not be without such a means to influence the future of the world.

Since the start of the atomic age four years earlier, people had said 'the old formulas are outmoded'. But there were no new formulas in Washington that winter to apply to this question, no new modern man to replace the old modern man, who might indeed be obsolete, no new answers to substitute for the familiar old answers that urged a nation to be secure by being strong, and to be strong by having all the destructive power possible. Set against these, there were only vague hopes of a new international agreement on control, a fear of gadget-mindedness, half-acknowledged moral scruples, and, perhaps, the inchoate tug of some wider loyalty.

The heat generated on this issue was being confined to a small area; the discussions were secret. So well was the secret kept that Enrico Fermi's wife Laura, who was close enough to her husband and his colleagues to write a book about his life as a scientist, knew nothing about the G.A.C. meeting in which he took part, or the statement he signed with Rabi. She first learned of the statement in 1962, shortly after it was declassified, when she read it in a book by Edward Teller. This was a few months after her husband died.

The big leak came in an accidental outburst by Senator Edwin Johnson of Colorado in a television panel discussion. Johnson was a member of the Joint Congressional Committee, and thus privy to the discussions. Incredibly, the Senator was arguing in favour of secrecy, and getting furious with liberal scientists who wanted less of it.

A questioner asked him whether it would not be safe to allow a freer flow of information now that the Russians had the atom bomb. By this time, he was so worked up about the need for secrecy that he gave out the secret that was to be kept.

'I'm glad you asked that question,' he said heatedly, 'because here's the thing that's top secret: our scientists, from the time that the bombs were detonated at Hiroshima and Nagasaki, have been trying to make what is known as the super-bomb. Our scientists have already created a bomb that has six times the effectiveness of the bomb that was dropped at Nagasaki, and they're not satisfied at all. They want one that has 1,000 times the effect of that terrible bomb that was dropped at Nagasaki, that snuffed out the lives of 50,000 people just like that. And that's the secret, that's the big secret, that the scientists in America are so anxious to divulge to the whole scientific world!'

This was on 1 November. For ten days nothing happened. The members of the A.E.C. held their breaths, and hoped no one had noticed. Then the *Washington Post* ran an editorial on Johnson and the super-bomb, and other newspapers picked it up.

Truman summoned the Senator to the White House for a private talk that reporters presumed was about blurting out State secrets. At any rate, the Attorney-General, James Mc-Grath, was present. (Johnson tried to recover his poise by accusing Lilienthal publicly of a 'nefarious plot' to give away atomic secrets to Britain.) The Federation of Atomic Scientists issued a statement praising Johnson for his outspokenness, which he probably did not frame on his wall.

After this, there were some stories in the Press, but they were not many and they did not indicate that a decision on the super was going to change the world. But on 18 January 1950, when the issue was still to be decided, Joseph and Stewart Alsop, then a team of syndicated columnists, devoted a column to the question. They referred to studies on whether a thermonuclear explosion would poison the atmosphere and end life on the planet, and said that though the answer had turned out to be negative, the mere fact that the question was asked signified that a new situation had arisen:

Harnessing creation's inner secrets for purposes of destruction is a terrible act, whose consequences cannot be foreseen. In one way or another, it is a menace to the order of nature.

This, in turn, creates a cruel, circular dilemma. On the one hand, it is intolerable to let the Soviets build hydrogen bombs while we shrink back, because this amounts to acceptance of ultimate surrender to the Soviet Union. On the other hand, it is equally intolerable for such a weapon to be competitively manufactured by two hostile world-systems. And it is because they offer no way out of this dilemma that the old assumptions of world politics and strategy are now obsolescent.

A possible menace to the order of nature was not on Truman's mind when he considered the matter. He wrote in his memoirs that, so far as he was concerned, 'America's security and the security of the free world depend to a large degree on our leadership in the field of atomic energy.' His sole concern now was whether this leadership would be enhanced by a crash programme on a super.

He was troubled by an indication in the G.A.C. report that it might actually be reduced. This was the part that explained that uranium would have to be diverted from fission bomb production if a super were to be built.

Truman is not a man much awed. He received news of the successful test of the first atom bomb when he was at the Potsdam Conference, in July 1945. Oppenheimer may have been moved by the sight of this first atomic explosion, to quote the *Bhagavad Gita* on 'death, the destroyer of worlds'. Truman, 5,000 miles away, had a different reaction. Winston Churchill learned the news only the following day, and told Stimson: 'Now I know what happened to Truman yesterday. When he got to the meeting after having read the report, he was a changed man. He told the Russians just where they got off, and generally bossed the whole meeting.' (Stimson recalls this episode in his published diary.) His reaction to the Hiroshima bombing was more sombre, but he still left the decision on Nagasaki up to the military chiefs in the theatre, as a military operational matter.

In early November, the problems of the super landed on Truman's desk from several directions. He received the G.A.C. recommendations with its plea for a gesture of renunciation, the multi-faceted A.E.C. report, and the report of the Joint Committee urging a super programme. He was also being subjected to separate efforts at persuasion by McMahon, Strauss and some of the military chiefs.

He was impressed by the A.E.C. reminder that a decision on the question would have the broadest political and strategic implications. Nine months earlier, he had formed a three-man Special Committee of the National Security Council, specifically to consider nuclear energy matters. It consisted of the Secretaries of State and Defense and the Chairman of the A.E.C. This seemed to be a question for them. On 10 November he wrote instructing this committee to consider it. He also asked the three men to have staff members of their agencies prepare any necessary studies, to 'analyze all phases of the question, particularly the technical, military and political factors'.

The Secretary of State, Dean Acheson, assigned a study of the implications of a super to George F. Kennan, whom he had recently appointed to head the State Department's new Policy

Planning Board. Kennan, a leading and thoughtful specialist in Soviet affairs, first became widely known outside official circles the previous year when his position paper on a 'containment' policy *vis-à-vis* Communism was published in the magazine *Foreign Affairs*.* Acheson called in Oppenheimer to brief Kennan on the super, and this was the first that Kennan heard of it.

The assignment gave Kennan, a scholarly thinker with a patrician cast of mind, a chance to spend some time clarifying the thoughts on nuclear weapons that had been troubling him for some time. The report he produced was remarkably radical in its contents, and asked questions that were to arise again later.

He warned that production of a super would 'deepen and make more inevitable the present dilemma of nuclear weapons'. Before embarking on such a momentous step, he said, the United States should make a new and more serious effort to reach an international agreement to outlaw them. As he saw it, the Baruch Plan had shortcomings. It would not ban nuclear weapons effectively, but would give the potential for making them to the United Nations, which the Russians regarded as American-dominated. Like Oppenheimer and Lilienthal, he worried that America was trying to solve problems by building new mechanical devices instead of by thinking through the problem. The United States should clarify its reasons for building up a stockpile of atom bombs before it could reach any rational decision on the super, he said. Were they intended to deter atomic attack, or to fight a war? He suggested that they be kept only for deterrence. He wanted the Government to renounce 'the pernicious doctrine of first use', and state that it would never use nuclear weapons unless an enemy used them first.

The Defense Department produced a series of new reports. They were lengthy and represented a lot of work, but Lilienthal found them less than precise, and summed up their view-

* Mr Kennan is now at the Institute for Advanced Study at Princeton, New Jersey.

point on the super privately as: 'It'll be a handy thing around the house.'

We are indebted again to Lilienthal's journal for the fullest account of the two key meetings of the three-man Special Committee.

The first was on 22 December. They agreed that they would not reach a decision on that day, but would simply share their thoughts. Lilienthal worried that a decision to go ahead might slam the door on any prospects of international agreement on control. General Bradley, who was accompanying Defense Secretary Johnson, said that, on the contrary, a super was so frightening that it might be a spur to international agreement.

Johnson said the Defense Department would be willing to forgo the super only if the Russians agreed first to the Baruch Plan. He and an aide outlined the military uses of the bomb. Lilienthal broke in to exclaim that the whole course of mankind was involved in this question, that one could not treat the super as a gadget, unrelated to human objectives and philosophy. Johnson said they should not get 'philosophy' mixed up with the question. Smyth supported Lilienthal. Acheson took no position, and said very little.

The pressure on the President was continuing. In case Truman was restrained by moral scruples, McMahon wrote to say that there was no moral difference between annihilating people with one bomb and with many, that the mass air raids on Hamburg and Tokyo killed as many people as the Hiroshima bomb. Strauss, in a letter to the President, cited the G.A.C. report on feasibility as an indication that Russia might produce one. 'A government of atheists is not likely to be dissuaded from producing this weapon on moral grounds,' he wrote.

Truman was waiting for the Special Committee to report, and he simply asked them to please hurry.

Towards the end of January, something happened in Britain that altered the climate of opinion in which the discussion was taking place. Klaus Fuchs, a physicist with the wartime British team at Los Alamos, then Deputy Scientific Director at

Britain's Atomic Energy Research Establishment at Harwell, confessed to police officers that he had been passing information to Soviet agents for several years. This was not announced until 2 February, when Fuchs was arrested and charged, but official Washington was informed immediately. Fuchs had sat in on meetings at which the super was discussed, including a symposium at Los Alamos in 1946 at which all available knowledge of the subject was summarized.

The three members of the Committee met again on the morning of 31 January, in the old State Department building, along with several aides. This time, Acheson spoke first and most.

He had prepared a paper that contained elements of a compromise. It recommended a programme to develop the super but not produce it as a weapon; that is, to determine its technical feasibility. This paper also called for a re-examination by the Secretaries of State and Defense of the national objective 'in peace and war', in the light of the Soviet Union's atomic and possible thermonuclear capability. It recommended that, pending this re-examination, the President defer any decision to produce thermonuclear bombs, except for testing.

Lilienthal put his own reservations. Now he said that moral questions, and the question of international control, were not central to the issue. What was central was the United States' dependence on nuclear weapons for defence, which seemed to him a serious weakness. A public decision to go ahead on the super would appear to the world to confirm this weakness and turn it into a policy. He wanted a re-examination of American policies, and a delay in any decision at all on the super until this was completed. Unless one believed that war with Russia soon was inevitable, he said, America could afford to wait for a few months.

Acheson said he agreed with most of this, but that the pressure for a decision was so great that he could not recommend a delay. He said a negative decision would set off a furore in which rational re-examination of defence policies would be impossible.

37

They then drafted a statement for the President to make. They intended it to play down the importance of the decision, to make it seem less than dramatic.

When they finished their meeting, they went in to see the President. Acheson handed over the recommendations, with the proposed Presidential statement for him to sign.

Lilienthal put to Truman now his reservations, with his fears about American reliance on atomic weapons. Truman interrupted him. He said there was so much talk in Congress and elsewhere now that he had no choice but to go ahead.

He signed the statement they had prepared without a single alteration, and that afternoon a mimeographed copy was issued by the White House Press office. It read:

It is part of my responsibility as Commander-in-Chief of the Armed Forces to see to it that our country is able to defend itself against any possible aggressor. Accordingly, I have directed the Atomic Energy Commission to continue its work on all forms of atomic weapons, including the so-called hydrogen, or super bomb.

Like all other work in the field of atomic weapons it is being and will be carried forward on a basis consistent with the overall objectives of our program for peace and security.

This we shall continue to do until a satisfactory plan for international control of atomic energy is achieved. We shall also continue to examine all those factors that affect our program for peace and for this country's security.*

In the Capitol building McMahon hurried along to Chet Holifield's office to tell him the glad news. It was an emotional moment. 'I didn't know whether to laugh or to cry,' Holifield recalled later. He knew now that America would not lose the race for a super by default. Some years afterwards, when he was asked to contribute to an anthology entitled *The Day I was Proudest to Be an American,* Holifield told the story of his

*The re-examination of defence-foreign policy was undertaken in the following months by the National Security Council. It resulted in a report known as N.S.C. 68, calling for increased military forces. This was produced just in time for the Korean War.

recommendation on the hydrogen bomb, and cited the day of the White House announcement as his red-letter day.

Oppenheimer wanted to resign, since his advice had been so decisively rejected. Lilienthal asked him to stay on, as a resignation at this moment would be divisive, and he did.

The *Bulletin of the Atomic Scientists* asked a number of eminent men of science for their comments. Albert Einstein was eloquent and sombre. 'If successful,' he wrote of the fusion bomb programme, 'radioactive poisoning of the atmosphere and hence annihilation of any life on earth has been brought within the realm of technical possibilities. The ghostlike character of this development lies in its apparently compulsory trend. Every step appears as the unavoidable consequence of the preceding one. In the end, there beckons more and more clearly general annihilation.'

He offered a kind of a solution: lessen international fear, establish institutions of co-operation. International control he saw as only a secondary measure, at best.

The Special Committee had intended this to be an interim decision. As they saw it, the President had decided to explore the possibilities of a fusion bomb and perhaps to test one, not to build the weapon. But the brakes they had built in were weak, and it did not take much to snap them.

The Joint Chiefs of Staff were not satisfied with this half-way decision; now that they had been persuaded of the need for a super, they were not likely to be. At the end of February, the Joint Chiefs and the Defense Secretary sent another memorandum to the President. This urged the stepping-up of the super programme from research to weapons production, and on to 'all-out delivery of hydrogen bombs.'

Once again, Truman turned the matter over to the Special Committee. By now, Lilienthal had resigned and had been replaced as A.E.C. Chairman by Sumner Pike. They solicited advice from the General Advisory Committee, and learned that a thermonuclear explosive might be ready for testing by late 1952.

For all the talk of a re-examination of policies, there seemed no logical way now to defend the research but not the production. On 10 March Truman directed the A.E.C. to proceed to production of H-bombs in quantity. 'This was of 'the highest urgency', his directive said.

The world was on its way now, the General Advisory Committee finally answered. There would be no limit to the totality of war.

2. 'Something Technically Sweet'

Did he smile his work to see?
Did he who made the Lamb make thee?
The Tyger by William Blake

Some of the atomic scientists were dismayed by Truman's announcement, not only because it set off a crash programme to build a super, but because it signalled this so loudly. Isidor Rabi, who had expressed his concern in the G.A.C. about an intensified atomic arms race, thought the announcement was a disaster. 'However it's worded,' he told colleagues, 'this will be taken as a statement that we're going ahead and building a hydrogen bomb. The Russians are certainly going to take it that way. Only we're not building a hydrogen bomb, because we don't know how. We're going to try. We don't even know that it can be done. But the Russians will never believe that an American President could be so stupid as to say we're going to build the most powerful weapon in the world when we don't know how. We've got the worse of both worlds. We haven't got a super, but we've spurred the Russians on to an all-out effort to build one.'

For the atomic scientists, the settling of one super question was the opening of another: could they learn how to build a fusion explosive? For that matter, was it possible? And if it could be done, how could it be produced? One of the G.A.C. scientists' objections was that the only plan in existence for a fusion explosive envisaged the use of hydrogen isotopes at very low temperatures, close to absolute zero. Massive equipment is needed to keep them in this state, and you couldn't carry all this in an aeroplane and drop it. Teller and Alvarez both said a way could be found to dispense with the equipment, but this seemed to be a statement of faith.

The comparison was constantly made with the wartime fission bomb project: was there less or more chance now of producing a fusion bomb than there seemed to be of producing a fission bomb when that was started?

It is ironic that atomic physicists should be preoccupied with questions of what could be built and what could be made to work, put to them by government officials. For years, theirs had seemed the most abstract of the sciences, the most detached from human affairs.

Victor Weisskopf, the Austrian-born physicist who helped build the atom bomb, once said, 'When I was a student, I was very interested in politics, and concerned with what was going on in the world around me. It would have been difficult not to be, in Vienna between the wars. I had doubts about going into physics, only because of its remoteness from the important things that were happening in the world, its ivory-tower character. I'd have worried less about this if I'd known just how influential physics would be on world affairs.'

Since the Newtonian picture of a universe of immutable mass and motion began to crumble, in the last years of the last century, the physical sciences have been moving into abstract realms of thought, and away from the world of people's ordinary understanding. The quantities with which they deal are of a different order from those of our experience.

For instance, atomic scientists guessed that a fusion bomb might be a thousand times as powerful as a fission bomb. They often deal in increases by factors of thousands and millions. But an increase by a factor of even a thousand is beyond most people's experience. The speed at which a man walks along the street multiplied by a thousand is faster than the fastest jet plane.

Atomic scientists deal in billions. But even a million separate entities is beyond anyone's perception. Fewer than a million days have elapsed since the birth of Jesus.

Physicists who deal with the very big, astrophysics, and the very small, atomic physics, deal today not only in quantities, but also in concepts, which occupy a different realm from that which we experience with our senses. Cosmology, the physics of the cosmos, is seeking answers to questions which go beyond our perceptions, and are incomprehensible in its terms. How shall we measure the curve of space? (But how can space be curved or straight or *anything*?) How big is the universe? (How can it have a size? It's everything, isn't it? If not, what else is there?) How old is the universe? (But how can it have had a beginning? How can the infinite be measured in the finite? What was there *before*?)

The physics of sub-atomic particles also deals with things that are not only very much smaller than the objects we see around us, but conceptually different. The familiar picture of an atom is of balls rotating on fixed orbits around a nucleus, and this is a convenient and useful representation. It is not, however, an enlarged model of an atom, in the way that a model aeroplane is a small-scale model of the real, airborne machine. The atom, enlarged a few billion times, would not look like this.

The atom behaves in ways that are completely incompatible with this picture. For one thing, the German physicist Werner Heisenberg has shown in his Uncertainty Principle that we can never predict precisely where an individual particle will be at any given time. This is not because its movements are un-predictable, but because knowledge itself is too coarse-grained to make direct contact with the phenomenon. It is a problem not of observation, but of epistemology.

Moreover, it can be shown that in certain circumstances, the atom is nothing like a collection of particles rotating around a nucleus; it is a wave of pure energy, and can be refracted or deflected like any other wave. Common sense says the same entity cannot be a group of solid particles at one moment, and a wave of pure energy at the next. It must be one or the other. Modern physicists do not recognize the demands of common sense, and refuse to commit themselves to either a wave or a collection of particles; some have facetiously coined the word 'wavicle' to cover the phenomenon. They treat the atom as par-ticles or a wave as it suits them in a particular situation, and note that this is consistent with the world as they find it.

What, then, does an atom really look like? The question does not make sense in the terms of modern physics. The atom is represented for physicists by a collection of formulae.

The atomic physicist does not only know things that the rest of us do not know; he knows things in a different way.

No one, nor even the most sensitive machine, can single out an atom and tell what is happening within it. For the most part, we study them statistically. That is, machines can observe the behaviour of a large number of atoms, and tell us what is happening to some of them. A physics laboratory consists mostly of machines, machines which produce violent effects in a world beyond our reach, and others which measure these effects. To a crackle of power, electric charges are hurled along a 100-foot tube, which stretches out of the building and into an adjoining one. Numbers spin on fast-turning wheels as neutrons are counted. A geiger counter clicks away with the clean sound of billiard balls colliding. The things that are being counted seem to bear no relation to the things of the material universe, so that after we learn about the heaviness of uranium atoms, it comes as a shock to pick up a piece of uranium and find that it *feels* heavier than lead. One senses then that one really *is* holding in the hand a collection of heavy atoms. (Uranium is silvery in its pure state, but it is usually a gun-metal colour by the time one gets to pick it up because it oxidizes quickly.)

Ingenuity in experimentation consists mainly, not in achieving effects, but in detecting and measuring them. Otto Hahn and Friedrich Strassmann made the key discovery on splitting the uranium atom, in Berlin in 1938, showing the way to a chain reaction and a fission bomb. But physicists in other laboratories had split the uranium atom, most significantly Fermi in Rome. Hahn and Strassmann were chemists, concerned with analysing matter, and they were simply the first to work out what had happened in the process.

Paradoxically, as the objects of the physicists' attention became more and more minute, the physicists became more involved with big machines. Like the astronomers in the age of the first telescopes, they had to acquire technical inventiveness so that they could make more observations. In addition to asking 'What happens?' they had to ask 'How can we make it work?' This was a good preparation for the years when the atomic scientists of the Western world were asked to create an atom bomb.

By one experimental method or another, usually using the electrical properties of atomic particles as measuring rods, physicists deduced the nature of the atom in the first three decades of this century. They found (this is in the particle image) a nucleus consisting of protons with a positive charge surrounded by an equal number of electrons with a negative charge. They found neutrons in the nucleus, of the same weight as the proton, but with no electrical charge. Each element has a distinctive atom, and also, it was found later, one or several isotopes; these are variants of this atom, with the same number of electrons and protons but a slightly different number of neutrons. Starting with the discovery of radioactivity in 1896, they found out, too, about the immense amount of energy that is released by events in the nuclei of atoms, as matter changes into energy.

They were now in a position to think about the phenomenon of atomic fusion. Attention was directed to it by way of consideration of the sun and the stars. The ancient Greek scientists thought of the sun, the source of our heat and light, as a great big fire in the sky. By the end of the last century, scientists knew it was nothing of the sort. Any fire giving off that amount of heat would have burned itself out millions of years ago. By the 1930s, it was known that the energy of the sun, and therefore of all the other stars, came from atomic reactions, the fusion of very light atoms to release energy. As the result causes more light atoms to fuse, the process is self-perpetuating.

In 1938, George Gamow, a Russian physicist settled in America, explained this process in the greatest detail yet to a conference on atomic fusion at George Washington University in Washington D.C. In the ensuing months, Hans Bethe, one of the participants, worked out many possible fusion reactions, the course they would take, and the energy they would release.

These were fascinating discoveries, but nothing could seem more remote from human operation. Then, in 1942, something new entered the picture: the atomic bomb, by this time seriously in prospect. This would create a fission chain reaction in an isotope of uranium (or in plutonium, a similar, artificially-created element). Its explosion could create a heat of 50 million degrees centigrade, which is hotter than the sun.

Enrico Fermi made the connexion one day early in the year, as he and Teller walked back after lunch to their laboratory at Columbia University, where they were then employed on the bomb project. 'Couldn't such an explosion be used to start reactions similar to the reactions of the sun?' he asked. Fermi made some rough calculations of the fusion of hydrogen atoms, then of atoms of hydrogen-2, or deuterium, an isotope of hydrogen with one neutron; ordinary hydrogen has none. From these, he did not see how it could work.

Others had the same idea. Oppenheimer and some others discussed it at a workshop that summer on the Berkeley campus in California, and Bethe agreed to carry out some experiments. A team went from his laboratory at Cornell to Purdue University in Indiana to perform them.

This was the kind of experiment where you set a machine to do something and another to find out what you have done. The idea was to project particles against others and find out what percentage of the atoms fuse, and with what effect. The statistical probability that an atomic reaction will produce certain effects is calculated as a cross-section. From now on, the fate of any atomic fusion project would be told by the cross-sections.

The cross-sections for deuterium were discouraging – Fermi was right about this. But cross-sections were ten to twenty times higher for deuterium plus tritium, or hydrogen-3, an artificially created isotope, and this merited further study. It was taken up at Los Alamos in 1943 in a section called Advanced Development. But it soon became clear that further study would take a very long time, and that even the fission bomb, the necessary preliminary, was many steps off. Oppenheimer decided to shelve the matter of atomic fusion for the duration, to concentrate on the urgent wartime task of building a fission bomb.

After the war, scientists at Los Alamos worked out more cross-sections, and learned more about the fusion process. Hopes for a fusion explosive were raised by the increasing power of fission bombs. The higher the temperature, and the longer it was sustained, the more chance there was of achieving self-sustaining fusion. (The short times that are being dealt with here are around a millionth of a second.)

Tritium and deuterium atoms together are the easiest to fuse, that is, they require the lowest temperatures, around 80 million degrees centigrade. Deuterium alone requires about 350 million degrees. Tritium is so costly to produce in materials that it is uneconomical as an explosive; but a small quantity fusing might raise the temperature to 350 million degrees, so that deuterium atoms would fuse with one another.

The atom bomb is the match to light the log fire, the tritium the kindling, and the deuterium the logs. The fire was still not hot enough, nor the kindling arranged in an inflammable pattern, when Truman made his announcement, and sent his directive on production of fusion bombs to the A.E.C.

Truman followed this order with a large and necessary investment in the programme. He ordered the construction, at a cost of 200 million dollars, of a plant on the Savannah River in South Carolina, to produce tritium from uranium piles. He hedged his investment by ascertaining in advance that if a fusion bomb proved impossible to build, the factory could produce plutonium for fission bombs from these uranium piles.

The next step was to recruit more scientists to work on the project. Only a half-dozen or so scientists had done any real work on a fusion explosive. Recruitment was undertaken within the scientific community itself, informally, as often happens. The community of physics is a close one, in which most members share interests outside their absorbing professional ones, many are good friends, and there is a very free flow of ideas. Those interested in the super sought out colleagues, or sometimes recommended young graduates.

They met with a negative response much of the time, just as the inner group had earlier when they tried to drum up support for a crash programme. Apart from any moral doubts about the super, there was not much that was attractive to most physicists in the prospect of going to Los Alamos to work on weapons. Los Alamos during the war was a stimulating place for a scientist to work, because of the presence of so many of the world's leading nuclear physicists, but it was not entirely a pleasant one.

It had its good points even then. Thirty miles out of Santa Fe in the New Mexico desert, seventy miles from Albuquerque, it is in one of the most beautiful parts of the North American continent. The desert there is volcanic, and riven by huge rocks and sand-coloured, winding canyons thousands of feet deep, interspersed with flat-topped mesas, as if some god had doodled in wet clay with a mile-long finger. This yellow-brown landscape of sumptuous irregularity, contained between wide, clear horizons, is the scenery beloved of directors of Western films. And indeed, this is the home of the Pueblo Indians, whose abandoned cliff homes dot the area. Los Alamos is one of the mesas, at an altitude of 7,000 feet. It is flanked on one side by pine-covered hillsides; on the western horizon lie the Sangre de Cristo Mountains, the 'Blood of Christ' Mountains, given that name by the first Spanish explorers of the area because of the blood-red glow that emanates from the peaks in the setting sun. Some people find all this irresistibly attractive, and a good reason to make their home and career at Los Alamos rather than in some metropolitan area or university town.

The mesa was chosen in 1943 as the site for the laboratory where the atom bomb was to be designed and constructed because it was isolated, easily guarded, and there was already a ranch school there with a few buildings. The dwelling places thrown up for the laboratory workers and their families during the war were crowded and uncomfortable, and the heat and water supply was often faulty. Social life was confined. What was most irksome, the place was run by the military. The military administration allocated houses or apartments. It censored mail. People there were not allowed to leave without official permission, which was not given lightly. They could not, of course, publish any of their findings, and publication in professional journals is the way a scientist normally earns recognition. Furthermore, most top-grade scientists do not find work on nuclear weapons very interesting, particularly after the basic problems have been solved and it is only a matter of improving performance and efficiency.

This was their war work. When the war was over, most wanted to go back to their careers in universities, and they did. The A.E.C. kept the services of most of the wartime team only by asking them to do consultancy work part-time, at salaries of up to 500 dollars a week. Work at Los Alamos is stepped up during the summer months, when men come in from universities during their vacations. There are few leading physicists in America who have not done some work at Los Alamos at one time or another. The community there was improved after the war: dirt tracks were replaced by proper roads, canteens by restaurants, more comfortable homes were built, and the military were less in evidence.

All the same, in the moral climate of early 1950, not very many scientists felt like answering the call to go to Los Alamos and help try to build a new and more powerful kind of nuclear bomb.

Among some of the wartime scientists, there was also an element of disillusion. Scientists like to feel that they are dedicated to their calling. During the war, most thought they were placing science at the service not of a government, but of an overriding cause, the defeat of Nazism, that seemed identical with civilization and human decency. Like many others at the time, they felt that the political and military leaders they served shared with them a common purpose and common values. A wartime spirit encourages feelings of unity, dedication and resolve, rather than critical faculties. Later, they came to question this purity of purpose, and to fear that the products of their science would be used not only for the overriding cause, but as an instrument of power politics, old-fashioned statecraft. This doubt began to develop towards the end of the war, when some of the scientists in contact with military and political men noticed that they had some different attitudes towards the enemy and towards their allies.

One episode will illustrate this difference. It was known to some scientists because it involved Alsos, a scientific intelligence unit assigned to find out what the Germans were doing in the field of atomic energy, which tapped the brains of the physicists. In the last few weeks of the war in Europe, Alsos found that there was a factory producing uranium from ore in Oranienburg, just north of Berlin. As advancing Soviet forces drew close to the town, an air raid on Oranienburg was ordered by the military, and 612 Flying Fortresses of the Eighth Air Force pulverized it with 1,500 tons of high explosives and 178 tons of incendiary bombs. This attack was carried out not against the remnants of the enemy's war effort, but to deny a uranium factory to an ally. This was not the war effort in which the atomic scientists felt they were enlisted.

After the Truman announcement, Teller gave talks at several universities to audiences of young scientists, and invited applications to join, emphasizing the urgent patriotic purpose of work on the super. There was little positive response to his call.

John Wheeler, one of the wartime Los Alamos group, was pursued to Paris, where he was taking a sabbatical year from his post at Princeton University and working on electromagnetic theory. Smyth telephoned him long-distance from Princeton to talk about the super. Then Frederic de Hoffman, a physicist who was on brief leave from Los Alamos for a trip to Europe, arranged to meet Wheeler in the South of France, where he was taking a holiday with his wife. Wheeler had travelled in Europe during the past few months, and he was concerned now about the threat of Communism and Europe's weakness. In Copenhagen, he called on Niels Bohr, one of the great pioneers of modern physics, and his teacher and collaborator in the past. In the course of their talk, the old man said to him, 'You don't really think, do you, that Europe would be free today if it weren't for the American atom bomb?'

De Hoffman told him when they met on the Riviera that they were trying to get together a team to build a fusion bomb before the Russians did. Wheeler agreed to cut short his sabbatical, and come back to join it.

The man they wanted most to get on the super project was Hans Bethe, who was head of the Theoretical Physics Division at Los Alamos during the war. This was partly because he has a powerful mind, and had been coming up with good ideas on atomic fusion since the George Washington University meeting in 1938. It was partly, too, because of his standing among other scientists, as a man of intelligence and integrity. He was held in the same kind of regard by many scientists as Oppenheimer. If Bethe joined the project, this would help break down resistance.

One of his best-known papers on particle physics began as an academic prank. Ernest Alpher and George Gamow came to him one day with a proposition: the three of them would collaborate on a paper to be published in the April issue of a learned journal as a mild April Fool joke, to be called the Alpher–Bethe–Gamow paper. They thought up a subject: the nuclear reactions in the primal explosion that, according to one theory, created the universe. Bethe pursued the subject with quickening interest, and the Alpher–Bethe–Gamow paper appeared in the *Physical Review* in April 1948.

Hans Bethe has qualities of cheerfulness, patience and helpfulness that have endeared him to colleagues and students alike. He left Germany in 1935, when he had already earned some reputation, took a post at Cornell University in New York State, and has remained on its huge, leafy campus ever since, apart from his wartime period in the desert at Los Alamos.

Teller went up to Cornell to see Bethe in October 1949, when the super programme was still in the balance. He urged him to come back to Los Alamos to work on the super. Bethe promised to think about it. For him, this was certainly a moral issue, and he was in a state of terrible indecision. It seemed to

51

him that the destructive power of a super was so great that no civilized power should ever use it. But, he recalls, 'I worried that the Russians might get the bomb. This was a critical time in world affairs, and the Russians might blackmail the world if they alone had it.'

He talked it over with his wife, and she seemed to be against his helping to build the super. She reminded him that he had worked on the atom bomb only because they were at war with Nazi Germany, and Germany might build one. She indicated their two small children asleep in the next room, and asked whether he wanted them to grow up in a world with the hydrogen bomb.

Bethe decided to ask Oppenheimer's counsel, and went to Princeton the next day. Oppenheimer had been moving in Government circles in the postwar years, while he had stayed in his laboratory. Oppenheimer discussed with Bethe several details about how a super programme should be run, but, as he so often did, he remained non-committal on the main question. However, he pulled out of a drawer Conant's letter to him expressing repugnance at the idea of a super, and dropped it on the desk for Bethe to read, without comment.

It so happened that another old friend and colleague was also visiting Princeton, Victor Weisskopf. They drove together to New York, across the flat, iron-scarred landscape of eastern New Jersey, and talked about this question. Weisskopf had already made up his mind. When he left Los Alamos after the war, he decided, in his own words, that 'Hiroshima was a blunder, and Nagasaki a crime', and he vowed never again to help build nuclear weapons. He stuck to this, and is one of the few senior American atomic physicists who have never done any weapons work since the war, full-time or part-time. During the two-hour drive, Weisskopf argued that Bethe's fears of Soviet blackmail were exaggerated. He said that even if the worst came to the worst, and America did not build a bomb and Russia did, the Russians would not be in a position to dominate the world, and America would still have time to catch up. He asked him to envisage what a war with fusion bombs would be like. Could he imagine wanting to live in the kind of world there would be after such a war?

By the time they reached New York, Bethe was decided. He telephoned Teller, and told him, 'Edward, I've been thinking it over. I can't come.'

At Los Alamos, after the President's directive, people working on fusion went on to a six-day week, and more work was given to outside contractors. A few more scientists joined the team working on the super.

In June 1950 the Korean War broke out; from then on, scruples about working on a fusion bomb were more easily overcome, and there were more volunteers. Under the pressure of world events, Bethe agreed to do some limited work at Cornell on problems connected with the super.

Discussions of the design of a fusion explosive in those days were random. People would throw out ideas, and work on one thing after another. Experiments had something of the same character. When Wheeler came back from Europe to join the Los Alamos laboratory, he was offered a post as group leader, and declined it. 'There's no direction to lead in,' he said. 'No one knows where we're going.' The scientists at Los Alamos created atomic reactions as the experimenters had at Purdue eight years earlier, using pure tritium which had not been available at Purdue, and more refined methods. They worked out cross-sections, rearranging the factors and trying it again. The electrical machines did their powerful work, and the dials spun with their messages from the inside of the atoms. When the figures were calculated, the cross-sections always turned out to be too low.

Most of the calculations were assigned to Stanislaw Ulam, a mathematician and physicist from Poland. Ulam was unhappy about the prospect of having a fusion bomb in the world, and hoped that the most important consequence of his research would be the peaceful application of thermonuclear energy. But he took no part in the arguments about a super, and did not see any point to them. 'If a super can be built, somebody is going to build one,' he said. 'It's only a matter of time.' That summer, he was beginning to get the idea that perhaps a super could *not* be built. With John Everett, he wrote a paper summarizing his calculations. They said that all the experiments led to the conclusion that a self-sustaining fusion reaction could not be achieved at atom bomb temperatures. The kindling would not light. This was confirmed by an electronic computer when the figures were fed in.

Ulam showed the figures to Bethe when he came to Los Alamos on some consultancy work, and he agreed with the conclusions. Bethe noted that a number of the scientists did not seem at all unhappy that nature herself seemed to have cast a veto on the super. Teller, however, was dejected. He was frustrated as a scientist, and he worried furiously that there might be a way around the difficulty, and that somebody in Russia would find it.

All through the last months of 1950, Teller, Fermi, Ulam and others played around with new designs, configurations and combinations. The dials on the machines gave the same negative answers: the cross-sections were too low. Then, early in the following year, Ulam had an idea about a different kind of fusion process. He talked it over with de Hoffman and Teller. Teller quickly worked out a way from this to a fusion explosion, and gave de Hoffman the calculations to do.

This was the way to the bomb. It was an entirely new approach, a daring new idea, yet also a very simple one, that made many of the experiments and calculations of the past year irrelevant. As Wheeler explained it later, 'All our ideas about how to create a fusion explosion were based on one premise. Within a fixed framework, we went through unbelievably clever and subtle distortions to try to make it work, and we couldn't. This new idea changed the framework.'

The new way was even economical, and it dispensed with the need for a tritium-producing factory. The big new Savannah River plant that Truman had authorized was not needed; much of it was turned over to making plutonium and heavy water.

In those weeks, in April 1951, Bethe was paying another visit to the mesa. Teller told him the new idea excitedly, and promised to follow it up with the figures. But when Bethe heard the idea, he did not need the figures; he knew it could be done. He went back to Cornell and told a colleague that there was now a way in which the hydrogen atoms would fuse explosively, and he added, 'We're all victims of a freak of nature.'

Los Alamos reported progress to the A.E.C., and Henry Smyth called a meeting for June to discuss the thermonuclear programme, at the Institute for Advanced Study in Princeton. Almost everyone who was or might be associated with the programme was there: the A.E.C. commissioners, Oppenheimer and most of the G.A.C., all the key people from Los Alamos, Fermi, Bethe, Wheeler.

The Institute, built as a quiet haven for thinkers (Albert Einstein was then its most famous resident), consists of pink brick, clean-lined, Colonial-style buildings, around green lawns and shady paths. It was a balmy, summery weekend when the conference met in a ground-floor lecture room, and several of the participants fidgeted as they looked out of the window, and wondered whether they could not discuss the matter better strolling under the trees in the warm breeze.

Then Teller stood up and explained his new plan for a thermonuclear explosion, illustrating it with figures on the blackboard. Now the attention of the scientists in the audience was riveted. They were carried away by the ingenuity of the idea. This was not a new concept of the order of nature, one of those intellectual revelations that can be, for the scientist, an experience of an almost religious quality. But it was a cunning trick to bend nature to Man's will. 'It's cute,' exclaimed one scientist, 'it's beautifully cute!'

It was an exciting moment. But this kind of excitement, like some other kinds, can ignore the consequences. Three years later, when Oppenheimer gave evidence at his security hearings, he said:

It is my judgement in these things that when you see something that is technically sweet, you go ahead and do it, and you argue

55

about what to do about it only after you have had your technical success. That is the way it was with the atomic bomb. I don't think anybody opposed making it; there were some doubts about what to do with it after it was made. I cannot very well imagine that if we [the G.A.C.] had known in late 1949 what we had got to know by early 1951 that the tone of our report would have been the same.

He added that he was not sure that all the other members of the G.A.C. would agree with this. Some of them certainly do not.

Hans Bethe worried a lot in the next few weeks that if this was thought up at Los Alamos, it could easily be thought up by some Soviet scientists. He decided that there was no longer a case for not working whole-heartedly on it, and he spent eight months of the following year at Los Alamos on the super project. But his conscience still troubled him, and he wondered sometimes whether his anxieties about the Russians might not have been rationalizing a simple desire to take part in this clever trick on nature.

The next few months at Los Alamos were a time of calculations. John Von Neumann, the Hungarian-born mathematician and physicist, had turned his enormous energies to computers in recent years, and he developed a fast computer big enough to handle the fusion equations. He presented it as the Mathematical Analyser, Numerical Integrator and Computer. It was only after this name was printed that the other scientists noted Von Neumann's humorous touch: the initials, by which it would inevitably be known, spelled MANIAC. Von Neumann taught the physicists at Los Alamos to be computer programmers, and they fed their equations into MANIAC, permuting all the factors until the optimal design was worked out. This could not have been done without MANIAC, and without it, the scientists could not have known with the same degree of certainty what would happen at the first test.

In a test in the central Pacific the previous spring, which most of the key men at Los Alamos attended, an atomic explosion had produced a deuterium-tritium reaction. This was code-named Operation Greenhouse. The fusion reaction was tiny, and of purely experimental significance, but Greenhouse showed that fusion was possible.

The first real thermonuclear test was scheduled for November 1952. The site chosen was the same as that of Greenhouse: Eniwetok, in the Marshall Islands, one of those tiny Pacific atolls that first came to the world's attention during the Second World War as the scene of brief, furious battles between United States Marines and Japanese troops. Now the Marshalls were United States trust territory, and some of the islands had been the site of atomic bomb tests. This test was code-named Ivy, or Mike.

At this point, a group of men entered the scene who were to have a far-reaching and quite unexpected influence on the way the world adapted to the hydrogen bomb. This was the Rand Corporation, a non-profit organization of professional intellectuals and scientists which does contract work for Government agencies. Rand men were to learn to encompass the thermonuclear bomb, if not in their imaginations, at any rate in their calculations, and to teach governments to do the same.

The name Rand is a contraction of 'r and d', which stands for Research and Development, and this was its original function. It was set up by the Air Force in 1946 as a branch of the Douglas Aircraft Corporation in Los Angeles; the Air Force wanted to retain the services of some of the engineers and scientists who were going back into civilian life now that the war was over. Rand's orientation was long-range and visionary, but it was also technical: the first paper was on a plan for stationary earth satellites.

Soon, the men at Rand revealed intellectual ambitions beyond its station. The President, Frank Collbohm, encouraged social scientists to join, and John Williams, a mathematician and astronomer, went to New York to recruit some: men with academic backgrounds in political science, economics and psychology. This may have been justifiable in terms of Rand's brief, in that war and preparation for war might involve these fields. Then Rand spread its net wider, and drew in people involved with emerging but highly academic ideas: some anthropologists, semanticists working on information theory, even a couple of linguistic philosophers. The Air Force put up with this, partly because Rand had done some useful engineering work and it wanted to keep them happy, partly because it was grasping the new idea that brains of any kind are a national asset. Rand was becoming an intellectually convivial band of lively minds with no exclusively military or even practical orientation.

Very soon, Rand men chafed at their organization's position within the Douglas Aircraft Corporation. They might have to advise the Air Force on procurement, and the association could seem invidious, they explained. There were other anomalies, particularly for some of the recent arrivals from university posts. John Williams recalled some in a personal memoir of the early days at Rand:

Academic people are like gypsies in some respects, so if you haven't seen a man for a few years, it is perfectly legitimate to ask, 'Where are you now?' And just the bare statement 'Douglas Aircraft' is likely to be met with 'How quaint.' Then, of course, he wants to know what you do there, and you say you do philosophy. ... You can imagine the rest of it. This sounds humorous, but there was nothing humorous about it when you lived it.

In 1948, Rand borrowed a million dollars from the Ford Foundation and declared its independence. Like a migrating group of scholars in the Middle Ages leaving one university to found another, Rand moved to near-by Santa Monica, bought a large, low, toffee-coloured building on the ocean front as offices, and came to a satisfactory financial arrangement with the Air Force, which agreed to provide a large retainer in exchange for continuing services. It was still unknown to the general public, and even to most of the academic world.

In 1950, the Los Alamos laboratory gave a contract to Rand's Physics Division to do research on thermonuclear fusion, and this continued through the following year. Because of this, when the Ulam–Teller invention on a fusion bomb came, one

58

of the few outside the A.E.C. and its scientists who learned about it was Ernest Plessett, the head of the Physics Division.

Plessett, a talented and shrewd physicist who now heads his own investment analysis firm in Los Angeles, decided that Rand could give advice on this development on a higher level than that of technical detail. They were supposed to be thinking about war and peace, after all. The matter was still secret, so he asked Norris Badbury, the Director of Los Alamos, whether he might discuss it with some other members of the Rand staff. (The Physics Division was an exception to the Rand rule that, as everyone is security-cleared, anyone can discuss anything with anybody, an exception resented by the other divisions.) Bradbury gave his permission.

Plessett got together Charles Hitch, an economist, and Bernard Brodie, a political scientist, and suggested that they think about the thermonuclear bomb, and prepare briefings for members of the Government on what the new weapon would be like and some of its implications. They made up a set briefing with charts and tables, and, after preparing the way through Government contacts, they went to Washington. They gave this briefing to members of the Air Force Council, then to the Secretary of Defense, Robert Lovett, Secretary of State Dean Acheson, and other high officials. The head of Rand's Washington office, Lawrence Henderson, sat in on many of the briefings, and by then knew them well enough to brief President Truman in February 1952. For an organization with ambitions to influence, this was something of a coup.

The tone of the briefings was cool and unemotional. The trio decided that the facts themselves were sensational enough. Plessett, speaking as a physicist, explained the primary effects of the bomb: the fireball that could burn up a large town, the blast, the radiation. (He did not mention fallout; he missed out on that.) He also explained why it was easier to produce the bomb than had been expected now that tritium factories were no longer needed. Charles Hitch gave figures on the damage that a thermonuclear bomb could cause to a society, of casualties, damage and long-term economic effects.

Bernard Brodie was one of the few among those at Rand thinking about strategy who had some experience in the field, having written two books of military history. He also wrote a short book about the atom bomb in 1946 called *The Absolute Weapon*, and as they prepared these briefings Hitch told him, 'You know, you've already written the book about this weapon. Only you were talking about the wrong one.'

Brodie talked about the strategic implications of the hydrogen bomb, and his thoughts on this subject were an intimation of wider debate in years to come. He began by saying that this was not an improved weapon but something quite different from other bombs, a quantum jump in military power. (He did not know that Strauss had used the same phrase in urging a crash programme.) He took it as a reasonable assumption that both sides in a major war in the future would have thermonuclear weapons. In that case, he said, it would be important for each to accept certain restraints; not to use thermonuclear bombs on each other's territory, and, in fact, to get war back to the battlefield.

Shortly after this, another man had thoughts on the hydrogen bomb that were later to be shared by others as they came to know what he knew. Vanevvar Bush, the wartime director of U.S. scientific research and now a member of several Government advisory panels, knew about the test being planned for November, and the destructive potential. He went to Acheson with a proposal to be passed on to the White House: make a new approach to Russia before November, and ask for an agreement not to *test* any more nuclear bombs. This first test-ban suggestion was turned down.

The test armada for Mike moved into the Central Pacific to carry out one of its periodic transformations. Army and Navy engineers and civilian contractors landed by ship and helicopter on the coral atolls around the lagoon, twenty-five miles long and twenty-five miles wide. They built sleeping shacks, mess halls, scientific laboratories, cinemas, baseball fields, and homes for the animals that were to be exposed to the test explosion. Ships moved into place. The explosive device was set up on the island of Elugelab, in a huge protective shed. Meteorologists made wind forecasts, to determine when the winds would be sure to blow the radioactive cloud away from the other islands, and chose 1 November as the best date.

Back in Washington, Gordon Dean, now Chairman of the A.E.C., had a sudden thought about this date, and he took it to President Truman. 3 November was election day, when the American people would choose Dwight Eisenhower or Adlai Stevenson as their President. Dean wondered whether the world's first thermonuclear explosion two days before might not seem like an election stunt by the Democratic Administration. Truman asked whether it would be difficult and costly to postpone the test. The answer was that it might be; there were only one or two suitable days in a month. He told them to go ahead and not let election considerations affect the choice of date.

Shortly before dawn on 1 November, Eniwetok lagoon was lit up by the brightest light ever seen on earth. The thermonuclear device exploded in a fireball that ballooned out in less than a second until it was three miles in diameter.

The closest observers were forty miles away, and they watched through smoked glasses a fantastic transformation scene. Millions of gallons of water were turned into steam, and part of the ocean boiled away within seconds. When the vapour cleared, the island of Elugelab had disappeared. A crater was torn in the ocean bed a mile wide and two miles deep.

Analysis of the explosion showed that it had a power of ten megatons (this means the equivalent in explosive power of 10 million tons of TNT), which made it about 700 times as powerful as the bomb that was dropped on Hiroshima.*

President Truman heralded the opening of the thermo-

---

*The official announcement of the atom bomb raid on Hiroshima said the bomb had the explosive power of 20,000 tons of TNT, or, in the terminology that grew up later, twenty kilotons. But later measurements put it at about thirteen kilotons.

nuclear age grimly and accurately in his last State of the Union message to Congress, in January 1953. 'From now on,' he said, 'Man moves into a new era of destructive power, capable of creating explosions of a new order of magnitude. ... The war of the future would be one in which Man could extinguish millions of lives at one blow, wipe out the cultural achievements of the past, and destroy the very structure of civilization. Such a war is not a possible policy for rational men.'

But when it came to details of the event that opened this new age, the U.S. Government was reticent. Its announcement in November, after the end of the series of test explosions of which the fusion blast was by far the biggest, said only: 'The test program included experiments contributing to thermonuclear weapons research.' After General Eisenhower took office, he confirmed on 2 February that the test was 'the first full-scale thermonuclear explosion in history'.

The words were chosen carefully. Officials talked of a thermonuclear explosion, and a successful fusion device; they did not mention the word 'bomb'. The explosive device that eliminated Elugelab was not a bomb, nor could it be used as one. It was an array of delicate equipment that may have weighed as much as sixty-five tons, built around an atom bomb, more like a whole laboratory. This was a distinction that was not often made in public discussion at the time; newspapers usually spoke of the American hydrogen bomb.

Tritium has to be stored in liquid form and at temperatures close to absolute zero. It can be stored only for a few days. The equipment on Elugelab was refrigeration machinery. There was some talk of miniaturizing this mass of equipment, but this seemed very difficult.

Actually, before 1 November, though too late to apply it to Mike, scientists at Los Alamos had already devised a way to turn the explosive laboratory into a compact, simple device that could be dropped from an aeroplane. It sounds ingenious, but they say this trick is only a short step from the fusion explosion.

One way tritium is created is by bombarding lithium-6, an

isotope of the metal lithium, with neutrons. Lithium-6 is easy to handle: it is the lightest of the metals, and can be packed into any space like rock salt. The idea was to pack around the atom bomb, not deuterium and tritium, but deuterium and lithium-6, combined as lithium deuteride. The explosion of an atom bomb sends out a shower of low-energy neutrons, which would create tritium from the lithium. The tritium would fuse with the deuterium explosively at the same moment as it was created.

After Mike, Los Alamos went to work to turn the thermo-nuclear explosion into a hydrogen bomb. The feeling was that Russia must be working on a hydrogen bomb, that now they were in an East–West atomic arms race. They already had years of warning of what would happen if the Communist power won.

Soviet interest in atomic energy has a long history. In the lean years of the 1930s, the Soviet Government kept nuclear physics research laboratories going.

George Gamow often told an interesting story. In 1927, six years before he left Russia, he gave a lecture at the Soviet Academy of Sciences on the fusion of atoms to provide the energy of the stars, which was then a new theory. At the end of the lecture, he was approached by Nikolai Bukharin, an overseer of Soviet scientific development who was later to become head of the Comintern (and to die a victim of one of Stalin's purges). Bukharin asked him whether it might be possible to create this source of energy on earth. Gamow said he did not see how. Bukharin offered to turn over to him the Leningrad Electrical Power Station for a few hours a night if he could use it towards this end.

The Soviet Government began its atomic bomb programme in early 1943, taking scientists off other kinds of war work to join an institute established for the purpose in Moscow under Igor Kurchatov, a leading nuclear physicist. At a time when German armies were deep in Russia and resources of every kind were desperately short, this is an extraordinary testimony to their sense of the importance of this long-term project.

The stimulus was probably a report from intelligence agents that an Anglo-American bomb programme was under way. There is an indication of this in the first published account in Russia of Soviet nuclear weapons development. It is contained in a biography of Kurchatov by Igor Golovin called *Father of the Soviet Bomb*, that appeared in 1966. This book says that when the decision to go ahead was taken, 'The Government was already aware that, under conditions of the utmost secrecy, work was going ahead urgently both in Germany and in the United States on the creation of a new and super-powerful weapon.'

The work of the atomic spies has been given extravagant treatment in some quarters. Low-grade technicians were said to have given the Russians 'the secret of the atomic bomb'. On the other hand, some of the atomic scientists, as part of a running battle against a narrow, militaristic view of science, have said, not only that the stolen secret formula belongs to a comic book world, and the principles of the atom bomb were public knowledge, which is true, but also that there was no secret of the atomic bomb. However, the most important secret of the atomic bomb during the war years was that it was being built, and this was a very simple one.

Actually, the detailed information stolen from the United States and Britain could also have helped Soviet development. Klaus Fuchs has said that he passed over documents explaining the principles of the plutonium bomb (though he was surprised that the Russians exploded their atomic bomb as soon as they did).

After the dropping of the American atom bombs in 1945, the Soviet Government stepped up its programme to the kind of urgent effort that America and Britain put into the wartime atom bomb. Most Western physicists with some knowledge of Soviet nuclear weapons believe that Russian scientists were working on a thermonuclear bomb before they completed their fission bomb and before President Truman made his announcement; that, therefore, during those months of private debate in America on whether to build a super and what effect this would have on Russia, some kind of decision had been made already.

In conversation with Westerners, some Soviet scientists have indicated that they, too, had serious doubts about the morality of building a hydrogen bomb, and that they discussed it among themselves. But the years of Stalin's rule hardly encouraged individual interpretations of morality. In any case, there were few doubts in the early 1950s. By that time, America was building a hydrogen bomb – Truman had said so. The question was not whether there would be hydrogen bombs in the world, but whether the U.S. Government would be the sole possessor.

There is little substance with which to speculate on whether a different American decision might have altered Soviet intentions, because so little is known in the West about the discussion of a super in Soviet official circles. It seems obvious that the Truman announcement must have given a new impetus to the Soviet programme, and that if the American decision could have been taken in secret as the Russian was, with no public word of the hydrogen bomb until it was completed, Soviet development might well have been slower.

An announcement by the President that America would not build a super would obviously have strengthened any doubts that existed in Russia about building a bomb. It might even have hardened some of them into resolve. Whether an American renunciation, perhaps coupled with reactions in the Soviet Union, would have meant a different Soviet Government policy is a subject on which one can only guess wildly. If it would have had this effect, then the issue that was being decided in Washington at the end of 1949 may not have been one of American policy, but whether the world would have hydrogen bombs.

On 8 August 1953, nine months after Mike, the then Soviet Prime Minister, Georgi Malenkov, announced that Russia now had a thermonuclear bomb. He did so in a back-handed sort of a way, on the last day of a four-day meeting of the Supreme Soviet, in the middle of a long discourse on foreign policy. After recalling that the U.S. monopoly of the atomic bomb had been broken, he said, 'The Government deems it necessary to report to the Supreme Soviet that the United States has no monopoly in the production of the hydrogen bomb either.' The delegates broke into applause at this statement.

As he spoke, Soviet scientists were putting the finishing touches to preparations for a test explosion of the hydrogen bomb in Siberia. This took place four days later, on the morning of 12 August. The test was not announced until 20 August, and then it was without any fanfare. *Pravda*, the Communist Party newspaper, reported it in a news story buried on an inside page. In Washington, the A.E.C. confirmed this. The test had been monitored by planes of the radiation detection patrol.

There was consternation among the American public. Some newspaper editorials said that the United States had embarked on a hydrogen bomb programme in the nick of time, that she had beaten the Russians to the H-bomb by only a few months.

A.E.C. officials knew differently. The dust brought back from the stratosphere by the detection aircraft carried particles of lithium-6. Soviet scientists had already worked the lithium-6 trick. Russia, it seemed, had a usable hydrogen bomb. The United States did not.

3. The Scientist: the Obsession of Edward Teller

If science gave the world the hydrogen bomb, Edward Teller is the scientist who contributed the most to it. His dual role in both arguing the need for the bomb and making a vital contribution to its creation is unique. Newspapers, following Lewis Strauss's lead, dubbed him 'the father of the H-bomb', and the phrase has more truth than most such newspaper epithets. Teller disclaims the title, but out of modesty rather than distaste.

To some, Teller typifies the scientist pursuing new technical tricks, full of his own curiosity and ingenuity, not caring that the result may imperil half of humanity. His main contribution to the development even has something of the vulgar notion of science as a succession of dramatic discoveries, a 'Eureka I've found it!' quality. Except that, to Teller, the destructive power of the thermonuclear bomb is not an incidental by-product of his virtuosity; it is the point of the trick.

Edward Teller is a stocky, rumpled figure with tousled hair, a long nose, shaggy eyebrows and powerful blue eyes that seem to be focused with sombre gaze upon serious things. He is anything but a representative contemporary scientist; in fact, he is the most controversial figure in the scientific world. He has been the object of uniquely personal attacks within the scientific community; he has been denounced as an egomaniac, a paranoid, a seller-out to the military. He is a *bête noire* to the liberals and the U.S. Air Force's favourite scientists, and he also has his friends and admirers among other scientists.

What his critics among the scientists charge most bitterly is that he split the world of science in America, which was bound together by dedication, professionalism and mutual respect. This survived the wide public disagreements of the postwar years when scientists took stands on national issues, and ranged as far apart as Leo Szilard and Linus Pauling with their peace lobby on the left, and Ernest O. Lawrence and Luis Alvarez on the right. Teller and Weisskopf, differing as widely as they did, could still collaborate fruitfully along with Fermi to produce a paper on proton-neutron vibrations. Some feel that Teller betrayed this spirit by his lobbying tactics on the H-bomb issue, by waging personal feuds, and, most of all, by his testimony in the Oppenheimer hearing.

He is the object of some unfair criticism. Small vanities which are likeable weaknesses in others become unforgivable sins when they are seen in Teller.

Teller is deeply hurt by this; he could hardly not be. The world of atomic physics in the 1930s and 40s was a small one, and most of the professionals in the field knew one another. The men who turned against him were his friends and colleagues since student days, his intellectual peers, the small minority with whom he shares the language of modern physics.

As so often happens, since he became involved in a lot of arguments he has become more argumentative. He is an abrasive, hyper-sensitive personality, and tolerates little disagreement. With Teller, every issue rapidly becomes personal. Recently, a scientist found himself differing with him on a narrow technical point about which reactor to use for a certain purpose. He pressed his own opinions firmly, and was amazed when Teller responded with: 'We used to get along well together! Why don't you like me now?'

When he is not facing a challenge, when there is no expectation of disagreement, then qualities of warmth, kindness and gentleness emerge from behind his defences. A few people who have disagreed with Teller's politics have managed to remain friends with him, and enjoy his companionship and his home. At Berkeley, where he is professor-at-large and lectures mainly to graduate students on advanced subjects, he sometimes gives a series of elementary lectures on physics to first-year students – he says they are on 'physics appreciation'. These are always an enormous success. One San Francisco reporter who hates his politics went to scoff and stayed to praise. He described Teller as 'gentle, tender and loving', as he put across the beauty of modern physics.

Teller likes children, and they like him. At Los Alamos during the war, the parents organized story-reading sessions with a rota of readers. Teller was the most popular reader with the children, vivid, warm and dramatic. When his own son and daughter were learning to read, he composed for them a verse for each letter of the alphabet.

Sometimes, Teller can assume an air of extraordinary innocence when he talks of his own role. He will write in an article that a scientist should not try to influence political decisions, and he would not dream of doing so; he should merely be prepared to give his judgement on scientific matters when this is requested. Or he will pay tribute in print to scientists with whom he has disagreed and quarrelled. At times like this, he portrays the kind of man he half wishes, and half imagines, himself to be: detached, objective, equitable. Like many desperately wilful people, he quotes approvingly Lao-Tzu, the Chinese philosopher of quietism, of 'letting things happen'.

The thermonuclear explosive, for which Teller struggled so heroically with nature and with other men, has come to occupy more and more of his thoughts. It seems to be the solution that occurs to him to one problem after another, the technical trick to suit any occasion. After he was appointed to Governor Nelson Rockefeller's New York State panel on air pollution, and he considered fuel policy, he suggested storing gas underground in holes to be blasted by hydrogen bombs. When Queen Frederika of Greece met him on a visit to the University of California, he told her that hydrogen explosives could be used to blast new harbours in Greece's coastline.

Later in the visit, Queen Frederika asked Stanislaw Ulam for his opinion of the idea. Ulam remarked merely that he thought Greece had enough harbours already, and, for that matter, enough picturesque ruins.

Edward Teller was born in Budapest in 1908, the son of a comfortably well-off lawyer. He was taught by a tutor at home until he was ten, turned to science at an early age, and in his teens went to the Institute of Technology in Budapest. There is a widespread impression that Teller's anti-Communism stems from terrible childhood memories of the Communist uprising under Béla Kun in Hungary in 1919. He has allowed the impression to remain, but he is never specific about his experiences. In fact, the suppression of the short-lived Communist regime by Admiral Horthy's forces was much more bloody than the revolution; furthermore, they were anti-Semitic, and the Tellers were Jewish.

Like many Hungarian intellectuals, Teller gravitated to Germany as a cultural pole. He studied at Karlsruhe, Munich and Leipzig, where he earned his doctorate under Werner Heisenberg, and at Gottingen.

When he was twenty, he was knocked down by a tram in Munich, and his right foot had to be amputated. This was a severe blow to the young Teller, a keen swimmer and mountain climber. He has overcome it to the extent that he walks with only a slight limp, and with an artificial foot still climbed mountains in his sixties.

When Hitler came to power, Teller went to Copenhagen, where the university had become a centre of nuclear physics because of the presence of Niels Bohr. In Denmark, he married a childhood friend from Budapest, Mici (pronounced 'Mitzi'), with whom he has had a happy and stable home life. He went to the University of London on a Rockefeller Foundation grant, and then to George Washington University in 1935, when he was offered a post there.

At this time, Teller was an ebullient, zestful, young man, with enthusiasm for whatever he was doing and a ravenous intellectual appetite. He used to translate poetry from Hungarian into German. He also played the piano, as he does today, and, like many scientists, became a serious and accomplished amateur musician.

Otto Frisch, now a professor at Cambridge University, one of the many physicists who was a colleague both at the German universities and at Los Alamos, says Teller has more powerful 'intellectual muscles' than anyone else he has ever known, and gives a picture of him in his Copenhagen period, when he was in his twenties.

They had gone to Bohr's country house for the weekend, and on the train ride back, Teller was restless because he had not worked for two days. He said, 'Have you got a problem for me to solve?' Frisch told him to place eight queens on a chess board so that none could take another. Teller was silent for twenty minutes, then came up with the answer, giving the squares by numbers. Stimulated by this exercise, he asked Frisch to play mental chess with him. They started, calling out the moves by numbers, but Frisch could not hold in his mind the position of all the pieces, and had to give up. So Teller demanded another problem. 'All right,' said Frisch. 'Tell me the regular polyhedra in four-dimensional geometry.' This is a problem that Frisch worked out for the fun of it when he was sixteen, when, he says, one's brain is at the peak of its strength, and it had taken him several months. There are six of them. Once again, Teller fell silent. Frisch dozed off, and when he woke up, Teller had worked out four.

During these years, Teller acquired his characteristic style as a scientist. He is an ideas man, whose talent lies in original ideas or discoveries rather than following through with the detailed work. His mind works with dazzling swiftness, though sometimes carelessly. Fermi often said of Teller, 'If only he could find one thing to concentrate on!'

He very often discusses his ideas with someone else at a very early stage, striking sparks, getting new thoughts and insights from the other's reactions, slapping his forehead as he corrects his own error, discarding his first idea as ridiculous, dashing off on another. This mental process explains a peculiarity of Teller's scientific career: though he has published many papers, none of them bears his name alone; all are collaborations. He is known for some of his discoveries on molecular vibrations, and the chemical bonds between molecules, and also spectroscopy.

In 1939, Teller took a drive in the country that would guarantee him at least a footnote in history. Leo Szilard and Eugene Wigner had become alarmed at the possibility of a nuclear bomb that had been opened up by the Hahn–Strassmann findings in Berlin, and wanted to alert the American Government. Though they were both distinguished men in the field of physics, neither had any standing outside it. So they asked Albert Einstein to write a letter to President Roosevelt, sure that a letter from such an eminent man would be read.

When Szilard went to see Einstein for the second time, to get the letter approved and signed, Wigner was away on a trip to California, and Einstein was staying in a rented summer house on Long Island. Szilard took along Teller, his junior in years and scientific standing, because he himself did not have a driver's licence and Teller could drive. It was this letter that started the American atom bomb project. (It may interest students of ethnic characteristics that Szilard, Wigner and Teller all come from Budapest.)

Teller joined the Manhattan Project at Columbia University in New York, and later moved out to Los Alamos when the laboratory was started there in 1943. He became a group leader in the Theoretical Physics Division, headed by Bethe.

Teller was happy at Los Alamos for a while, and the Tellers' apartment there was a happy place. Mici had devoted some effort and imagination to furnishing it. When a hotel in Santa Fe redecorated and sold its old furniture, Mici bought some heavy oak Spanish-style pieces and had them sent to the mesa. The living room was dominated by a grand piano; under the piano there was always a pan of water to moisten the atmosphere, for heating came from a boiler which tended to dry out the air. Politics were discussed among the scientists, naturally, but in the Tellers' home less than in most. Teller was always anti-Communist; he never shared the sympathy for the 'Soviet experiment' that many intellectuals felt in the 1930s. But politics was not a major preoccupation; if he talked about European affairs in those early days at Los Alamos, it was usually about the accounts of massacre and cruelty that were coming out of Nazi-occupied Europe, which upset him deeply.

He used to argue that scientists should stay out of politics, and beware of forming any lobby to tell politicians what they should do. To some European colleagues, he told a homely story to illustrate his point: the Greek sculptor Phidias once created a statue of Jupiter, put it on display, and then hid behind it to hear what people were saying. Several people praised it highly, but then a cobbler came along and said that one foot did not seem natural, it was too long. That night, Phidias made the foot shorter. The next day, the cobbler came by again, and said, 'I see that he's altered the foot, and that's good. But that elbow doesn't look right.' Phidias ran out of his hiding place and said, 'You're a cobbler, so I'll listen when you talk about feet, but not when you talk about elbows.'

Nevertheless, Teller was in favour of circulating at Los Alamos the letter from the chemist James Franck signed by several scientists in the Chicago laboratory of the project, urging that the bomb be demonstrated to the Japanese and not dropped on a target. He says Oppenheimer dissuaded him, telling him these matters were best left to the wise and conscientious men in authority. He regrets today not having disregarded Oppenheimer's counsel, and believes that the United States would have won a moral victory if it had followed this policy.

Teller was at the 1942 summer conference at Berkeley, and was one of the group that discussed the thermonuclear project. He was fascinated by the discussion, and, back at Los Alamos, began to pursue research on his own. At last, Teller had found something he could concentrate on.

After a while, he stepped up his work at Los Alamos on thermonuclear fusion, in defiance of the work programme. He had his group working out cross-sections of fusion reactions. Oppenheimer felt that time was being devoted to this that should be spent on the immediate fission bomb effort.

Bethe, his section leader, argued with him frequently, and these arguments became quite emotional. Bethe would say 'Look, Edward, we have a tremendously important job to do. We're short of people. Please come back and work on the main problem.' But Teller went on with his fusion calculations. Bethe felt Teller was not doing his part in the war effort, and he was angry. The Bethes and Tellers had been friends for years, in Europe and America, and they had gone on holidays together. But relations between them were cooler from now on.

Oppenheimer's authority could not prevail against Teller's will. There is a limit to the extent to which you can compel a scientist to do effective work, and firing Teller from Los Alamos would have caused a rift among the staff. From mid 1944 onwards, Teller's small group was doing calculations exclusively on fusion reactions. One of the group, trying to explain his boss's attitude at the time, said 'To Edward, the atom bomb is a lead pipe cinch now. There's no challenge in it. Only the details remain to be worked out, and that just doesn't suit his temperament.'

In the last year of the war, Teller started worrying about the Russians developing an atom bomb or even a hydrogen bomb. He told a young couple in his home one evening that he was more afraid now of the Russians getting the bomb first than of the Germans doing so, since there seemed little risk of that. 'You must understand,' he told them, 'Communism is a religion. These people are fanatics. They're our allies only for convenience, and they'll turn against us later.'

Already, Teller found the problem of thermonuclear fusion intellectually fascinating, and he saw a need for it in the international situation. It is possible that one of these motivations rode on the back of the other. Combined, they were to be, in the years to come, the ruling passion of his life.

There was an element of ego in this, and Teller's associates disagree about how much. A number of people at Los Alamos had more authority and standing than Teller, notably Oppenheimer, with his esteem and his easy charm. Others, like Fermi and Gamow, whom he admired and liked, had great discoveries to their credit. The thermonuclear project was his bailiwick, the territory he had staked out for his own very early on, where he could make his own conquests.

By the war's end, Teller was identifying himself with the thermonuclear. He had begun to polarize the world into those on his side, and those who had objections to the super, or thought it did not merit an all-out effort, or believed that it could not be built; these latter tended to become the same in his mind.

Oppenheimer resigned as Director of the laboratory soon after the war ended, and was replaced by Norris Bradbury, a professor of physics and naval reserve officer, who set about improving the output and efficiency of weapons despite the exodus of scientists. Teller was dissatisfied with his zeal, nevertheless. He said he was thinking of leaving, but would stay if fission bomb production were pursued so vigorously that they could test twelve bombs a year, or else if an all-out effort were put into exploring the super. This was out of the question given the resources available, and Bradbury told him so.

Teller asked Oppenheimer's advice, and Oppenheimer said he thought he could be more useful to the atomic energy programme somewhere else later on. So he handed in his resignation to Bradbury. That evening, at a party, Oppenheimer asked him whether he did not feel better now that he had made up his mind to leave. Teller said no.

He was offered a post at the University of Chicago, where a number of the atomic scientists were going, so he packed his things in his car, arranged for the grand piano to follow by rail, and drove north-east.

In Chicago, the Tellers ran into the postwar housing shortage, and they shared a house for most of their first year there with Robert Christy and his wife. Christy, a physicist a few years younger than Teller, had been a student of his at George Washington and a friend at Los Alamos.

In Chicago, Teller seemed for a while to espouse liberal attitudes. He helped to launch the *Bulletin of the Atomic Scientists*, and remains an occasional contributor; he endorsed the Baruch Plan. But soon, the anti-Communist strain in his thinking about the world became dominant.

He went back to Washington frequently, not, this time, to George Washington University, but to talk to congressmen and military chiefs. He was nervous at first about the kind of impression he would make at these sessions, but soon developed more self-confidence and ease of manner. He renewed his acquaintance with Strauss, and was a frequent guest at Strauss's home near by in Brandy Station, Virginia. He cultivated Senator McMahon, then Chairman of the Joint Committee on Atomic Energy, and convinced him early on of the importance of fusion work. He also sat on the Air Force's Scientific Advisory Panel, and later became its Chairman. His advice on scientific-strategic matters was trenchant and perceptive.

Apart from McMahon, most of his friends in Congress were Republicans. A particular friend was Senator Bourke Hickenlooper, the Republican from Iowa and a member of the Committee on Atomic Energy. They made an unlikely pair, the cosmopolitan scientist and the primitive isolationist from the Corn Belt, but Teller rarely visited Washington without seeing Hickenlooper, and often lunched with him. When Hickenlooper discussed atomic energy matters with other committee members, Teller's word was gospel so far as he was concerned.

By the time the struggle for the all-out super project began in the autumn of 1949, Oppenheimer could describe him, waspishly but not altogether inaccurately, as an 'experienced promoter'.

After Truman's go-ahead, he went to Los Alamos with the title of Assistant Director for Weapon Development, and his special responsibility was the chairmanship of the committee supervising work on the H-bomb, called, for some reason that no one can remember, the 'family committee.' There was struggle and frustration.

The Princeton meeting in June 1951 was Teller's hour of triumph. So many people had said it could not be done, gloatingly, it seemed to Teller. Now he triumphed over all his foes. As he explained his plan for a super, and won over a sceptical audience, he was elated and jubilant.

Back at Los Alamos, not everything was done as he wanted it. As he had done at the war's end, he made demands that even some of his friends found unreasonable. He suspected darkly a lack of zeal in pressing for the H-bomb. He had a new idea: he wanted a separate laboratory to pursue work on fusion reactions where he could set the pace himself. He began to propagandize for this, with Lewis Strauss, who was now A.E.C. Chairman, with his friends on the Joint Congressional Committee, and in the Air Force. He complained to them of a lack of enthusiasm at Los Alamos; this angered some of his colleagues there, who accused him of disloyalty. He left Los Alamos at the end of 1951.

By the time of Mike, the first thermonuclear explosion, in November 1952, relations between Teller and the leadership at Los Alamos were strained, and he did not go out to the Pacific for the test – he had been out the previous year, for Greenhouse. This, too, was his triumph; but his success with nature was matched by a failure in handling human relations, and ensured that he would savour it alone. He waited for the explosion in a darkened seismograph room at Berkeley. A successful thermonuclear explosion at Eniwetok would be recorded on the seismograph as an earth tremor, by a fine beam of light that played constantly on photographic paper.

He describes his excitement in an article on the H-bomb in the magazine *Science*, 25 February 1955:

I waited with little patience, the seismograph making at each minute a clearly visible vibration which served as a time signal.

At last, the time signal came that had to be followed by the shock from the explosion and there it seemed to be: the luminous point appeared to dance wildly and irregularly. Was it only that the pencil which I held as a marker trembled in my hand?

I waited many more minutes to be sure that the record did not miss any of the shocks that might follow the first. Then finally the film was taken off and developed. By that time, I had almost convinced myself that what I saw was the motion from my own hand rather than the signal from the first hydrogen bomb.

Then the trace appeared on the photographic plate. It was clear and unmistakable. It had been made by the wave of compression that had travelled for thousands of miles and brought the positive assurance that 'Mike' was a success.

Teller sent a gleeful telegram to Los Alamos saying: 'It's a boy', and went back to the new laboratory. For he had won his battle for a new A.E.C. laboratory, and it was opened the month before at Livermore, some thirty miles from Berkeley. (It was actually set up by the University of California, which is also responsible for the administration of the Los Alamos laboratory.) Teller and Ernest Lawrence recruited a team of young scientists.

The two laboratories were rivals, and sometimes lobbied the Air Force competitively for contracts like industrial corporations. Livermore specialized in weapons work in the first years. They did a lot of work on miniaturizing equipment; their crowning achievement in this field was the H-bomb warhead of the Polaris rocket.

In those early days, Livermore scientists tended to have different attitudes from Los Alamos scientists. The Livermore men were younger – the first director, Dr Herbert York, was thirty-one – and they felt a need to prove themselves as a group. They had a go-ahead air, a self-conscious dynamism about them. They did not see themselves serving the higher interests of science so much as the interests of their country, and they usually got on well with the military. By comparison, there seemed something almost bohemian about Los Alamos people. Livermore men were unsympathetic to what they considered their intellectual pretensions, and their frequent chafings at the rulings of security officers, as if it were crass and ignoble to apply these to men of science.

The differences in location may have something to do with the distinctive characters of the laboratories in those early days: the one beside the fast, worldly highways of the San Francisco Bay area, the other amidst the dreamy, empty vistas of the desert. But as one scientist said, 'It's really quite simple. It goes back to the fact the one was started by Robert Oppenheimer and the other by Edward Teller.'

At the end of 1953, the F.B.I. sent a detrimental security file on Oppenheimer to President Eisenhower. Oppenheimer's security clearance was suspended, and he was told that he could no longer act as a consultant. Stunned, Oppenheimer demanded a hearing, and it took place over several days in April 1954.

Most of the scientific community were outraged at Oppenheimer's suspension. Many blamed Strauss for it, and saw this as his revenge for past disagreements. These were the days when Senator Joseph McCarthy and his Investigations Sub-committee were casting their hue over much of American life. Strict enforcement of the 1952 McCarran-Walter Immigration Act made it difficult to hold academic conferences in the United States because many foreign scholars were barred from entering by their politics, and Linus Pauling was denied a passport to travel abroad. The philistines seemed to be riding high. To most scientists, the defence of Oppenheimer seemed as natural and obvious an obligation for a member of the intelligentsia as would have been the defence of ancient Athens against the Persian hordes.

In the charges against Oppenheimer, old left-wing associations were brought up, and a clumsy attempt (which he himself described as idiotic) to cover up for an old friend who was a Communist, and who had hinted that Oppenheimer might pass on scientific secrets. When the three-man board met to hear the charges, his judgements were also brought up and cast in a sinister light.

As old issues were reviewed, two sides shaped up in retrospect, and they turned out to be the big bomb versus the small bomb. The big bomb men, who appeared to dominate the Air Force, wanted to rely on the power to obliterate with nuclear bombs for America's strength. Oppenheimer was on the other side. The most damaging item in Oppenheimer's record, in their view, was the G.A.C. recommendation against a super programme. It had recommended that the President desist from building a new weapon that would increase America's military power, and in their eyes this was by definition a form of treason.

Since then, Oppenheimer had taken part in producing two studies on defence which seemed to the Air Force chiefs not to give sufficient emphasis to strategic nuclear bombing; one advocated a European defence relying on tactical nuclear weapons. They suspected him of a strong bias against the big bombs.

Several scientists gave evidence. Bethe came to Washington to testify, and so did Teller. They met in a hotel room, and Bethe tried to persuade him that he should testify in Oppenheimer's favour. Teller said he would not, and started listing the occasions on which he thought Oppenheimer had acted against the best interests of the United States. These turned out to be the same things that had angered the Air Force's strategic bombing advocates. Bethe argued Oppenheimer's merits as an individual, and he argued, too, that Oppenheimer was right on the issues. He did not get around to saying that whether Oppenheimer was right or wrong was not the question, only whether he had acted for the good of his country as he saw it.

Teller's testimony before the board was curious. First, he gave his own account of his differences with Oppenheimer, at Los Alamos at the war's end, over the super, over the new laboratory. Then Roger Robb, the lawyer representing the A.E.C., asked Teller – and no other scientist was asked this – whether he considered Oppenheimer loyal to the United States.

Teller said he found Oppenheimer a 'complicated' person, and went on: 'But I have always assumed, and I now assume, that he is loyal to the United States. I shall believe it until I see very conclusive proof to the opposite.'

So far so good. Robb asked him next whether he believed Oppenheimer was a security risk – a similar but significantly different question (the board decided finally that Oppenheimer was loyal but a security risk). Then Teller spoke the words that, more than anything else he ever did, estranged him from his scientific colleagues:

'In a great number of cases, I have seen Dr Oppenheimer act – I understood Dr Oppenheimer acted – in a way which for me was exceedingly hard to understand. I thoroughly disagreed with him in numerous issues, and his actions frankly appeared to me confused and complicated.

'To this extent, I feel that I would like to see the vital issues of this country in hands which I understand better, and therefore trust more. In this very limited sense, I would like to express a feeling that I would feel personally more secure if public matters could rest in other hands.'

But this is not what is meant by security. Teller gave reasons for voting against a candidate in an election: you don't agree with him, or understand his judgement on vital issues. But this is hardly saying that you would not give him the key to the safe because he might sell it, or pass it to an enemy, or let it fall from his pocket during a bout of moral or physical laxity. Yet this is what a security issue is about.

Teller said the same thing in different words later on, when he was asked if he thought it would be dangerous to give Oppenheimer his security clearance; he trusted Oppenheimer's good intentions towards his country, but not his judgement.

The board would have been quite justified in taking Teller's testimony as his personal opinion that Oppenheimer was not a security risk, but they did not seem likely to do so. Ambiguity, as Oppenheimer's friends saw it, was betrayal.

When Teller had finished, he went over to Oppenheimer, and told him: 'I'm sorry.'

'You only did your duty,' said Oppenheimer.

'Good luck,' said Teller, and left the room.

The hearings of the board were secret at the time, but word of what went on there travelled quickly within the scientific community.

A few weeks after his testimony, Teller was at Los Angeles Airport when he saw across the lounge Robert Christy, the younger friend and colleague with whom he had shared a house in Chicago. 'Bob, how are you?' he called out, and walked over with outstretched hand. Christy turned on his heel stiffly and walked away. Teller stood there, astonished. Christy had earned his doctorate under Oppenheimer at Berkeley.

A week after this, Teller paid a routine visit to Los Alamos, and on his arrival he telephoned Harold Argo. Harold and Jane Argo were both students of Teller at George Washington, and he had brought them to Los Alamos during the war ('There was a shortage of apartments there, and he knew he could get two physicists for the price of one apartment,' Argo says jocularly).

The Argos were very fond of Teller, and they still are. They were having a social gathering that evening, and normally, nothing would be more natural than to ask Teller to come along, since nearly everyone there would be old friends. But they knew the feeling about his testimony on Oppenheimer, and they hesitated before deciding that they could not avoid doing so. There were no unpleasant scenes, which they had feared, but there was a frosty, distant politeness. Teller recognized this, and he did not come back to Los Alamos for ten years, not until 1964, when he delivered a lecture on a technical subject.

The hostility of most of the scientific community closed in on Teller in the next few months. Lifelong colleagues all but ignored him when they met at conferences. They seemed to be saying that he belonged with Strauss and the big bomb generals, not with scientists. But some scientists sided with Teller, among them the Livermore leaders and some others who had always pushed for the H-bomb, and there was a deep rift.

Teller sees himself as a victim of disputes rather than an initiator. He spoke later of his respect for Oppenheimer, and asked, 'What else could I do at the hearing? What else could I say?' His wife was angry at the criticisms. He once told a friend in a good-humoured complaint, 'I can forget about all this for a while by plunging myself into physics work. But Mici won't let me. She'll come running up with some item from a newspaper or magazine and say, "Now look what they're saying about you!"'

A kind of an end to the Teller–Oppenheimer story came in December 1963, when Oppenheimer was not officially reinstated – this would have necessitated a new hearing – but rehabilitated. The A.E.C. awarded him the annual Enrico Fermi award for contributions to nuclear physics (Teller was the recipient the previous year), a gold medal and a 50,000 dollar cheque. President Johnson himself went to Princeton to present it. Some of Oppenheimer's old friends and allies in past struggles were there: Lilienthal, Smyth, some who served under him on the G.A.C. and some Democratic members of the Joint Congressional Committee on Atomic Energy, but none of the Republicans.

Thanking the President for the award, Oppenheimer took note of the changed climate of opinion when he said: 'I think it is just possible, Mr President, that it has taken some charity and some courage for you to make the award today. That would seem to me a good augury for all our futures.'

Teller was present too, and when Oppenheimer finished his speech, he walked forward with outstretched hand and said, 'I enjoyed what you had to say.' Oppenheimer shook his hand, and said something to him. When photographers moved forward to catch the moment, Teller eagerly shook his hand again. Mrs Katherine Oppenheimer, however, was unforgiving, and would not speak to him.*

In a rare quip, Lewis Strauss said once that there are three kinds of physicists: theoretical, applied and political. Teller

*Dr Oppenheimer died in February 1967, at the age of sixty-seven.

became the most political of all. Generally taking a right-wing line, he has argued mostly in favour of nuclear weapons: big bombs, small, tactical bombs, bomb tests, and even bombs for peaceful purposes. He collaborated with a journalist, Allen Brown, to collect a series of essays into a book, *The Legacy of Hiroshima*. This regrettable legacy, as he saw it, was not the threat of the bomb hanging over the world; it was the fears and inhibitions about atomic power resulting from the Hiroshima raid that he found deplorable. Hiroshima, he said, had distorted the judgement of policy-makers on the subject of nuclear weapons, and 'fixed the idea in the minds of our people that atomic weapons are weapons of indiscriminate destruction'.

Teller wants the taboo removed from nuclear weapons, so that they can be seen as instruments of power like any other. 'The distinction between a nuclear weapon and a conventional weapon is only the distinction between an effective weapon and an outmoded weapon,' he wrote in *Our Nuclear Future* with Albert Latter.

He came to feel that only a preponderance of American power held in check a Soviet attempt to conquer the world. He worried about any moves towards disarmament or co-operation that might weaken the West's guard, and opposed moves towards a *détente*. In the early 1960s, when both super-powers were building long-range missiles and H-bomb stockpiles, Teller suggested to a friend two strategies that he thought would be rational for the Soviet Union, based on Soviet attitudes. One would be to make an H-bomb attack on America at any time that they could wipe out all of America's population with a loss of one third of their own. Another would be to make a sudden and devastating attack that would wipe out America's cities, and then count on Western morality to restrain surviving American forces from striking back at Russia's cities with an attack for which there could be no purpose other than revenge.

When fallout became an issue, Teller made speeches and wrote articles playing it down. This was one more stigma attached to nuclear weapons. With Allen Brown, he wrote a series of articles for the *Saturday Evening Post* designed to counter the world-wide alarm over fallout and the agitation for a test ban. 'Fallout from nuclear testing is not worth worrying about,' they wrote. 'Its effect on human beings, if there is an effect, is insignificant. Yet fear of test fallout is real and widespread. This fear is influencing national policies in dangerous ways.'

He devised new ways to test weapons underground undetected to demonstrate that it would be possible to cheat on a test ban, and he played a significant part in preventing agreement on a ban on all tests, surface and underground. Dr Harrison Brown, the Columbia University physicist, accused Teller of 'wilfully distorting the realities of the situation' in an article on tests in the *New Leader*. This kind of accusation was rarely made by scientists in public argument before this time. State Department men working on drafts of a test-ban treaty were told 'Remember, this has got to get by a Senate Committee briefed by Edward Teller.'

His testimony before the Senate Subcommittee hearings on the test-ban treaty in August 1963 was a *tour de force*. His intellectual muscles were as powerful as ever, but they were working in a different direction now. For a whole day, he answered questions about his opposition. His objections were many: the Russians could cheat and perhaps remain undetected; the United States needed to explode weapons at missile sites to test a missile's vulnerability; a treaty would seem not to allow nuclear explosions for peaceful purposes; it would impede anti-missile-missile developments. He warned the Senators gravely: 'If you ratify this treaty, you will have given away the future safety of our country, and increased the danger of war.'

The next day, President Kennedy was asked at a news conference about Teller's objection to the proposed treaty, and he said simply, 'It would be very difficult, I think, to satisfy Dr Teller in this field.'

More recently, he has issued warnings of the dangers of

arms control talks with Russia, and he has been prominent among those arguing for the development in America of new weapons, and for the deployment of anti-missile missiles.

Teller's position has hardened, his polarization of his surroundings intensified, and under the pressure of criticism and hostility, he has become suspicious of people who are not committed friends and allies. He refused an interview to a journalist, Arthur Herzog, until Herzog told him where he stood on the test-ban treaty. When Herzog said he tried to be objective, Teller replied, 'There's no such thing as objectivity on these questions. Feeling runs strong.' (Herzog recounts this in his book *The War/Peace Establishment*.)

He refused to grant the author an interview. When we were introduced, at a luncheon, he offered to answer one question only. He chose the first of several I had written in one of a number of letters to him. This was whether his early enthusiasm for the hydrogen bomb had been prompted by intellectual curiosity or his feelings about national security. He said simply that it was first scientific curiosity, and later the needs of national security.

Intensity has become his style. Smouldering passion emerges when he is putting forward arguments, even when he is making a speech from a platform and has no opposition. His voice and body both heave with emotion, whether he is talking about the fate of America or the need to adopt the metric system. Confronted by opposition, he bristles and can be fierce. But no one can be as effective as Teller has been without tactics as well as energy. When his argument meets an obstacle that cannot be taken by storm, such as a valid objection before a reasonable audience, he can be disarming, switching his manner to some light, self-deprecating joke.

As his commitment becomes more total, the tone of his utterances has become more strident, and they are often on an intellectual level unworthy of his scientific work. In *The Legacy of Hiroshima*, he wrote of nuclear disarmers: 'A surprising number of our people profess a preference to crawling to Moscow in surrender rather than risk the dangers of nuclear war.'

In the 1964 election campaign, he served Senator Barry Goldwater as his adviser on scientific matters.

Anxious about the state of science teaching in America, he was instrumental in getting started a Division of Applied Science at the Davis-Livermore campuses of the University of California; he is the Chairman, and he also teaches there. One of his aims is to produce more people with training in both science and engineering. He plays a part in the Livermore work, and has an office at the Lawrence Radiation Laboratory there (named after Ernest O. Lawrence, who died in 1956). He also serves as consultant to industrial corporations from time to time.

He once testified to a Senate Subcommittee on the many fields in which America was in danger of falling behind Russia, and warned that if Soviet science outpaced American, Russia might be able to control the world's weather.

The Livermore laboratory has branched out from weapons work, with his encouragement. It has a major long-term project going to try to develop atomic fusion for peaceful purposes. It has new plans for peaceful nuclear explosions, and lists many possible uses, the most spectacular being to blast a new canal through Central America. Teller is enthusiastic about these. He really would like to be able to control the weather, and to control the environment in other ways as well.

He is continually optimistic about the future of a world improved by science. He can paint glowing visions of underground nuclear explosions creating new mineral deposits and new sources of power, or scientists solving the food problem by controlling the weather so as to irrigate the world's deserts, and cultivating edible fish on a global scale.

In this optimism lies one key to Teller's position. Another is found in the one issue on which he differs most sharply from the standard right-wing nationalist line, scientific secrecy. Rightwingers generally want scientific research to be guarded jealously, like any other source of military power, and argue strongly against those liberal scientists who think the requirements of security are over-stressed, to the detriment of progress and science's spirit of internationalism. On this issue, Teller is a radical. He wants no secrecy whatever. He wants all laboratories, all scientific research to be open, for friends and enemies to see. He argues that there is not much to be gained by secrecy anyway since science everywhere is discovering the same things at about the same time, and that any gain is more than offset by the cramping effect on the spirit of scientific inquiry.

Teller, usually seen by those on the Left as a figure of black reaction, is actually a man of the Enlightenment. He lives still in that spirit that has dominated Western civilization since the late eighteenth century, equating human good with education, reason and the spread of knowledge into dark places, the spirit that has underlaid and motivated scientific progress.

Some lost the optimism that stemmed from this attitude and these values on the Somme or in Flanders. Many Europeans lost it when the most educated and socially ordered country in Europe apparently chose barbarism, others when they saw the rise in crime and violence that accompanied increasing education and prosperity.

The atomic scientists lost it with Hiroshima and Nagasaki. As one talks to those who began their careers in the 1920s and 30s, one thought arises again and again, expressed in similar phrases. It goes something like this: 'When I was a child, I always believed that science was a noble thing, that a scientist was somebody who contributed to the advancement and the welfare of mankind. To increase human knowledge seemed a very worthy aim. When I found myself and other scientists building these instruments of mass slaughter, I felt it was ironic and sad that this was where our pursuit of knowledge had led us. I wondered what had gone wrong. I had terrible doubts about whether we were doing the right thing.'

Teller never lost his optimistic faith in the values of the Enlightenment. No doubts or scruples slowed his resolve to build the hydrogen bomb. He is the physicist before the Fall, who has not known sin.

For Teller, widespread protests about radiation are the voice of superstition, to be answered with reason and knowledge, and resisted all the way by the scientist. A nuclear bomb test is a scientific experiment, and the test ban seems like the equivalent of putting a padlock on a laboratory, or burning a book, a gain for obscurantism. He looks on the test-ban advocates as a biological experimenter looks on the antivivisectionists. Furthermore, in Teller's mind, the principal defence of the free and enlightened spirit in a threatening world is the power of the United States.

Teller had no thought of drawing back from arrogating power over man and nature for fear of playing God, since new knowledge of nature, power over our environment, the power to change worlds, can be knowledge and power for good in the right hands. As an optimist, he has no doubt that the right hands exist

4. Eastward and Onward from Bikini Atoll

In the winter of 1953, President Eisenhower asked for and received an intelligence report on whether Russia had the capacity to wage thermonuclear war against the United States. It was reassuring. It said Russia had no stockpile of H-bombs, nor the ability to build up one quickly. Later and more detailed analysis of the debris from the 'dry' Soviet thermonuclear explosion confirmed this. It was true that the explosion employed lithium-6 as a source of tritium, which was the method by which American scientists were planning to build a bomb. But the bomb they had exploded was quite different from the one the United States would soon have, it was not the efficient, practical weapon it was first thought to be, and it did not give them any military lead.

At that time, there was almost no public mention of the fact that the Soviet Union might have achieved anything first. The Secretary of Defense, Charles E. Wilson, told reporters that Russia was three years behind the United States in the development of nuclear weapons. This stung Andrei Vishinsky, Russia's chief U.N. delegate, to deny the claim, saying pointedly on 27 November, 'Why don't you listen to your own specialists, chemists, physicists, etc.? What good is it to talk like this, when the U.S.S.R. possesses the atomic bomb and the hydrogen bomb, when the U.S.S.R. in no way lags behind other countries, and these possibly do not even have all the weapons that the U.S.S.R. has?'

The A.E.C. went ahead with the test in the Pacific of the first real American thermonuclear bomb, made to the lithium-6 formula and not requiring any refrigeration. The test was scheduled for 1 March, and the site selected was Bikini Atoll, like Eniwetok one of the Marshall Islands group. Bikini also consists of a necklace of coral islands surrounding a lagoon roughly twenty-five miles long and wide.

Again, the military and civilian teams descended on the coral islands to erect there a temporary veneer of modern civilization. Again, there were weeks of preparation and waiting for the right winds, for there were populated islands in the vicinity.

The scientists stayed mostly on Parry Island, and those who were veterans of other Pacific tests noted that the food provided by the catering contractor was the best yet in the Marshall Islands. It was warm weather but the sea breezes kept the heat comfortable, and there were some enjoyable pastimes. They could go out fishing in rowing boats, and catch yellowtails, grupas and langoustes. Most enjoyed underwater swimming with snorkel masks; the tropical fish presented a gorgeous spectacle of colours, particularly inside the lagoon. A favourite sport was dropping over the side of a rowing boat in a snorkel mask, and allowing oneself to be carried by the current under water into the lagoon, often along with a shoal of fish. In this way, and with a good deal of work, they waited for the bomb.

The first American H-bomb was not dropped from an aircraft, though it could have been. It was fixed to a tower on Bikini Atoll, so that its precise location would be known at the moment of explosion, and calculations could be made very finely. The scientific teams making the measurements were told to expect an explosive force of seven megatons, twice the power of Mike, and the biggest explosion ever.

Roy Reider, the safety director with the scientific team, had been seeing atomic explosions since 1946. He is a plump, cheery and usually matter-of-fact individual. But when, watching from Parry Island in the pre-dawn darkness, he saw that gigantic fireball balloon out in the shape of a flattened sphere, larger than any fireball he had ever seen, and then grow larger still, the terrifying thought flashed into his mind that it might swallow up the whole world, and he asked himself 'Isn't that fireball ever going to stop?' Then, he recalls, he performed an act of imagination which surprised him. As he tells it, 'I had been to planetariums in New York and Philadelphia. And you know how you look all around you at the horizon, and there's the outline of a city, in silhouette? I sketched in my mind the outline of a city against that fireball, in silhouette. And I thought, "Oh my God!"'

The explosion was twice as big as expected. It turned out to be not seven megatons, but fifteen. A plan for another, larger explosion in a few days' time was called off, because of the unexpected power of the bomb.

Nor did the wind behave as anticipated. It was predicted that it would blow in a north-easterly direction from Bikini. But just after the explosion, the wind shifted south of this line. It blew radioactive debris on to an American destroyer in its path, and on to three tiny Marshall islands that were nearly 100 miles away to the east: Uterik, Rongerik and Rongelaap.

What was being blown in this ill wind was minute, dust-like particles of matter that were scooped up with the sea and the coral dust by the explosion, and made radioactive. Back in the 1930s, when scientists were learning new tricks they could play with the atom, Frédéric and Irène Joliot-Curie were awarded a Nobel Prize for creating new radioactive isotopes by bombarding aluminium and other elements with electrons and neutrons. In the following years, physicists created radioactive isotopes of most elements. The dust and ash drifting eastwards from Bikini Atoll was just that: many different radioactive isotopes, created by the bombardment of small pieces of matter with sub-atomic particles. This is what is known now as fallout.

The first indication that something went wrong at Bikini was a brief announcement by the A.E.C. that twenty-six Americans and 236 Marshall Islanders (the order in which it put them) had been 'unexpectedly exposed to radiation' There were not many other announcements by the A.E.C. after that. The big bang of the bomb had a certain boyish appeal, but there was something nasty and insidious about radiation, and it was much more likely to cause profound and even irrational fears.

None of those injured was on the destroyer that was in the path of the fallout. The destroyer crew had their test drill for exposure to radioactive debris, and when the cloud of ash and dust appeared, the order went out: 'Button down!' All the crew disappeared below deck, hatches were battened, and hoses fixed on the deck swept all the surface space over and over again for hours, washing away the dust. No one on the ship was injured. But on the islands, it was different.

The twenty-six Americans were sailors stationed on Rongerik to make weather observations. The others were more permanent inhabitants of the three islands, who lived in palm huts on stilts, and earned a living by fishing, and farming copra and coconuts.

When the sailors on Rongerik noticed the haze of dust settling some six hours after the explosion, they washed themselves, put on extra clothes and stayed in their tents, as they had been taught, to keep themselves as free of the dust as possible. None of them became more than slightly ill.

The Marshallese islanders had not been taught anything like that. They did not know about radioactivity, nor that this dust and ash that drifted in from the sea carried the power to injure and cause disease, and to kill. Two days after the explosion, the Navy flew all the islanders by helicopter to Kwajelein, an island where a medical centre was set up. In the next few days, they all fell ill. They vomited, and their skins itched and burned, and most developed sores. They were suffering from radiation burns and radiation sickness.

The Rongerik and Uterik islanders were all cured after six weeks. Rongelaap received more fallout, and the eighty-two inhabitants remained ill for longer. A.E.C. scientists who measured the radioactivity on Rongelaap, an island some thirty miles long, found that the islanders were lucky as it was. Radiation is measured in roentgens, a unit named after Wilhelm Roentgen, the discoverer of X-rays. The northern tip of Rongelaap received 1,000 roentgens from fallout in the two days after the explosion, which would have meant almost certain death for anyone who lived there; the count at the centre of the island was 400 roentgens, and this would have meant serious illness for all those exposed, and probably death for many. All the islanders were on the southern end, which got 175 roentgens.

They received a great deal of attention on Kwajelein, and later, as the world's first victims of fallout, they were medical celebrities. Members of Congress serving on the Joint Committee on Atomic Energy, who had come out to watch the test, were brought to see them. These men had visited laboratories where rabbits had been exposed to radiation, and had observed the animals' injuries; this was a part of their job of informing themselves about nuclear weapons and their consequences. Now, fortuitously, they could have an even more precise picture of the consequences, and they saw on these human victims the same sores, peeling skin and falling hair that they had seen on the rabbits.

Four women of Rongelaap were pregnant when they were showered with fallout. Three of the births were normal; one was a stillbirth. Ten of the islanders were brought to the United States for further examination with growths on their thyroid glands. In one, the growth was found to be malignant, and was removed by an operation.

Rongelaap remained radioactive for a while, and it was three years before the islanders were able to return. By then, their palm leaf huts had rotted on their stilts and crumbled, and the Navy built them new ones, made of aluminium and painted grey, but in the same style.

A team of A.E.C. doctors has visited Rongelaap every year since then, in case they need to know one day just what fallout does to people. Two islanders who were infants at the time of the explosion were found to be suffering from arrested growth as youngsters, because of a thyroid condition. They were cured by the injection of a synthetic hormone.

The Marshall Islanders were not the only victims of the Bikini Atoll bomb, though this was not known at first. The Japanese trawler *Fukuryu Maru* – the name means 'Lucky Dragon' – with twenty-three crewmen on board was around the delineated edge of the danger zone, also somewhere east of Bikini, trawling for tuna on the morning of 1 March. The crew had heard on their radio about the scheduled tests, but there was nothing said about one on that date. U.S. planes scouring the area had unaccountably missed the *Fukuryu Maru*.

Just before dawn, a twenty-eight-year-old seaman, Shinzo Suyuki, unable to sleep, stood on the bobbing deck staring out at the calm sea. Suddenly, the whole western horizon lit up with a whitish yellow glow that, after a few moments, turned to orange. He rushed down to the cabin where some others were dressing, and said in bewilderment, 'The sun's rising in the west!' They heard the report minutes afterwards.

A few hours later, white ash drifted down on to the deck, and into the seamen's hair and clothes. At lunch, some of them found they had surprisingly little appetite, and in the evening, two of them were dizzy and vomiting. On the third day, several were ill with itching skin and eye ache. They hauled in their nets and headed for home. By the time their ship arrived at the Japanese port of Yaizu, two weeks later, they were all ill. They went to hospital, and were found to have a low blood count, and to be contaminated with radioactive material.

The Marshall Islanders suffered and were treated in relative obscurity, and the public did not know at the time about their injuries and sickness. But the arrival in port of the *Fukuryu Maru* was a sensation, and it was this that brought fallout to the attention of the world, weeks after the explosion. Understandably, any injury from nuclear bombs touches nerve ends in the Japanese nation, and nine years after Hiroshima and Nagasaki, the nerve ends were more raw than they are today. The seamen's illness received enormous Press attention, and set off anti-American demonstrations in Japan. Some fish from the Marshall Islands area was examined when it was brought in for the market and found to be radioactive, and dumped. At this, there was widespread alarm, and more anti-American protests. The U.S. Government agreed to pay indemnities, for the seamen's injuries and for the fish.

Men Who Play God

A German newspaper correspondent, Hilenar Pabel, went to see the *Fukuryu Maru* crewmen in hospital, and one, Misaki, gave him a message as he lay there weak and shivering: 'Our fate menaces mankind. God grant that they may listen.'

Six months after the explosion, some were still in hospital. One who seemed the most ill was the radio operator, Aiticki Kuboyama, whom the others had always looked upon as one of the strongest in the crew, as well as one of the cleverest. A hard, wiry man, a veteran seaman at thirty-nine, and the father of three small children, Kuboyama was an extrovert who liked to eat, to drink and to talk. It was he who first guessed that the explosion that showered ash on them was a nuclear test at Bikini, and, by working out the time between the flash and the noise, calculated the distance at somewhere around 100 miles. He was too active a man to take well to hospital life, and, bored and sometimes morose between the visits of his children, he even took up knitting as a pastime. In the late summer, he suffered an attack of jaundice, his blood count fell, and on 23 September he died. A.E.C. officials say Kuboyama died of hepatitis contracted in hospital, not from the effects of the fallout. But he was in hospital because of his exposure to the fallout, and it was fallout that made him ill and weak. To the Japanese people, and to many others, Kuboyama is the world's first H-bomb victim. Unless – and this rests only on a statistical probability – you count the unborn child of that Marshallese woman.

The fallout puzzled scientists who were not a part of the bomb project. Atomic fusion does not create radioactive isotopes, so a fusion bomb should not produce much fallout. The U.S. Government gave out very little information on the bomb, and it was left to scientists with no official connexions to play detective with the available evidence.

In Japan, the country's leading nuclear physicist, Dr K. Kimura of the Institute of Scientific Research, examined the ash from the *Fukuryu Maru*. At the end of May, he told a meeting of the Japanese Chemical Society in Osaka that he had found in the ash traces of uranium-237, but he could not understand how it got there. Coincidentally, he himself was the first person to create u-237, an artificial isotope of uranium, in the 1930s; he did it by bombarding ordinary, natural uranium with high-energy neutrons. But a fusion bomb does not contain natural uranium. Nor does the fission bomb that acts as its trigger: its fissile material is uranium-235, the radioactive isotope. He was mystified.

In August, Professor Nishiwaki, who had been at the Osaka meeting, went to Europe to attend a conference on radiation biology in Liège. There, he talked about the u-237 puzzle to a Briton, Josef Rotblat, Professor of Physics at St Bartholomew's Hospital, London, who had some knowledge of nuclear explosions.

Professor Rotblat is an unusual man, with an unusual career behind him. As a young Polish nuclear physicist studying at Liverpool University in England when war broke out, he was an early participant in the British atom bomb effort, and he went with the British team to America. Like many other atomic scientists, he was motivated by the fear that Nazi Germany would produce an atom bomb, but unlike any other, he acted on this position. In January 1945, when it was clear that Germany was beaten and that she would not produce an atom bomb, he decided there was no longer a justification for building one, and he quit Los Alamos, despite strenuous objections from security officials, and returned to Liverpool University. He sought some non-military use to which he could put his learning, and he decided upon radiation medicine. There were two sides to this: understanding and treating radiation injuries, and using radiation to effect cures. Over the years, he became an authority in this new field.

When Professor Nishiwaki told him in Liège about the u-237, he tried to work out whether there could be natural uranium in the bomb, and what it could be used for. Dr Kimura had already made calculations of the amount of u-237 that was released. Rotblat made some rough notes, and came up with an answer to the puzzle: the Bikini bomb was not just a fusion bomb. It had a large quantity of natural uranium, which would be fissioned by the fast neutrons shooting out from a fusion explosion, and would produce u-237 as a by-product. Back in London, he worked this out in detail. The more he thought about it, the more likely and ingenious the explanation became. He put the idea to a physicist who was then a leading figure in Britain's independent nuclear bomb programme.

The physicist said to him, in effect: 'It looks as if you're right. But please don't say anything about it. Even though you worked this out entirely by yourself, there'll be a frightful row with the Americans if it's published by an Englishman. We've had a lot of security leaks lately – Fuchs, the missing diplomats, and Pontecorvo. With your own past disagreements with American security men, if you publish this it will make relations between us worse. Some people will call it a security leak.'

At his urging, Rotblat kept his idea to himself. But in America Ralph Lapp, the scientist and author, had already come to a similar conclusion; so had a Japanese physicist, Professor Mituo Tarketain. It was being talked of in scientific circles. There was also some alarmist speculation about the effects of fallout in the United States from several atom bomb tests in Nevada over the years, and throughout the world from the Bikini explosion.

In February 1955 the A.E.C. released its report on the effects of fallout as observed at Bikini. In this, it admitted an area of uncertainty about the genetic effects, but played down the alarm prevalent in some quarters. 'It is important to recognize', it said, 'that the average amount of radiation exposure received by residents of the United States from all nuclear detonations to date has been about the same as the exposure received from one chest X-ray.'

This was intended to be reassuring, but it alarmed Rotblat. He regarded this amount of radiation as dangerous. A chest X-ray, he reasoned, is concentrated in one part of the body; it does not affect the reproductive organs, and so produces no genetic damage. Nor would any part of it go into the womb of a pregnant woman, where it could damage the foetus. Furthermore, it was already known that the distribution of fallout is irregular; if this radiation was the average dose, then some places and some people received more.

After this, he decided to make known his conclusions about the Bikini bomb. It seemed a secret that would not be kept anyway. He wrote an article that appeared in Britain in the *Journal of Atomic Scientists*, and in America in the *Bulletin of the Atomic Scientists*. More details were worked out later, with still fuller information.

It was clear now that the Bikini bomb was more powerful and nastier than anyone had anticipated. It sowed death and illness into the wind, and, because it did genetic damage, its power reached into another dimension.

It was what came to be known as a three-stage bomb, a fission-fusion-fission bomb. The first stage was a u-235 fission bomb that served as a trigger; the second was the fusion part, about 200 pounds of lithium deuteride, to provide the fusion explosion. This was the hydrogen bomb as conceived. The third stage was an ingenious afterthought, a large quantity of natural uranium, wrapped as an envelope around the fusion bomb. This produced a powerful fission explosion under the impact of the high-energy neutrons released in the fusion process. The three explosions are almost simultaneous.

The natural uranium envelope is the cheapest nuclear explosive ever devised. U-235, until then the only kind that would serve as a fission explosive, constitutes only ·7 per cent of natural uranium. Separating the one from the other is a major industrial operation, the most expensive part of producing a nuclear weapon. Natural uranium is, by comparison, plentiful and cheap, costing around 10,000 dollars a ton.

In a fission bomb, the power is limited by the critical mass; it can never be more than one megaton. In the Bikini bomb, there were probably several tons of uranium wrapped around the fusion bomb. The explosion by fission of this uranium probably contributed twelve megatons of the fifteen-megaton power of the bomb.

In the days after the Bikini test, newspapers all over the world carried accounts of the terrible power of the explosion, with diagrams and sketches showing how many square miles the fireball would burn up, and how far the mushroom cloud spread its shadow. They fully justified the statement by Lewis Strauss at a news conference in Washington that the H-bomb would 'take out a city'. (A reporter: 'How big a city?' Strauss: 'Any city.') Then the *Fukuryu Maru* sailed into port with the rest of the bad news.

This, then, was the hydrogen bomb. Reading newspaper editorials in the following weeks, it seems hardly a figure of speech to say that the world shuddered.

Fallout was a new problem for the scientists, which posed new questions for which they were not well prepared. They had always known about the possibility. At the test of the first atom bomb at Alamagordo, New Mexico, in 1945, army lorries stood by ready to evacuate a tiny hamlet of fifty people out in the desert, if winds should blow fallout that far away. But fallout from fission bombs was insignificant compared to other, more direct effects, and there was little serious study of the phenomenon until the Mike test. Then Government laboratories set about working out how much fallout nuclear explosions produce, what happens to it, and how much harm it does.

Only a part of the fallout drifts away in the wind, while the rest goes up in the stratosphere, to be distributed throughout the world. Actually, high-level winds tend to follow the lines of latitude, so most fallout from tests settles in the same area of latitude around the globe in which the test took place.

It comes down in the ensuing months and years in rain, and it drifts down, imperceptible except to the most sensitive geiger counters.

It is made up of many different kinds of radioactive substances. Some retain their radioactivity for thousands of years, some lose it in a few months, days or even minutes. Some are closely related to substances that are naturally absorbed into the body, and these tend to lodge in human beings. Strontium-90 is the most notorious. Similar to calcium, it is absorbed into the bone. Its radiation consists of beta rays, which have a range of only a few inches and are easily stopped, but from inside the organism it can damage the bone tissue and cause leukaemia or bone cancer. Because it is found in milk, and because it affects most of all bones that are not yet fully formed, babies and small children are most likely to be affected by strontium-90.

Many of these radioactive isotopes do not exist in nature. Or rather – and this depends what one means by 'nature' – they *did* not. Now, in minute quantities, the longer-lived among them are a part of the physical world. In a minuscule way, the H-bomb has already fulfilled its promise of changing mankind's environment.

Those isotopes that lodge in the human body are passed on, in quantities so minute as often to be undetectable, into every baby from its first month. The ubiquity of fallout is a new idea, and it took most people some time to grasp it. Even years later, President Kennedy, after he took office, called in his Science Adviser, Jerome Wiesner, and asked him to explain fallout from tests. When Wiesner had given his explanation, Kennedy looked out of the window, where a drizzle was coming down, and asked, 'You mean that stuff is in the rain out there?' Wiesner told him it was.

Kennedy stood there staring out at the light rain drifting down on the White House lawn, silently and thoughtfully, for some minutes.*

The argument over testing began very soon after Bikini, and continued with increasing intensity over the next eight years. It was first raised at a high level in the British House of Commons. On 25 March 1954 Philip Noel-Baker asked the Foreign Secretary, Anthony Eden, to propose to the U.S. and Soviet Governments a suspension of tests. Five days later, 104 Labour Party members of parliament signed a motion calling for an end to tests. In Golders Green, the North London suburb,

* Arthur Schlesinger Jr tells this story in *A Thousand Days*.

some local housewives and a Quaker formed, in the following months, the Golders Green Committee for the Abolition of Nuclear Weapons Tests, probably the first organization in the world devoted to this end, a root which later flowered into the Campaign for Nuclear Disarmament.

President Eisenhower did consider a suggestion at this time that he propose a test ban to Russia, but he turned down the idea after the A.E.C. and the Defense Department told him a ban would hamstring America's nuclear weapons development. This was disclosed only two years later, when a test ban became an issue in the 1956 election campaign.

The arguments in the first two years or so after Bikini were mostly differences of principle. The principles involved, like many raised by the existence of the H-bomb, were new ones, and men had not grappled with them before. This was a new kind of violence that was being committed, different to Cain's kind. The victims were anonymous people, here and there, anywhere. They may be people not yet born, who will not be born for decades, or centuries. Like atomic particles, they cannot be identified individually, but only in statistical terms.

The number of cases of leukaemia in the world is increased by x per cent (the percentage is certainly very small). The number of stillbirths, or deformed children, is increased by y per cent. Did that woman of Rongelaap lose her baby because of fallout? She was one of four, and the other women all had normal births. Find out the usual percentage of stillbirths among Rongelaap islanders. The ratio between these two figures gives the probability that her birth was due to fallout.

The A.E.C., now the possessor and manufacturer of H-bombs, became their defenders, and fought against any who cried alarm over radiation from tests. (This is in itself a testimony to the new kind of power in the hydrogen bomb. As Robert Gilpin pointed out in *American Scientists and Nuclear Weapons Policy*, the hydrogen bomb was the first weapon of which the opponents exaggerated the power and the advocates understated it.)

When the A.E.C. joined the Rand Corporation in a study of

radioactive fallout, they named the study Project Sunshine; for the measuring unit of strontium-90, they coined the term 'sunshine unit'. This emerged at a hearing of the Joint Committee on Atomic Energy, and the members of the committee proved resistant. Representative Chet Holifield said doubtfully, when the terms were used: 'The word "sunshine" has a cheery note to it, and I was just wondering if we were allowing, let us say, propaganda to creep into our scientific terminology. Why did you not put it "happy" units, or something like that?'

Senator Clint Anderson chimed in: 'They've put out Project Sunshine as the most enlightened and happiest look on radiation damage.' Dr Willard Libby, the chemist and A.E.C. commissioner, protested that the choice of name was haphazard and had no propaganda purpose, and was not altogether inappropriate because the subject did relate to sunshine. Nevertheless, no more was heard of the sunshine unit after this.

From a public relations point of view, the A.E.C. could have done worse. Another study of fallout was originally given the name Project Gabriel, but this name was dropped because it had unnecessarily apocalyptic overtones.

The A.E.C. talked of 'safe levels', and gave out assurances that the radiation was well below safe levels. But this level is a purely relative standard. By 1949, tests on animals had shown conclusively that there is no threshold for radiation below which no dose does any harm, somatic or genetic, as there is with some drugs. All radiation inflicts some damage on living tissues, and the amount is proportional to the dosage. (The A.E.C. no longer uses the term 'safe level'.)

Linus Pauling warned that a new and uncertain situation had been created by the tests, and no scientist knew what the final effects would be. This seemed to be underlined by the A.E.C.'s announcement on 28 January 1955 that laboratory tests with mice showed that the genetic effects of radiation were ten times as great as was previously thought. The A.E.C. added in the same statement, 'The amount of radiation people have so far been exposed to from atomic tests is still not important as a genetic hazard.' Clearly, this last is not a statement of fact; it is a value judgement. It depends what you regard as important.

There was argument in those days over how much damage radiation does to living cells – there is still a wide range of uncertainty. But most of the argument was not over the figures but over their significance, and the way they should be used, as people faced this totally new situation. A. H. Sturtevant, an American geneticist very concerned about tests, warned in a public speech that 1,800 children born in 1954 would suffer illness because of fallout. The pro-test scientists said that illness would not be increased by more than a minute fraction of 1 per cent. The statements are not incompatible.

Edward Teller and Albert Latter said the radiation from fallout was only 5 per cent of the natural radiation from cosmic rays, and less than the difference between radiation at sea-level and in Denver, Colorado, which is at an altitude of 5,000 feet. If you are really interested in cutting down on the harmful effects of radiation, they said, persuade people to move out of Denver. Teller came up with another, more bizarre alternative. The chances of deformed birth are reduced, he said, if the sperm, and hence the reproductive organs, are kept cool. You could do more to cut down the number of deformities by insisting that all men wear kilts than by stopping nuclear tests.

There was, here, a wide gulf in attitudes between many scientists and ordinary intelligent people.

The ordinary person hears that several thousand people might die of leukaemia in the coming years because of nuclear tests, and several thousand babies will be born defective. He thinks of this as an enormous tragedy, to be avoided at any cost. The scientist sees the casualties in numerical terms, as a part of a vast pattern of interwoven benefits and costs, a tiny percentage of the illnesses that will occur in any case, too tiny a percentage to get very alarmed about.

The ordinary man says each of these people is an individual, even if you never know his name. The percentage of which their illness is a part has nothing to do with it. If you see a man drowning, you don't pass on, remarking that the world is full of woe and thousands of people drown every year. He may go on to say that each human tragedy, each person's suffering, is unique, and exists in a universe of its own, that they cannot be added together to make a sum which can be balanced against some other figure. Feeling deeply that this is true, he may quote a line from a poem by Dylan Thomas: 'After the first death, there is no other.'*

The scientist replies that this kind of addition is done all the time, and must be. You put an enormous effort into combating a disease if it is likely to reach epidemic proportions, but not if it kills or maims only a few. A nation enters a small war more readily than a large one. He may even get testy, and see an element of hypocrisy in the other man's attitude. He is aware of the cost in lives that society extracts for its comforts. Why this outrage at killing people by testing nuclear weapons, which, after all, has a purpose? If each life is so uniquely precious, you could save far more of them by outlawing the internal combustion engine, or simply setting a universal speed limit of thirty miles an hour. Or, for that matter, by devoting a larger proportion of the national budget to overseas medical aid.

Furthermore, he continues, the argument about there being no safe levels works both ways. If you say that because of the kind of damage that radiation does, no amount is tolerable, will you ban luminous watches? And what about X-rays? Are you not willing to set off their medical benefits against the minute amount of damage they undoubtedly do to the human race's genes? Is this kind of arithmetic also immoral?

It is interesting that some of those scientists who argued most earnestly and effectively for a ban on testing, like Hans Bethe, were not motivated by concern over fallout, but were worried only about the danger of nuclear war, and saw the test ban as a first step back from the nuclear confrontation.

Behind most of the replies to the numerical arguments on this question is a deep-rooted, almost instinctual value judge-

*From *A Refusal to Mourn the Death by Fire of a Child in London*, 1940.

ment, though even this is not inviolable to the arguments. It is one that was manifested, though rarely expressed, when the H-bomb was first proposed. This judgement is that there are some things men must not poison for any gain; that we live on this planet not as possessors, but as tenants and trustees; that we may have obligations towards the human race that go beyond our immediate acquaintance with it or our immediate concerns; that there are things before which we should be humble.

The explosion of the American and Soviet hydrogen bombs coincided with the beginning of a new period in America's international relations: for the first time, she was now vulnerable to serious aerial bombardment. Since the end of 1949, the Soviet Air Force had a long-range bomber that could reach the United States on a return mission with the aid of in-flight refuelling, the TU-4, modelled after the American B-29.

In September 1953 the Defense Department released to the Press new kinds of maps. On these maps, with their unfamiliar angle of vision, some far-off points seemed nearer, and American cities far inland were closer to an overseas power than some cities on the sea coast. These showed the routes to America over the North Polar region, by which Chicago and Denver are 5,000 miles from central Siberia, and Los Angeles 4,500 miles from Novaya Zemlya.

This was a time when war between the blocs seemed very possible, and the nations were prepared for it, psychologically and militarily. American military men at bases overseas held in mind the distance from the nearest Communist bloc border. There were crises from time to time in the Far East and in Germany. Communist doctrine still taught that war between the Communist and capitalist worlds was inevitable, though there was now an escape clause that said the strength of peace-lovers and proletarians in the capitalist world might possibly prevent it. The cold, grey figure of John Foster Dulles spoke for America in the world; he built up new anti-Soviet military alliances, and said this was a global conflict between Good and

Evil, and every nation must choose its side (this was merely the rhetoric of the Dulles era; in practice, when it seemed opportune, Dulles supported with economic aid Yugoslav neutrality and Polish Communism. But the rhetoric creates the mood, and the fears).

In their 1955 May Day parade, the Russians worried Western military attachés with a fly-past of squadrons of intercontinental jet bombers, to be called Badgers in NATO nomenclature. Actually, there is some evidence that the Western attachés were tricked into thinking that there were more of these than there were. In retrospect, it is clear that during those years the Soviet Government did not make a major effort to bring the United States into bombing range. They did not develop in-flight refuelling, which would have made the TU-4 a real intercontinental bomber, nor did they make a major production effort to turn out the Badgers. Their big aircraft production programme was on Mig fighters to defend their frontiers – an ineffective programme, because the Migs had very poor performance at night.

To the Soviet military, the enemy lay in Europe, as it had before. They developed medium-range rockets by the mid 1950s, and targeted them on Western Europe. Nikita Khrushchev gave an indication of their further expectation, however, when he said during his visit to England in May 1954, 'I am certain that we shall quite soon have a ballistic missile with a hydrogen bomb that can fall anywhere in the world.'

The advent of the hydrogen bomb changed drastically the meaning and uses of military power in a number of ways. America's new vulnerability made one of these ways starkly apparent. In the time of the H-bomb, military power could do all sorts of things, but it could not protect. In past times, the power to attack an enemy has been the same as the power to defend one's country against him. The stronger force could defend a country from attack and, if this was required of it, overcome the enemy's forces and capture or lay waste his territory; but the enemy's forces had to be overcome first.

In the H-bomb age, however, military strength is no sure

107

defence against destruction. A weaker power with H-bombs can destroy a stronger. It does not have to overcome the enemy's forces, on the ground or even in the air, but only to get a few planes loaded with H-bombs over his territory once.

Forecasts of casualties in a future war could be made more precisely, and were made more publicly, than in previous times. These were usually expressed in clinical language. There was talk of 'taking out' a city, and destroying a country, of acceptable and unacceptable losses. As the losses that were calculated became greater, so, seen through the distorting prism of language, they came to seem less painful, and easier to contemplate. A thousand people killed can conjure up a picture of tragedy, but a city being 'taken out' sounds neutral, and antiseptic. It seems a loss that is numerical in nature, like so many chips in a poker game, or an indemnity that a country is forced to pay. It has a sound of something done with surgical neatness. If you live in the city in question, you are dead; if outside it, you are not. There is no hint of the process of dying, the millions outside the fireball burned or irradiated or crushed to death, the hundreds of square miles of half-destruction and half-death, or slow death, or delayed death.

Operating strictly within their sphere, military men could encompass the H-bomb by multiplying or increasing exponentially the destructive power available to them, and go on thinking in the same way that they are accustomed to. This was particularly easy for airmen, who tend to see the enemy as a series of targets to be attacked. Airmen do not deal with the enemy as people, as an army on the ground does; they never take prisoners of war, or occupy territory. Target destruction is stupendously effective with hydrogen bombs; their military problems seemed simpler rather than more complicated. A Navy press release extolling the value of carrier-borne bombers said that even if the United States were completely wiped out by a nuclear attack, carrier-based planes at sea could go on to win the war. It did not say what they would win; this, presumably, was a political question, and outside the Navy's sphere.

Some months after Bikini, James Fisk, an A.E.C. consultant, was paying a visit to the Boston area, and he offered to brief some old friends and colleagues on the Massachusetts Institute of Technology faculty on what had been learned about fallout. These were among the new breed of American scientist who were becoming used to advising the government on matters scientific or related to science. Most of them had their introduction to government during the war; now they were called upon for advice occasionally, and always had the ear of people in government if they felt like giving some. They sat on scientific advisory panels, like the G.A.C., or else on *ad hoc* studies on particular subjects.

One such study, on air defence, was carried out earlier at M.I.T. in the summer of 1952, at the request of the Air Force. It was called Project Charles (Cambridge, Mass., is on the Charles River). The study expressed concern at America's coming vulnerability, and recommended some vigorous defence measures, including a chain of radar stations in the Far North to warn of an attack across the Polar regions. Then the participants went back to their classrooms, and construction began of the 1,500-million-dollar Distant Early Warning Line.

Among the dozen or so M.I.T. scientists who gathered to hear Fisk on fallout were several who had been on Project Charles, and three men who were later to fill the office of Science Adviser to the President: George Kistiakowsky, James Killian and Jerome Wiesner. They found the talk profoundly worrying. The problem of air defence took on a new and even more foreboding aspect. It meant preventing an enemy not only from dropping a single bomb on a city, but also from dropping one 150 miles or more on the leeward side.

Later, someone asked Jerome Wiesner what he did when he first learned what the full effects of fallout were. 'I bought a farm,' he said promptly.

It happened this way. A short time after the meeting with Fisk, he and Jerrold Zacharias, who was also at the meeting, whiled away a couple of hours working out idly what kind of retreat would be a safe haven in a nuclear attack. They decided that it must be away from a major city and away from a fallout pattern. It should also have a source of fresh water, and should not be near a main road leading out of a city, where it would be in the path of a flood of refugees. Wiesner had earned a lot of money in recent years by patenting some inventions, and he was thinking of buying a place in the country as a second home. That summer, he and his family took their holiday in rural New Hampshire, and on an afternoon's drive, they saw a farm for sale. It met all the requirements of a haven, and he bought it. As he tells it, 'I didn't rush out and buy a farm immediately I heard about the fallout. But I wouldn't have bought that particular farm if it hadn't been for the fallout picture, and that talk with Zacharias.'

Officials of the Civil Defense Administration in Washington wanted to make public their findings about the threat of fallout, since alerting the public to the dangers of nuclear war was one of their functions. At first, they were not allowed to do so. The State Department was worried about the effects these would have, not so much on the American people as on America's allies in Western Europe. They would show that near annihilation awaited the people of this crowded continent in the event of attack with a large number of hydrogen bombs. To the discerning among the Western Europeans, they would show also that an American H-bomb attack on military targets in the Communist bloc could kill by fallout a large number of people in Western Europe, the area to be defended. The Project Charles scientists thought the public should be told, and agitated behind the scenes for full disclosure of the facts. Out front, the *Bulletin of the Atomic Scientists* called for more candour.

The A.E.C. published its report on the effects of fallout in February 1955. This showed that a Bikini-type bomb exploding on an American city would kill anyone remaining in the open 120 miles downwind, and half the people 160 miles away. This was putting things at their hypothetical worst; most people do not live in the open. As the report said, simple protective measures can cut down the exposure to fallout. Staying inside a brick or stone house would cut down the radiation received by about 50 per cent; sheltering in a basement might reduce it by 90 per cent. After one emerged, there would still be radiation; how much would depend on how many days or weeks had elapsed since the bomb fell.

Most people agreed that the hydrogen bomb was something radically new on the world scene, but governments, like military men, could only use it to pursue their old, customary purposes. The American Government's principal foreign policy aim in the years since 1947 was the containment of Communism. The Eisenhower Administration set out to use nuclear weapons to pursue this aim with a minimum of cost, and also a minimum risk of war.

A common-sense view of any risk situation is that you can vary the odds and the amount risked inversely, increasing the one by reducing the other. You can take long odds for the chance of a big win, or short odds for a less spectacular prize. This is also a common attitude to modern war: that you can make war more unlikely by making it unimaginably terrible, or else make it more bearable, and probably also more likely. The Eisenhower Administration set out to do the former: to reduce the risk of war by increasing its consequences.

When General Eisenhower was waging the 1952 election campaign with John Foster Dulles as his chief foreign affairs spokesman, they criticized the Democratic Administration for its 'timid' dealing with the Communist bloc, and looked forward to a 'rollback' of the Communists and a 'crusade for freedom' in Europe. Whatever this meant, it was soon forgotten. The promise to end the Korean War and bring the boys home was remembered, however. The Korean War was terminated in 1953, and two American divisions were pulled out of that country by the end of the year. Other troops were brought back from Japan. Then began the run-down of the army that usually follows an armistice. The defence budget was reduced satisfactorily, from 42,000 million dollars in 1953 to 29,000 million in 1954, despite the continuing Cold War.

111

The new defence policy was to rely on nuclear weapons to deter any attack rather than troops to repel one. As President Eisenhower explained in his State of the Union message in January 1954, 'Our great and growing number of nuclear weapons permit economies in the use of men.' This was the policy that Charles E. Wilson, the economy-minded Secretary of Defense, dubbed the 'new look'.

The genealogy of the new look contains some British ancestry. A Global Strategy Paper was produced by the three British chiefs of staff in 1952, also for an economy-minded government. This was the Conservative Government that had recently taken office, and was struggling with a balance of payments deficit. It decided that it could not afford to build up British forces to the level agreed upon at the NATO meeting in Lisbon the previous year.

Unasked, the three service chiefs went into seclusion at Easter 1952 to work on this problem. For their week of deliberations, they chose the Naval Staff College at Greenwich, which was deserted for the mid-term holiday. The three were Admiral Sir Roderick McGrigor, Field-Marshal Sir William Slim, and Air Marshal Sir John Slessor. They had with them only a few aides, and also Sir Pierson Dixon, a useful addition since he was both Deputy Permanent Under-Secretary at the Foreign Office and also an old friend of Air Marshal Slessor. They decided that if forces had to be cut back, Britain should make the nuclear bombs which she was just developing the principal weapon in her armoury. In the event of a major attack in Europe, the ground forces would fight a delaying action while the R.A.F. destroyed Russia's cities and industries with nuclear bombs.

They incorporated this idea into a Global Strategy Paper, and presented it to the Cabinet. The Prime Minister, Sir Winston Churchill, was pleased with it, but this was clearly a policy for the Western Alliance, not only for Britain. He sent Air Marshal Slessor to Washington to explain it to the U.S. Joint Chiefs of Staff. Lord Franks, then British ambassador, sat in on the explanations. The Americans gave the paper respectful consideration; Britain was taken seriously as a world power in those days. But under an Army Chairman, General Bradley, the Joint Chiefs were resistant to an Air Force-orientated strategy, and anyway the Korean War was still on. The paper was brought out again in Washington and studied when plans were being made for the 'new look', and Churchill's approval of this paper was cited as an argument in favour of the new policy.

In the twenty-one months after the Eisenhower Administration took office, while the Army was cut down in manpower, the Air Force was expanded from 99 partially equipped wings to 115 combat-ready wings. Administration spokesmen emphasized often the need for economy in military spending. President Eisenhower said in several speeches that economic strength was as important as military strength, and that weakening the one was as dangerous as weakening the other.

The statement of the new policy that resounded most around the world was Dulles' famous 'massive retaliation' speech on 12 January 1954 to the Council on Foreign Relations in New York. In this, he explained the change of policy.

If the enemy could pick his time and his place and his method of warfare, and if our policy was to remain the traditional one of meeting aggression by direct and local opposition, then we had to be ready to fight in the Arctic and in the tropics, in Asia, in the Near East and in Europe; by sea, by land, by air; by old weapons and by new weapons. ... The President and his advisers, represented by the National Security Council, had to make some basic policy decisions. This has been done. And the basic decision was ... to depend primarily upon a capacity to retaliate instantly, by means and at places of our choosing.

Naturally, the newspapers emphasized phrases like 'instant' and 'massive' retaliation (the 'massive' comes from another part of the speech), and 'means and places of our choosing'. Adlai Stevenson, a critic of the new look, gave it an extreme interpretation but a widely held one, in a speech two months later. 'All this means, if it means anything,' he said, 'is that if the Communists try another Korea, we will retaliate by dropping atom bombs on Moscow or Peking or wherever we choose – or else we will concede the loss of another Korea.'

Dulles made some qualifications following these criticisms. In an article in the monthly *Foreign Affairs*, he said that the new policy had been 'misconstrued', that there was not only one kind of military response envisaged. 'Some suggested', he wrote, 'that the United States intended to rely wholly on large-scale strategic bombing as the sole means to deter and counter aggression. What has already been said should dispose of this erroneous idea. The potential of massive attack will always be kept in a state of instant readiness, but our program will remain a wide variety of means and scope for responding to aggression.'

Dulles' speech was actually intended as an open-ended warning that the United States was prepared to escalate any war, either by the use of nuclear weapons, or by expanding the war territorially, or both. If the term 'escalation' had been in use then, and the concept a part of the currency of strategic discussion, his pronouncement might have been better understood.

His protest that the United States retained 'a wide variety of means and scope for responding to aggression' was not universally accepted, partly because of the frequent emphasis by Administration spokesmen on economy, and the cutdown of ground and naval forces.

The most conspicuous part of American military power was the B-47s with their three-man crews and 2,000-mile range stationed in increasing numbers at bases around the Soviet perimeter, and the promise of the B-52, the first real intercontinental jet bomber, then in production. The A.E.C. gave contracts for production of H-bombs in 1954, and these were now rolling out of factories, to replace the fission bombs in the Strategic Air Command's armoury. Atomic bombs were now even stored on aircraft carriers, for use by carrier-based planes.

Even to the extent that this 'variety of means' existed, there was some doubt about the will to use it. For the new look was a reaction to the Korean War, a profoundly disturbing experience for the American nation, with apparent anomalies that seemed new in those pre-Vietnam days. It was costly in lives, it dragged on for three years, and it was without that righteous, wrathful, all-out effort to destroy the enemy that Americans traditionally expect from a war, and that seems justified by any wrong great enough to require the sacrifice of young Americans.

There was much grumbling, among military and civilians, about the restraints in operation and the sanctuary allowed the Chinese. The complainers usually forgot that restraints operated on both sides, and that the United States had a sanctuary in Japan, where military operations were mounted and from which its planes flew missions. General Douglas MacArthur expressed the frustration of the military when he told a Senate Committee, after his abrupt dismissal, that the Administration's policy in Korea 'seems to me to introduce a new concept into military operations ... the concept that when you use force, you can limit that force'. This is not, of course, a new concept, but it was new then to many Americans.

The idea of massive retaliation – the very words, even, with their ring of vigour and rough justice – was more suited to the traditional American attitude to international affairs. This holds that there are two distinct and totally different situations: peace, when countries live together and obey the rules of the international community; and war, when the rules are transgressed violently, and all-out conflict ensues until the transgressor triumphs or is conquered.

It suited, too, the widely-held American picture of Communism: cruel, aggressive, monolithic, restrained only by the permanent threat of violent retaliation. Suited it and reinforced it, also. As the British physicist P. M. S. Blackett observed, in an article in the *New Statesman* (5 December 1959), 'Once a nation pledges its safety to an absolute weapon, it becomes emotionally essential to believe in an absolute enemy.'

If the policy matched the mood of Americans, it matched also the rather different mood of Europeans. Under American pressure, the European NATO governments agreed at their 1951 meeting in Lisbon to build up NATO's strength to ninety active and reserve divisions. This figure was a standard for

115

pious hopes and academic arguments for the next ten years, but it was never reached, and, after a while, people ceased to believe that it ever would be. What Western European governments wanted was protection by a permanent American nuclear threat to the Soviet Union, and this the Eisenhower policy provided. Their only fear was that this guarantee might be weakened some day.

Within the limits of the Administration's economies, the United States did try to achieve a variety of forces, and constantly pressed her NATO allies to strengthen their ground forces for the defence of Europe. But, more unequivocally than the United States, the Western European governments stood for deterrence rather than defence. The inter-allied arguments over what force levels were required in Europe were political rather than military. So far as Europeans were concerned, the military force that counted was the American Air Force with its nuclear bombs.

The massive retaliation policy in practice also reassured those Europeans who worried about the fervour with which the Eisenhower Administration might press its 'crusade against Communism'. The strategy of deterrence was not suited to a crusade. It meant sheltering behind the invisible barricade of the thermonuclear threat, and remaining there.

In the contested areas of Asia, there were crises which brought the possibility of American involvement. In Indochina, as the battle of Dien Bien Phu entered its final stage, some in Paris and Washington urged American intervention, including the then Vice-President, Richard Nixon; these were defeated with stalwart help from the U.S. Army top brass, who warned that no massive retaliation was possible against the Vietminh, and that any American participation would be down in the mud, and costly. There were crises in the Formosa Straits.

But in Europe, the policy was rigidly defensive. An anti-Communist uprising was crushed swiftly in East Berlin with no interference from American forces stationed in the Western half of the city. A short-lived government in Hungary cried out for United Nations protection as Soviet troops attacked, and its cries went unanswered. When the United States made a move towards the East, it was with radio propaganda and economic aid. This was not rollback; it was co-existence, across the barrier of mutual deterrence. Eisenhower even used the word 'stalemate' in his State of the Union message in 1955. He said the Communists must be assured that any attempt to gain their ends by aggression would be fruitless, and added, 'Now this, of course, is a form of world stalemate.'

Opposition to the massive retaliation policy in America came from two directions. Liberals, constitutionally nervous about any threat to use national power, objected to the particularly bellicose threat implicit in this strategic posture. There was also, here, the usual confusion of value judgements with analytical judgements. Liberals tend to see some positive values, however corrupted, in Communism, which shares some of their political premises. However much they might dislike the policies of a Communist government, many drew back from the idea of total and unqualified war on a Communist country as they would from total and unqualified condemnation of Communist principles. In the war against Nazi Germany, they reacted with alarm to talk of anything less than total war with unconditional surrender as the aim.

Others with a more pragmatic, Clausewitzian view of international affairs than most of the American public were brought to opposition to the 'massive retaliation' policy through the workings of a different political temperament. These men dislike and distrust attempts at total solutions to world problems, just as they distrusted the idealistic absolutism behind the unconditional surrender policy in the Second World War. What they deplored in the Dulles policy was not the threat to use terrible force, but the apparent renunciation of the use of force in a measured way for measured, realistic objectives.

The simplest and most practical criticism of the policy was that it was promulgated at a time when the Russians were acquiring the ability to inflict their own massive retaliation on the United States. As Representative George Mahon said in

Congress on 1 February 1956: 'Massive retaliation is rapidly becoming a two-way street.'

Dean Acheson gave a pragmatic view when he answered the often-heard comment that 'We can't afford another Korea' in an article in the *New York Times Magazine,* three weeks after the Bikini Atoll explosion: 'Such a war is the only kind that we or anyone else can afford.' This kind of harsh realism was unwelcome. Arguments over the validity of the defence policy diminished, and by the 1956 election campaign, it was no longer an issue. The savings in the defence budgets were palpable, the risk remote.

The political difficulties of questioning massive retaliation were demonstrated to Eric Larrabee, the author and editor, when he put the issue to one of Governor Adlai Stevenson's campaign aides, John Bartlow Martin. Larrabee saw dangers in the current situation, and thought Stevenson should argue for an alternative policy, with larger armed forces and less reliance on the H-bomb. Martin heard him out, then said: 'Let me see if I get this straight. You want the Governor to claim that he knows more about war than Eisenhower, and then come out in favour of an increased draft, plus a few hundred thousand aircraft workers laid off on the West coast, and all this in order to get ready for another Korea. Somehow, I don't think it will work.'

Ever since the Baruch Plan for the international control of atomic energy was rejected in the early postwar years, there was always one plan or another for nuclear disarmament before the United Nations or its Disarmament Subcommittee. Ever since the Baruch Plan was rejected, none was taken very seriously.

In June 1954, at the London Disarmament Conference held under U.N. auspices, the British and French representatives put forward a plan for the abolition of nuclear weapons and the drastic reduction of conventional forces, under an international control and inspection body. The United States accepted the plan so quickly as to make it clear that it had agreed beforehand and was virtually a sponsor. In May of the following year, the Soviet Union accepted the plan. This was a surprising about-face, since, up to that time, Russia had refused to consider any inspection of her territory, at least until after all nuclear weapons were abolished. In September of that year, the Americans withdrew their offer.

Not surprisingly, Andrei Gromyko, the Soviet Foreign Minister, pointed to this as proof that the U.S. Government was utterly insincere about disarmament. It was not, but it was almost certainly insincere about this proposal. It backed the plan as a gesture only, at a time when most disarmament proposals were gestures. The Soviet acceptance forced some American officials to think again and think hard about the requirements for nuclear disarmament.

The American view of this plan – and this was accepted by the Russians soon – was that now there were too many nuclear bombs to ban them all. When the Baruch Plan was first proposed, in 1946, there were very few atom bombs in existence, and few facilities for making them. Tight control of the world's supply was plausible. Like a new and rare disease germ that has just made its appearance, the atom bomb could be isolated and removed. By the middle 1950s, there were hundreds and probably thousands of nuclear bombs in existence. No control body could find them all if one government wanted to hide a few; no check could be made on the numbers. Any government which cheated on an agreement and concealed a few hydrogen bombs while its enemy destroyed all of its own would be in a dominating position militarily. The Soviet Government was to meet this situation in 1960 with a plan for nuclear disarmament beginning with the abolition, not of bombs, but of rockets and aircraft, which was more easily verifiable. But this plan did not get very far either. The withdrawal of the 1954 Anglo-French plan meant the abandonment by the governments of any serious hope of abolishing nuclear weapons.

In withdrawing American acceptance of the plan, Harold Stassen, the U.S. representative, revealed the new American thinking on the subject. He said that American policy no longer aimed at the elimination of all nuclear weapons, but at arms control measures. 'It is our view', he continued, 'that if armaments ... are brought down to too low a level, then instead of the prospects of peace being improved, the danger of war is increased.' To put it more concretely, if side A has 20 nuclear bombs, and side B has only 10, then in a very tense crisis in which both sides feel threatened, side A is more tempted to strike than it would be if the numbers were 400 and 200.

Stassen's position at the London conference was the first major American step towards replacing disarmament measures with arms control measures. Arms control belongs to a period when nuclear weapons are accepted; its aim is nothing so ambitious as to banish from the world the spectre of nuclear war, but only to steer a way through the years ahead. Its object is not the removal of all armaments, but stability in an armed world. Discussion of arms control has a different atmosphere from discussion of disarmament. It tends to be technical rather than moral; it aims to make the world safer rather than better; it rests on assumptions of common interests rather than protestations of good faith.

During the later years of the Eisenhower Administration, the main effort in the arms control field was directed to achieving a test ban. This began with a letter from Eisenhower to Khrushchev in April 1958, after the Russians initiated the test moratorium, suggesting a technical conference on test-ban inspection systems. The talks began in Geneva in July, and they dragged on, with interruptions, for two years. No inspection system was needed for most tests, since they could be detected immediately by the increase in radiation. But the previous autumn, the A.E.C. had exploded small, tactical nuclear bombs in an underground cavern in Nevada. These produced no radioactivity in the atmosphere, and they could only be detected, if at all, by seismic stations. During the next two years, there were many complicated arguments over what was needed to detect an underground nuclear explosion, between the participants in the Geneva conference, within the United

States, and, almost certainly, in official and scientific circles within the Soviet Union.

In the United States, A.E.C. officials and some scientists who wanted to continue testing thought up new ways of concealing underground tests, to show that an inspection ban would not work. In Geneva, the Russians at first refused to allow foreigners any inspection rights on their territory, then agreed to allow three inspections a year. There were arguments about how many earthquakes per year in the Soviet Union could be distinguished from afar as earthquakes and how many might conceivably be underground nuclear explosions. Geologists and seismologists found themselves arguing politically sensitive problems.

By the end of Eisenhower's second term, no agreement had been reached. However, despite the jockeying for position that accompanied every session of the disarmament talks, some common ground was found, if only a common desire to avoid mutual annihilation, and a dialogue was established.

5. Men with a Mission

In the era of massive retaliation, the most extreme advocates of strategic bombing came into their own. For these, the multi-megaton bombs in their long steel containers resting in the bellies of the bombers were a final justification for their military philosophy.

Like so many features of modern warfare, this philosophy goes back to the American Civil War. It was the theory behind General Sherman's march through Georgia. Though Southerners reviled Sherman for waging war on civilians, Sherman reasoned that, by laying waste the land behind the Confederate armies, he would cut off their source of supplies and starve them into defeat. This was humane in the long run, he argued, because it would end the war more quickly and with less loss of life than a continuing struggle on the battlefields – this was after three years of fighting.

The twentieth-century version of this philosophy is attributed usually to Brigadier-General Giulio Douhet, the Italian military writer. Douhet, writing during and shortly after the attrition in the trenches of the First World War, argued that a war could be won without this slaughter by aircraft, striking swift, devastating blows at an enemy's cities, smashing his industries and demoralizing his population.

Others put forward a similar view: Lord Trenchard, the first Chief of Staff of the R.A.F.; and Brigadier-General Billy Mitchell, the American Air Force officer who broke so many rules in arguing for air power that he was court-martialled and discharged. A few American military writers reached similar conclusions by adapting the views of Admiral Thayer Mahan, the American neo-imperialist of the McKinley and Theodore

Roosevelt era. The theory lay behind the Anglo-American bomber offensive against Germany, and it became the dominant theory in the U.S. Air Force.

Military life nurtures the qualities of loyalty and determination more than intellectual flexibility. When military officers take up a theory, they tend not to use it so much as to adopt it as a cause, and dedicate themselves to its defence. At times, a statement of belief in a theory of strategy sounds less like a reasoned argument than a litany. Here is Major-General Roscoe Wilson, U.S. Air Force, testifying at the Oppenheimer hearings:

> I believe in the theories of Douhet and Mitchell and Admiral Mahan, as modified to fit the present war.
>
> This is a belief that the object of war is not the defeat of the enemy's army, but the defeat of the enemy's will to wage war.
>
> That this comes about only after the failure to win the real victory, which is the prevention of war....
>
> I am a dedicated airman. I believe that proper defense lies along the lines that the Air Force proposes.

The argument that the swift and devastating blow behind the lines is more humane in the long run can hardly be applied to the hydrogen bomb. No possible alternative could cause more bloodshed. But the argument was given a new twist by the strategy of deterrence. The H-bomb massive retaliation strategy was humane, it was said, because it deterred any possible aggressor, and ensured that war would never break out.

In the mid 1950s, it became the fashion for U.S. Air Force generals to speak in paradoxes. 'Peace Is Our Profession' was the slogan erected at every Strategic Air Command base where the bombers that carried nuclear bombs stood ready on the runways. 'If we ever have to go on our mission, it means we've failed,' one bomber general after another said, and 'These weapons are useful only if they're never used.'

Emotionally, these paradoxes permitted the containment of the most belligerent, militaristic feelings within a rigid framework of peaceful purpose. The Confederates, with their cavalier ideals, despised Sherman's army because, they said, it made war on women and children rather than on fighting men. The Air Force projected romantic ideals of boldness, dash and carry-the-war-to-the-enemy spirit on to its strategic bombing men. To the bomber men, theirs was the only strategy with the proper military qualities of aggressiveness. Any alternative smacked of weakness, timidity, and a lack of virility. In some eyes, advocating the use of tactical nuclear weapons before strategic ones was practically tantamount to being soft on Communism.

In 1950, when Russia did not yet have a stockpile of atomic bombs, SAC staff officers briefed some Rand men on their war plans. Bernard Brodie asked General Curtis LeMay, the SAC commander, why there was this stress on instant response to an attack by the fullest force possible, since planes at American bases were not in danger of being destroyed on the ground. He suggested that in many circumstances there might be an advantage in waiting, or perhaps in sending only a part of the ready force on bombing missions. LeMay insisted doggedly that any pause, or any response that was less than total, would be against proper military principles. Professor Brodie has an active interest in psychoanalysis as well as strategy, and he is a trustee of a psychoanalytic clinic in Los Angeles. He saw this attitude in psychological terms. Coining on the spot a phrase that was to come into the language of nuclear strategy, he said, 'Gentlemen, you don't have a war plan. You have a war spasm.'

In the H-bomb age as in any other, arguments among military officers over strategy are inter-service. A strategic theory is usually advocated by a particular service if it will give that service a more important role in the national defence effort. Here, for instance, is Admiral Oftsie, giving evidence before the House Committee on Armed Services, in October 1949: 'We [the Navy] consider that strategic air warfare as practised in the past is militarily unsound and of limited effect, morally wrong, and decidedly harmful to the stability of a possible world war.' Seven years later, when a Navy submarine was being built to carry Polaris rockets with nuclear warheads, Admiral Oftsie testified before Congress as an enthusiastic advocate of strategic attacks on the enemy's homeland, with Polaris rockets.

The services lobby competitively members of Congress and civil servants. Each has a sizeable budget devoted to this, under the heading 'legislative liaison'. In the early 1950s, to demonstrate the vulnerability of aircraft carriers, Air Force bombers 'attacked' the carriers with cameras, and the Air Force surreptitiously passed the photographs to newspapers. The Navy drew up figures to show weaknesses in the projected B-36 bomber, the price of which would cut down the number of carriers to be built.

It was a great day for the Air Force when Arthur Godfrey, the popular television personality who was in the Navy as a youth and often chatted fondly with viewers about the Navy, resigned his Naval Reserve commission and started talking about the Air Force. Senior officers had worked hard for this. General Hoyt Vandenberg, the Chief of Staff, made the first approach; General LeMay took Godfrey with him on a tour of overseas bases, and then went with him on a hunting trip in Africa, along with a reporter and photographer.

When the H-bomb deterrent came into being, the Air Force seemed to have won most of the arguments, strategic and budgetary. As the deterrent force, S A C came to feel itself the sole repository of its country's safety. General LeMay at one time resented the A.E.C.'s custody of nuclear weapons, and the fact that S A C had to ask for them. He was worried because some of the fissile material, which was then still fairly scarce, was going into making the new tactical nuclear weapons for battlefield use. He thought S A C should be the proprietor of all fissionable materials, should procure its own nuclear bombs, and decide how much uranium was left over for weapons for other services.

In the first postwar years, S A C was a successor to the wartime bombing force carrying more powerful bombs, and its pilots and crews prepared for a bomber's war. Then the picture of the coming war changed, as the destructive power available to both sides multiplied. It became one of swift, devastating blows struck in the first hour.

In this war, every minute is important, every plane, every bomb. Failure to reach a Soviet airfield, to manoeuvre precisely through a hole in the radar defences, might mean that several Western cities and the populations are wiped out. A delay of minutes in passing on an order, or in executing it, might mean unprecedented disaster and total defeat. LeMay, when he was commander of SAC, said, 'If war comes, we will fight and win, or fight and lose, with what we have at the time of the outbreak of war. The ultimate outcome will be decided by the men who are on duty at the time.'

This is a heavy responsibility for the men who are on duty. SAC prepared its men not to fight a war, but to carry out one mission, perfectly, at a moment's notice.

SAC was turned into this kind of military force by its first commander, General Curtis LeMay, a longtime bomber pilot who planned and led the incendiary raids on Japanese cities in the closing months of the Second World War, and turned his natural bellicosity into political channels briefly when, during the 1968 presidential election campaign, he became George Wallace's vice-presidential candidate. LeMay fashioned SAC for its deterrent role, and he once called the result, lovingly and not altogether inappropriately, 'a wonderful, complex and beautiful instrument'. When he left in 1957 to become Air Force Chief of Staff, he handed over his command to General Thomas Power, his old friend and deputy.

LeMay gave SAC its distinguishing characteristics: pride, *esprit de corps*, intense professionalism, tight discipline, and preparedness for war at every instant with an almost paranoid intensity. This last is not criticism; it is a part of a military man's job to be this way. The commanders at Pearl Harbor were court-martialled for negligence after the débâcle in a welter of civilian denunciations, and the memory of this may well be in military men's minds when they ignore civilian criticisms that they are over-imaginative about the dangers of sudden war.

During its formative years, S A C learned a great deal from the Rand Corporation's analyses of its operations. Rand acted as a sort of loyal opposition. Subsisting on money from Air Force contracts, they challenged some of S A C's proudest claims, such as the rapidity with which it could go to war.

Rand was developing a method of analysing problems known as systems analysis. Like folk songs and sex appeal, systems analysis is easier to recognize than to define. It is an outgrowth of the operational analysis developed in the British forces during the Second World War, but it considers a wider context. Some characteristics by which it can be recognized are the rigorous consideration of methods of operation in relation to the ultimate end in view, the establishment of numerical ratios between factors that are not usually considered in numerical terms, and the quantifying of alternatives.

The most important thing that Rand brought to S A C's attention was its destructibility. It turned out that civilians had to urge the airmen to be ready for an attack from the blue, not only on America but on themselves. Airmen tended to feel that worrying about this was defensive-mindedness. The destructibility of the force was demonstrated in several studies made by Albert Wohlstetter, an economist and mathematician at Rand with an original, searching and elegant style of analysis. He did several studies showing that S A C airfields were or soon would be vulnerable to nuclear bombing attacks. When he first gave a briefing on one of these to LeMay, LeMay snapped, 'This is the most important document in 175 years!' (Struck by the oddness of this figure, Wohlstetter did a rapid mental calculation on the spot and decided that this made it less important than the Declaration of Independence, but more important than the Constitution, which seems a likely military view.) The study urged concrete shelters for bombers and laid down some principles and criteria for these. LeMay seemed at first to favour the idea, but then went back to demanding more bombers as the solution to the vulnerability problem, as to most others.

The principles laid down for concrete shelters were followed later in the hardening of missile silos.

Herman Kahn, the physicist and strategist who worked as an assistant to Wohlstetter on some of these studies, pointed up SAC's vulnerability characteristically by depicting some lurid possibilities. He told SAC officers that soon, if the Soviet Air Force decided to wipe out SAC as a fighting force, it could do so with nuclear bomb attacks on twelve airfields, and could do so easily. If the Soviet Air Force made every mistake it could make, so that half the planes lost their way and the other half signalled their coming, it could *still* do it. In *fact*, he said, a Soviet bomber pilot could land his plane at one of these airfields, explain that he wanted to confirm that this was a SAC base because he did not want to waste an atom bomb, and take off again and *then* drop it, and no one would be able to stop him.

Wohlstetter's most important study was on the economics of choosing overseas bases, an unlikely medium for changing Air Force strategy. Rand was asked to produce a report on this; it sounded like a job for an accountant. The massive report that Wohlstetter produced eighteen months later concentrated on the damage that could be done to a base by enemy attack as an economic factor, one SAC had not considered. The policy recommended by this study was putting the main bomber bases in the United States and using overseas bases as staging airfields, and this was largely adopted. In the course of the study, Wohlstetter was amazed at the neglect of the vulnerability factor. He found, for instance, that one communications link depended on a radio serial at each base, and this could be snapped by an overpressure of two pounds per square inch, a light pressure that would be the effect of a ten-megaton bomb exploding ten miles away.

Out of this one report came many concepts that became basic to thinking about the strategy of nuclear weapons. The most important was the distinction between a first-strike and a second-strike force. The former is defined as one that can strike first, but would probably be destroyed before it went into action if the other side struck first. A second-strike force is one that can survive a nuclear attack and strike back.

The headquarters of S A C, the nerve centre of this complex instrument, was protected early on. It is deep underground, at Offutt Air Force Base near Omaha, Nebraska, a military base ever since it was a cavalry fort during the Indian wars, that happens to be about as far from America's borders as it is possible to get. It was put underground after Russia built her atom bomb, and given foot-thick, lead-and-concrete walls. An advanced feature is a set of blast doors that can slam shut in a fiftieth of a second, and are connected to a sensory device that shuts them the instant an increase in radioactivity is detected. This would be before the blast of a nuclear bomb reached it.

No place is H-bomb proof, and the S A C command post could be destroyed by the first bombs to land on the United States. So there is an alternative command post, in an aeroplane. At every minute of every day, a S A C command plane is flying over America. Inside is a S A C general with a small staff, and duplicates of all the radio and teleprinter communications equipment that are in S A C headquarters below, connecting him with S A C aircraft and missile bases and with the Pentagon. If a signal ever tells him that S A C headquarters has gone off the air, that general becomes the commander of S A C. There are several of these planes, and each is in the air for eight and a half hours, taking off a half-hour before the other lands, so that there is an overlap.

There is a staff at Offutt whose sole job is to choose targets to which nuclear weapons are assigned. For some years this was a S A C staff, but since 1960 the task has been shared with the other services. This group, sticking coloured drawing pins on a large map, is the Joint Strategic Target Planning Board (J.S.T.P.B.); the S A C commander is *ex officio* Chairman of the Board.

The J.S.T.P.B. has worked out a points system; it awards several points to a possible target for each characteristic that makes it desirable to destroy it, then adds up the points to see which targets have higher priorities. A town might be consigned to destruction in a war by the awarding of so many points for its railroad marshalling yards, so many points for its airfield, and so many for its army command headquarters. High-priority targets, with a large number of points, have several weapons assigned to them, giving an overkill capacity (that is, the capability of destroying completely a target twice over, or more) in case one or another does not reach the target. The Board revises its target list once a year. It has access to all pertinent intelligence data, and can make changes more frequently if a new situation warrants it.

On the lists these men draw up, no cities are named as targets. The J.S.T.P.B. would not put, for instance, Moscow on a target list. They might put on it the command room at the Soviet Ministry of Defence on Frunze Street, or the Moscow Railroad Station, or even the Kremlin.

There is a large element of hypocrisy in this, since the Air Force plans on city-destruction as a phase of a major war. But it continues an Air Force tradition, it helps keep up standards of accuracy, and it makes strategic bombing sound a little more like a military operation and less like a massacre.

The instrument that is S A C is controlled from Offutt through the most technically sophisticated communications system in the world. This has virtually abolished distance as a factor. When a S A C base communications officer wants to make sure that the line to the command post is still open, he lifts his red telephone and says, 'Are you hearing me?', and his voice sounds over a loudspeaker at Offutt command post just as clearly whether he is in an operations room overhead, or at a missile base in Texas, or an airfield in Alaska or Okinawa or Spain, and the response 'loud and clear' is just as swift and just as loud and clear. S A C's communications network is one vast inter-office telephone exchange. There are several communication systems functioning at the same time, at least one employing a communications satellite, in case one should fail, or one radio link should be blacked out by the radioactivity from a nuclear explosion. A teletype system runs from Offutt to the Far East, Europe, Alaska and Puerto Rico.

S A C flies two bombers: the long-range B-52, of which it has about 400, and the medium-range, supersonic B-58, the Hustler, of which it has about fifty. The F-111, the new, adaptable, 'swing-wing' plane, is supposed to serve as a strategic bomber in one of its metamorphoses. S A C also has one huge tanker plane for every two bombers, and electronic counter-measure aircraft, which carry equipment to baffle an enemy's electronic defences. For a while, the combination of anti-aircraft missiles and radar was becoming so effective that it seemed that the day of the heavy bomber had passed. In war plans, the bombers were to go in only after the first great phase of destruction had been carried out by missiles, and there were presumably few defences left. But recently, advanced airborne missiles which can travel more than 700 miles have brought the bomber back into a bigger role.

For a while, as part of their alert system, some S A C planes flew airborne patrols with bombs aboard, even though three crewmen together were needed to arm them. But after two accidents in which these planes crashed, in Spain and in Greenland, these flights were discontinued. S A C headquarters, or any base commander, can order a bravo exercise in which, at a klaxon sound, the men on alert status rush to their planes, take off and head towards their target. Twice, S A C headquarters has sent a crisis message saying there will be no more practice bravos until further notice, that any bravo order will be a real one. The first time was when U.S. marines landed in the Lebanon in 1957, the second during the Cuba missiles crisis in 1962. In the Cuba crisis, S A C carried out its red alert plan to disperse some bombers to civilian airports.

Once in the air on an alert exercise, the S A C crew will fly towards their target until they reach an irregular line that is on every S A C map. This is the famous fail-safe line. Unless they get the order to continue, they turn back. The order must come as a voice message in code. This, incidentally, was the flaw in the novel and film *Fail Safe*. The 'go' order is not an electronic signal that could go out accidentally.

The fail-safe rule is rammed home to candidates for SAC crew with the greatest emphasis. To show the inviolability of the rule, students are encouraged to dream up far-fetched situations in which it might seem that the rule would not apply rigidly. One example, from a student: My radio goes dead soon after take-off. Nuclear bombs are falling on the ground behind me, and I can see the mushroom clouds rising. I also see the other planes in my squadron going ahead. Don't I and my crew assume that the order to go has been given? Wouldn't we be evading our war mission if we turned back? The answer: No. You turn back at the fail-safe line.

They are told that high-priority targets have several weapons assigned to them anyway, and that whether there is a war or not, it is *always* better to turn back rather than take any chance of dropping a nuclear bomb that should not be dropped.

The most important place in any SAC airfield is the command building, which is category one restricted. It is guarded by armed sentries. The most important room in this building is the communications cab, the terminal point of all those control lines stretching out from Nebraska. In a typical design, this is one of two glass-walled rooms that look down on the command and briefing room.

Outside this room, you look into a mirror. This is, in fact, a two-way mirror; the people inside can see you. You ring a bell, and speak your business into a mouthpiece. If those inside want to admit you, they press a buzzer that releases a lock. Inside, the room is manned by two officers and an n.c.o. Two of the three must wear pistols at all times. On a shelf are four telephones, two plain black ones and two painted pillar-box red. The two red phones are connected to SAC h.q. in Offutt, one through the area h.q. and one directly. When SAC has an alert message one of the red telephones emits a warbling sound and the message crackles over the loudspeaker, and it is repeated on the teleprinter. If both the officers read it as a bravo order, they sound the klaxon. On the wall are clocks showing local time, G.M.T., and 'execution time', which is the time at Offutt.

As these match the operational rooms in S A C headquarters, so the administrative offices match the upper reaches of the S A C bureaucracy, with its rigid hierarchal structure, its image of an after-shave lotion sort of masculinity, and its nervous intensity about public relations. (This last is traditional in the Air Force. On the day after the bomb was dropped on Hiroshima, Air Force headquarters cabled General Carl Spaatz, the Pacific commander: 'atomic bombing story received largest and heaviest smash play of entire war with three deck banner headlines morning and evening papers stop radio networks gave national play'.)

The offices have their grey desks, their well-groomed secretaries, their coffee flowing. On the walls are usually colour photographs of S A C aircraft, the plane sometimes pictured as a sleek, cool beauty against the blue, sometimes zooming aggressively out of a dramatically dark sky, the pointed engines cutting across the wings like zig-zag lightning flashes. Sometimes, the picture on the wall is a photograph of the base commander. 'There were only a few of these, and I managed to snag one for my office,' says a captain, proudly, unctuously.

When a crew is on alert duty, which is normally for a week at a time, they are living three minutes from nuclear war. If their families live on base, they cannot be with them, but must live in a building facing the flight line, and known familiarly as the hurry-hut. They live and sleep in their flying suits. Each crew has the use of a car, with a yellow lightning flash along one side and the words 'Alert vehicle' written on it. They are permitted to go together two minutes' drive from the flight line, which usually takes in the post exchange and the base movie theatre and bowling alley. If they separate, they co-ordinate their movements. The one who goes farthest away takes the car, and arranges to pick up the others on the way to the aircraft. It is all quite a strain.

They have their target folders at hand, with up-to-the-minute details of their wartime target. Each crew is connected in their minds by invisible wires to this point in the Communist world, and when the klaxon sounds, they start moving along that wire. Lt-Colonel Jack Young, a lanky, cheery Missourian who piloted a B-47 until they were phased out, says, 'You move real fast when that klaxon sounds. Your reflexes get real good. You're out of bed and into your flying boots before you're awake. If all is calm in the world, we don't worry very much. We reckon it's just another practice. But if there's a crisis somewhere, the heart starts going pit-a-pat just a little more.'

SAC fliers do not always share the bellicose views usually attributed to the Air Force. Certainly they are not bellicose in manner. They tend to be relaxed, cool, friendly men, intelligent and responsible, with very high technical ability, though not on the imaginative side – imagination can be a burden if you're on alert duty. There is little to distinguish them from any other group of middle-class citizens, except that they are almost all crew-cut, and trim and in good condition.

Like all professionals, they are concerned with means rather than ends. They devote an enormous amount of effort to learning how to deliver a bomb to its target; they are content for the most part to leave it to others to decide whether it should be delivered. Lt-Colonel Wilbur C. Carraway, when he was Deputy Commander for Operations at a SAC base, put it this way: 'The President has got a lot of smart people advising him. If he gives the order, it means that he's decided it's necessary. It means they're going to hit us. The only question is, are we going to hit them? I've never lost any sleep over dropping a hydrogen bomb, and I never will. The only thing I'm going to lose any sleep over is whether I can get to the target and carry out my mission.

'Getting back? Well, that's my own business. We've got a saying in SAC, "You're working for General Power when you're on your way to a target, but you're working for yourself on the way back."'

Today's bomber pilot combines the adventurousness of anyone who wants to fly with a high degree of technical sophistication. He must go through a staggering amount of classroom and book work. He has to retain in his head more than most Second World War pilots ever had to learn. A pilot has a list of items to check over with his crew, in the plane before takeoff. The checklist is a loose-leaf book containing about 600 items, and running through it takes up to two hours. (When a plane is on alert status, the crew go over the checklist every morning, and keep it at the ready.)

A high-performance military aircraft today is a world of its own, demanding of its inhabitants but sustaining them, detached from the world in which other people live and the bomb would explode. Flying in a bomber eleven miles up, at almost the speed of sound, the crew member can hardly feel a part of the world outside the steel frame, where there is not enough air to breathe nor enough warmth to support life. The pilot and co-pilot alone look out, and this on a strange blue-black sky and clouds miles below. When you are a crew member of a modern jet bomber, you become a part of the aircraft, your body a part of the machine, strapped and clipped to your seat by your parachute pack, oxygen mask and helmet. The machine is your muscles, your sense organs. You move only by activating some part of its mechanism, not your own muscles. To turn around in your seat, you push a lever underneath it; to speak, you turn a switch on the oxygen mask and hear your voice over the earphones, metallic and clouded by static.

Most SAC fliers reckon in conversation that they have about a 50-per-cent chance of surviving their mission. Not unnaturally, this takes precedence in their minds over the lives of their potential victims, and they don't give much thought to them. Like most military men, they feel that risking one's life for one's country is unselfishness enough.

These men are dedicated to SAC, and proud to be a part of it. They believe firmly that SAC holds the peace of the world on its shoulders, and that if they were to falter, the peace would be endangered. After the Cuba missiles crisis, a lot of the fliers felt that the Navy and the marines received too much credit in the newspapers for America's strength in the crisis. In a conversation at a SAC base a few weeks afterwards, several of them insisted that it was SAC's instant readiness that counted. 'We were the hammer held over the Russians' heads,' one said, holding up his fist as if gripping a hammer, and the others nodding their agreement.

They like the other people in SAC. 'These are the finest bunch of guys in the world.' 'I haven't met one man in SAC that I don't like' – this kind of comment is heard often.

Sometimes, the bond between the men and their service seems almost like a psychoanalytic transference relationship. In one conversation, a co-pilot said that what he liked about SAC (he did not say the Air Force) was that if you had a crisis, it gave you whatever you needed: special leave, a doctor, a lawyer, a chaplain. The navigator of his crew, a balding, sandy-haired man puffing a pipe, slightly older than the others, supported him: 'I had a divorce. At first, I was pretty bitter. I thought it was the job. I was ready to quit SAC! But I talked to an Air Force chaplain, and my squadron commander, and they showed me that it wasn't the job, that it would have happened in any case, that it was *her*. I was real grateful.'

SAC doctors, and chaplains even, seem to share this dedication, and to feel that their vocation is to make men better members of SAC. One Protestant chaplain, an old Air Force man with two rows of ribbons, a sturdy erect crew-cut figure, fighting a heroic battle against the pains of multiple sclerosis, said that whereas lower-grade airmen often came to him with family and other problems, fliers rarely did. Anyone who was not a 'mature personality, well integrated' was soon weeded out. 'Mind you,' he went on, 'SAC fliers sometimes come to me on religious matters. These men follow their religion. I have pews in my chapel reserved for them. Occasionally, they have religious questions about their missions.'

What did he tell them? 'I tell them' – and here his brow lowered menacingly – 'the Bible says, "But if anyone provide not for his own, and especially for those of his own house, he hath denied the faith and is worse than an infidel." That's

Timothy 5, 8. They're defending their families and their way of life.

'I have had pilots, and trainee pilots, one or two, come to me and say their conscience does not permit them to fly with nuclear bombs and drop them. Well, the military doesn't require anybody to do anything that's against his conscience, so I tell the man's commanding officer and action is taken accordingly. What made them come to this view? I don't know,' he said indifferently, and shrugged. 'I haven't discussed it with them. Perhaps it was some article they read. Perhaps some religious fanatic got hold of them.'

The bombs that SAC deliver have become more powerful since the old fission bomb days, and the time when a fifteen-megaton explosion at Bikini seemed an incredible amount of destructive power. The B-52 bomber that crashed near Palomares in Spain in 1966, and the one that crashed in Greenland in January 1968 each carried four twenty-five-megaton bombs.

These bombs do not give the SAC pilot any great sense of power, nor does he want it. The power he wants is over his aircraft, the fine feeling of being able to control twenty-five tons of intricate machinery as a ballet dancer controls his body, to take it across a world he cannot see, through the clouds and over a precise point. He is equally remote from the human will that makes a decision on using or not using the bomb, and the human suffering that its use would cause. He sees himself as a part of a complex instrument, an agent between someone else's will and its effect. His pride is to function in this role perfectly. He has a sense of importance.

There is a similar instrument in the Soviet Union, and other pilots with missions. They, too, have developed technical skills of a high order, and they, too, are told that whether or not they complete their missions might decide the fate of their country.

But the Soviet bomber pilot has been trained in a different military tradition from the SAC pilot. Belief in the theories of Giulio Douhet is not a part of a Soviet Air Force litany. On the contrary, Douhet is often singled out as the prime example of a 'bourgeois adventurist military theorist', to quote the journal *Military Thought*.

In the past, Soviet military leaders never saw strategic bombing as the way to win wars. The major role of the Air Force, as they saw it, was to assist the ground forces, and most Soviet bombing during the Second World War was tactical. While the U.S. and British Air Forces proclaimed the number of tons of bombs they had dropped on cities, the Soviet Air Force counted up the number of tanks, trains and bridges destroyed behind the front line. After the war, students at Soviet military colleges were taught the lessons of the postwar Anglo-American Strategic Bombing Survey of Germany, which showed that the air raids did not damage the German war effort as much as was anticipated. So ingrained was this attitude that the coming of the atomic bomb did not change it, nor even, at first, the hydrogen bomb. The first nuclear war missions assigned to the Soviet Air Force were tactical ones, to support ground operations.

Soviet military writings in the middle and even late 1950s could hardly be more different from the dominant attitudes in the West at the time in their treatment of the role of nuclear weapons. 'Soviet military science decisively rejects any arbitrary fabrications that one could, as it were, achieve victory by the employment of one or another new weapon. There are no such weapons which possess exceptional and all-powerful qualities', wrote Marshal K. Moskalenko, in a fairly typical pronouncement of this period. 'Strategic bombing will not decide the outcome of a war, but soldiers on the battlefield', wrote Major-General B. Olisov, in another. The army was very much the senior service, as it is today.

After the creation of the long-range missile force, around 1960, the case for the effectiveness of strategic bombing became overpowering, and traditional military attitudes had to change. 'Only with the advent of missiles have unlimited prospects opened up for the employment of nuclear weapons', wrote the authors of *Military Strategy*, the standard Soviet textbook published in 1962.

Even then, strategic bombing was often accepted with reluctance rather than enthusiasm. 'It is clear to everyone that it is impossible under modern conditions to separate military from civilian targets. If war breaks out, the centre of armed struggle will shift inevitably from the "front lines" to the deep rear of the belligerent countries', wrote Lt-Colonel S. Barteney in *Red Star,* the Soviet Ministry of Defence paper.

This reluctance is partly ideological, a reflection of the humanitarian side of Marxism. In theory, all Soviet wars are wars of liberation; the Soviet Press still speaks of the 'liberation' by the Red Army of the Eastern part of Germany in 1945. The enemy is always an evil regime, and if the masses fight for this regime, they are misguided. But obliteration by nuclear bombs can hardly be represented as a form of liberation.

The Soviet nuclear bomber crews have not been imbued as deeply as their American counterparts with the belief that they are the primary military arm of their country. They probably do not think as rigidly as their Western counterparts of a one-mission war, but more in terms of a traditional, prolonged bomber's war, like the Second World War. There has been considerable discussion in the Soviet military Press about how long a nuclear war might last. There is no past doctrine of a spasm war.

They do not have the same intimate familiarity with nuclear weapons and their nuclear war mission. In the Soviet Air Force, tight control of nuclear bombs is favoured at the expense of readiness, even more than in the American services. The prevention measures have little of the sophistication of those in the American Air Force; there is no equivalent of the fail-safe procedure. Most nuclear weapons are simply locked away. Planes do not stand on the runways with nuclear bombs aboard, ready to roll towards their targets. (This may be due to fear of defection rather than of unauthorized use.) Probably, the crews do not know their targets; the details of the mission are sealed orders, to be opened by the squadron commander and distributed to the pilots if war breaks out or appears imminent. Even during the Cuba crisis, Soviet bombers were not dispersed as S.A.C's were.

As in the U.S. Air Force, the bombs they carry have become much more powerful over the years. They may even run up to sixty megatons, more powerful than any Western country has cared to make.

A few years ago, most people, if they could have seen into the future to the present day, would have wondered that these men and these bombers should be at air bases around the world, ready to carry out their missions against cities. If this seems to follow logically and inevitably from the past, it is only the very recent past that has prepared people for this phenomenon, softening up their moral sensibilities before nuclear bombs made their surprise appearance.

In most ways, the world has become more humane in the last two centuries or so. Slavery is unthinkable, physically cruel punishment is rare, the massacre of prisoners of war, common practice in past times if it suited the circumstances or the mood, is regarded as a war crime, and even animals come under the protective umbrella of our humane concern. In one important respect, however, people are probably more cruel in intent and certainly more so in practice than they were. Governments are willing to massacre huge numbers of civilians with fire and explosives in order to achieve their ends, and even in order to spare the lives of their soldiers.

This willingness to slaughter is so new that it is surprising that it came to be accepted so rapidly. It happened during the total-war mood of the Second World War. In 1938, the Secretary of State, Cordell Hull, denounced the Japanese bombing of Chinese cities, and called on aircraft companies to impose a 'moral embargo' on exports to countries that bombed civilians. In 1939, British leaders condemned the German mass bombings of Warsaw as a 'barbarous outrage', and President Roosevelt called for another 'moral embargo' on exports to Russia because Soviet planes bombed Helsinki in the Russo-Finnish war.

Yet within three years, the R.A.F. was raining down blockbusters, incendiaries and phosphorous bombs on German cities with the announced intention of 'saturating' them, the American Air Force went on to burn up whole sections of the main Japanese cities, and it finally dropped the two atom bombs on cities. In Korea, bombers and guns slaughtered civilians, 'enemy' and 'friendly', before advancing troops, so that far more civilians were killed than soldiers. The justification of these tactics with their terrible toll of women and children was that they saved the lives of fighting men, a striking inversion of the values of chivalry. Much of the war in Vietnam has been the same story. And today men of governments can, without noticeable shame, threaten to drop hydrogen bombs on cities.

When historians of some future period look back on this particular time, they may well decide that the bomber pilot is its representative figure: physically fit, mentally alert, brave, the master of fantastic technological creations, soaring high above earth as men once dreamed of doing on precision-tooled wings of metal alloy, inflicting death, injury and pain on people far below whom he does not know, cannot see, and for whom he feels neither hate nor any emotion whatsoever.

6. Third Party: Drifting into Deterrence

Britain's decision to build her own atomic bomb was not taken by Parliament, nor even by the Cabinet, but by the Prime Minister of the day, Clement Attlee, and a defence sub-committee of the Cabinet. The Secretary for War at the time, Emanuel Shinwell, has said he did not even know about it. It was communicated to the public on 12 May 1948, in a small phrase contained in a statement in Parliament by the Minister of Defence, A. V. Alexander. This was in answer to a question which he probably planted since it was asked by a member of his own party.

George Jeger asked at question-time whether the Minister was satisfied that adequate progress was being made in the development of the most modern type of weapons. Alexander replied: 'Yes, sir. As was made clear in the Statement Relating to Defence, 1948, research and development continue to receive the highest priority in the defence field, and all types of weapons, including atomic weapons, are being developed.'

Jeger: 'Can the Minister give any further information on the development of atomic weapons?'

Alexander: 'No. I do not think it would be in the public interest to do that.'

That phrase 'including atomic weapons' must be one of the great throwaway lines of British history.

If the intention in announcing the decision in this way was to pass it off as a technical military one, this was successful. In Britain, the country where the most articulate debate on the morality of nuclear weapons was to take place, there was very little discussion of the decision to build them outside specialized military circles, nor was any encouraged. Yet it had a significance reaching far beyond Britain. After the United States built nuclear weapons, it was inevitable that Russia would do so. These were the two giants that faced each other across a world of smaller nations. Britain's entry into the field opened the door for others. It meant that atomic bombs were not the prerogative of the giants, but part of the normal armoury of a powerful nation. In attempts to check the spread of nuclear weapons, it is difficult to find a logical reason to draw a line at any particular number of countries. But the Big Two would have been the easiest.

In Britain at the time, the decision was seen as a natural one. For one thing, most Britons still regarded their country then as a great world power, one of the Big Five victors of the Second World War. Of the others, France and China, occupied by the enemy and then rescued, were members of the Big Five only by courtesy. Britain manufactured every other piece of military equipment that the great powers had.

Also, the Government during the war had regarded Britain as an atomic power, in partnership with the United States. The first development programme for an atomic bomb was started in Britain, and when Harold Urey and George Pegram came over in early 1941 from the Chicago laboratory of the Manhattan Project, they were so encouraged by the progress being made towards separating u-235, and the seriousness with which it was taken, that they went back and urged successfully an advance to the next stage of the American programme. The British programme was merged with the American one, and moved to the United States to take advantage of the resources of America's industry and the safety from German bombing. It was seen from London as an Anglo-American partnership. The angriest exchanges of messages between Winston Churchill and President Roosevelt during the whole course of the wartime alliance were over the American refusal in the later stages to share information with British atomic scientists.

The wartime agreement, which included a mutual promise by the two partners that neither would use the bomb without the other's consent, was terminated in 1948. There was resentment on the British side, and it seemed natural to go ahead with the work that was begun in 1940.

Britons at that time were not in the self-doubting mood that was to overcome them some years later. They had a high opinion of their country, and this was shared by most others in the Western world. Britain alone had resisted Nazi Germany for the whole five-and-a-half years of war. Now she was dissolving an empire to give other peoples self-government, and, in a period of postwar shortage at home, she was trying to ensure fair shares for all. There were few fears about increasing Britain's national power.

The newly-established Atomic Energy Authority, Britain's equivalent of the A.E.C., embarked simultaneously on programmes to develop atomic weapons and also atomic power for civil use; in Britain as elsewhere, nuclear reactors were over-rated at first as a source of electricity-producing power. Harwell was set up in 1946 as the centre of the atomic power programme, on a wartime R.A.F. airfield some forty-five miles from London. A weapon factory was established at Aldermaston, also near the capital. All the decisions regarding nuclear weapons were taken inside the Government, and the weapons were built solely by scientists working for the A.E.A. Unlike America, most of the scientific and academic communities were not involved. Sir William Penney headed the team producing the nuclear bomb, and he personally devised a new implosion method, more efficient than the wartime one, for bringing the uranium together into a fissionable mass. Britain's first atomic bomb was tested in the Monte Bello Islands, off the coast of Australia, on 3 October 1952.

At the end of that year, after the United States had exploded the first thermonuclear device at Eniwetok, the Conservative Government decided to go ahead and build a British H-bomb. But this was only announced in the 1955 Defence White Paper. This, too, seemed a perfectly normal decision. There was no agonized debate on the issue, no sense that it was a momentous step. A senior service officer involved explained the attitude: 'There didn't seem any question about it. When the jet engine came along, and it was more powerful than the piston engine, we replaced the Lancaster bomber with a jet bomber. Nobody argued that we shouldn't. Well, in the same way, it seemed perfectly normal to replace the atomic bomb with the hydrogen bomb. After all, the Americans had them.'

But by the time the decision was announced, the Bikini explosion had taken place, and had been explained to the world. One man, at least, had the historic sensibility to see the hydrogen bomb as more than just an improved bomb. Nearly always, it has been younger men who have been able to break free from old conceptions and to grasp the newness of the hydrogen bomb. Yet this was a man eighty years old, whose personal military experience included the cavalry charge at the Battle of Omdurman in 1898. In the debate in Parliament on the 1955 Defence White Paper, Sir Winston Churchill, in one of his last speeches as Prime Minister, said:

There is an immense gulf between the atomic and hydrogen bombs. The atomic bomb, with all its terrors, did not carry us outside the scope of human control or manageable events, in thought or action, in peace or war. But when Mr Sterling Cole, the Chairman of the United States Congressional Committee, gave out, a year ago, the first comprehensive review of the hydrogen bomb, the entire foundation of human affairs was revolutionized, and mankind placed in a situation both measureless and laden with doom.

Sir Winston went on in this same speech to give his now famous vision of the age of mutual deterrence by H-bombs:

A paradox has emerged. Let me put it simply. After a certain point has been passed, the worse things get, the better. The broad effect of the latest development is to spread almost indefinitely, or at least to a great extent, the area of mortal danger. ... Then it might well be that, by a process of sublime irony, we shall have reached a stage in this story where safety will be the sturdy child of terror, and survival the twin brother of annihilation.

In the service of the H-bomb, Britain's nuclear power programme was given a bias towards the production of weapons material instead of electric power. The uranium diffusion plant at Capenhurst was set up to separate u-235 from natural uranium enriched to a low level; that is, uranium that contains 5 per cent u-235, seven times the amount in natural uranium. This is useful in power reactors. But when the Capenhurst plant was finished in 1954, it was turned into a high-enrichment separation plant to make almost pure u-235 for bombs. Later, is was made into a low-enrichment plant again, when Britain reached a secret agreement with the U.S. Government to get u-235 from America in exchange for plutonium.

Queen Elizabeth opened Calder Hall, on the bleak coast of Cumberland, as the world's first full-scale atomic power station, in a ribbon-cutting, speech-filled ceremony in October 1956. This was billed as Britain's great advance in 'atoms for peace'. It was not mentioned at the ceremony that the decision had been taken a short time before to optimize Calder Hall for the production of plutonium for bombs, rather than electricity. This is done by pulling the uranium rods out of the pile when a part of them has turned into useful plutonium, which would deteriorate if they were left in. This shuts down the pile for a while and cuts its output of power for the electricity generating station.

By 1957, Britain's first H-bomb was ready for testing, but now the Australian Government would not allow it to be tested in Australia because of the fallout danger. A test site was established at Christmas Island, a British-owned Pacific island even more remote than Bikini, with no inhabited islands within hundreds of miles. The British H-bomb was exploded there on 15 May 1957. It was a droppable bomb, using tritium in the lithium-6 method; there was little fallout, since it was a two-stage bomb, without any uranium-238 envelope.

Production of H-bombs was slow for a while. When the first processions filed past the wire fence that surrounds the Aldermaston factory, with their banners protesting against its manufacture of H-bombs, it was turning out only about five a year.

But production stepped up after two years, and as it did, the R.A.F.'s atom bombs were dismantled and replaced by H-bombs.

By the late 1950s, Britain had a powerful nuclear striking force. She had atom bombs and H-bombs, and modern, high-performance jet bombers. Principally, they were three types, called the V-bombers because of the initials: the Valiant, Vulcan and Victor. The Victor was the most advanced bomber in the world when it first flew in early 1953. Later, the Valiants were phased out of a nuclear war role, and the Victors converted to V-force tankers, leaving the Vulcan to carry the bomb. The Royal Navy had Buccaneers, which could fly off the decks of aircraft carriers with nuclear weapons.

This military power was of a novel kind. It was the ability to destroy; but it was not strength, in traditional international terms. Britain was not now a first-rank world power, along with the United States and the Soviet Union, by any conventional criterion. She could not hope to conquer, dominate or powerfully influence either one. But she had the power to inflict greater destruction on either one that it had ever known. With this potential for destruction went irremediable vulnerability. A Soviet general once told a British visitor, 'There are optimists and pessimists in Britain. The pessimists think five H-bombs will wipe out everyone in Britain, the optimists think it would take eight. We have 200.'

This contradiction was turned into a policy by Duncan Sandys, as Minister of Defence, in his 1957 White Paper. This is an extraordinary document, perhaps the most honest defence policy statement ever issued by a government up to that time. Sandys was certainly the first Defence Minister to tell his people that in a major war the Government cannot defend them. 'It must be frankly recognized that there is at present no means of providing adequate protection for the people of this country against the consequences of an attack with nuclear weapons', the White Paper said baldly.

The policy was massive retaliation, the American 'new look' in its starkest form. There were the same cuts in defence spending and rundown of conventional forces. Conscription would be ended in 1960; the armed services would be reduced from 690,000 to 375,000 by 1963. Forces in Germany would be reduced. Though some lip-service was paid to the need for defence on the ground in Europe, it was evident that the policy was to rely on deterrence, not defence.

The White Paper made it clear that if war ever came, the fighter planes would not even try to defend the cities. Their mission would be to defend the bomber bases for as long as possible, to give the bombers time to get on their way, carrying their nuclear stones from a glass house. To this day, the only places in Britain where there are signs pointing to fallout shelters are R.A.F. airfields.

In the theory of deterrence, Britain's nuclear striking force could match up to Russia's more powerful force. Air Marshal Sir Dermot Boyle explained this in a lecture. This was the new, clean kind of military arithmetic, in which losses are measured against one another in cities, or in countries or proportions of them. The addition and subtraction is easy, and even a civilian can do it.

'The size of a deterrent force,' said Sir Dermot, 'must be related to the value to an enemy of the prize being protected. For example, suppose – I repeat, suppose – Russian leaders were prepared to sacrifice half their country in exchange for the removal of the U.S.A. from the competitive scene. Then, for the American deterrent to be usable, it would have to be demonstrably capable of destroying far more than half Russia in retaliation. But Russia would not be prepared to accept anything like the same damage in exchange for the removal of the United Kingdom. Therefore, a much smaller retaliatory force can give us as much or greater security than the U.S.A. achieve with their vast nuclear capability.'

The V-bomber force was given two sets of war plans: one for a British war, and the other for a war as part of the N A T O alliance. For the latter, its target list was co-ordinated with the much larger S A C list made up at Offutt. The 1960 British Defence White Paper referred to it not as a British deterrent force, but as 'the United Kingdom's main contribution to the strategic nuclear power of the West'.

Those in Britain who argued against an independent nuclear force questioned whether any situation could ever arise in which it could serve a useful purpose. British defence specialists have worked out a few such situations, not in answer to these arguments, but for their own understanding. Here are two, devised not because they seem likely, but because they do indicate the *kind* of circumstance in which Britain might be protected by a nuclear retaliation force. The first was devised by Defence Ministry officials during Sir Alec Douglas-Home's premiership, the second at a seminar on defence at the London School of Economics.

British forces move into Kuwait to defend it against attack, at the request of the Kuwait Government, as provided by treaty. Russia sends in forces to help the attackers, and British troops are engaged in fighting against Russians. Russia then warns that if Britain does not withdraw, she will destroy a major British city – say, Manchester – with a nuclear bomb. This is a threat she would not make if Britain had a nuclear deterrent force.

The second: Race war breaks out in Africa, and Britain takes steps to protect white communities from massacre, shipping them arms and other supplies. The Soviet Union (or China), anxious to win favour with the Africans, supports their cause, and accuses Britain of imperialist aggression. After some days, she says that unless Britain ceases all support within twenty-four hours, she will drop a nuclear bomb on the port from which supplies are being sent, Southampton.

The implausibility of both these hypothetical cases lies in the assumption that an enemy would threaten to drop nuclear bombs on Britain over some peripheral issue. This seems extremely unlikely, in view of the international events of the H-bomb era. Russia could take very effective military action against Britain over a Kuwait or an African situation without resorting to nuclear weapons. To meet this threat, Britain

149

would need larger and more powerful forces, not a nuclear deterrent.

Sandys' 1957 Defence White Paper also contained an important technical decision. Plans for a supersonic bomber to succeed the V-bombers were scrapped. Instead, when advances in anti-aircraft rocketry made the V-bombers too vulnerable to be effective, a medium-range missile would carry the British nuclear bombs to their targets, to be called Blue Streak.

This was spoken of by the Government as a British-made rocket, but in fact it was to be Anglo-American. Britain lagged in missile technology; the British services had never really believed in missiles, despite the V-2 experience. Wernher Von Braun was brought to Britain after the war along with some other German rocket engineers from Peenemunde, but no work could be found for them. For the successful British missile projects – Sea Slug, Blue Steel – there are many that were cancelled. Under the aegis of the U.S. and British governments, firms in the two countries agreed to collaborate on the production of Blue Streak. The airframe and guidance system were to be American, the motors British.

The cost of the Blue Streak rose far above the planned figure, which was a feature of all missile projects at that time, British and American. When it was cancelled in April 1960, it was not primarily because of rising costs, but because it was obsolete before it was completed. Liquid-fuelled, taking two hours to fire, and without protection, it was a generation behind the new missiles being built, quick-firing from underground concrete silos, or else from nuclear-powered submarines.

Before the Government announced cancellation, it obtained the agreement of the U.S. Government to the purchase of an American airborne missile, Skybolt, then being developed by the Douglas Aircraft Corporation. This had a range of 1,000 miles or more, and could be launched from a plane this side of an enemy's defences. It would put off for years the obsolescence of the bombers. With this agreement, Britain ceased the effort to keep up with the advancing technology of missiles. From now on, Britain could have a nuclear striking force to last into the future only with American help.

In Parliament, the Labour Opposition scoffed at the Conservative Government's dependence on the United States for a nuclear deterrent in the future, and even doubted whether Skybolt would be delivered. They had some reasons for doing so. After Kennedy took office in January 1961 the United States entered a new phase of defence strategy, when it wanted all Western nuclear forces concentrated in its own hands, and it no longer had the same high regard for British power that previous administrations had shown.

There were also serious technical doubts about Skybolt; launching accurately a rocket from a speeding bomber was proving a more difficult feat technically than had been expected. There were reassuring words from the manufacturers, but after an abortive test in April 1962, Robert McNamara, the Defense Secretary, said publicly, 'Skybolt still has serious development problems. I'm less optimistic than either the Air Force or Douglas.' If the British Government still insisted in Parliament that it would have Skybolt, this was partly wishful thinking.

When word came in late 1962 that Skybolt was to be cancelled, it caused a political crisis in Britain, to the amazement of the Kennedy Administration, and an outburst of anti-Americanism on the nationalistic right wing. These suspected that the cancellation was not on technical grounds, but part of a plot to rob Britain of her nuclear-power status. The British Defence Minister, Peter Thorneycroft, telephoned McNamara, and told him that cancellation of Skybolt without the provision of a practical alternative would be a serious blow to Anglo-American relations. Macmillan spelled this out in a message to Lord Harlech, the ambassador in Washington, to pass on to the State Department. They had already decided what they wanted as the alternative: submarine-launched Polaris rockets. They took this request to the Anglo-American summit meeting in the Bahamas, which had been planned long before.

The gap between attitudes towards nuclear weapons was revealed when Thorneycroft and McNamara sat down together at Nassau for the first time. McNamara had come prepared, with graphs and charts of the figures on Skybolt, showing why the decision to cancel had been reached. Thorneycroft was puzzled when he saw these papers, and waved them aside. He could leave the nuts-and-bolts stuff to the boffins. He wanted to talk about what it meant *politically*.

Macmillan came away from Nassau with an agreement to buy Polaris rockets and firing sections for five nuclear-powered submarines, on generous terms. The submarines themselves were to be built in British shipyards. This was to be Britain's nuclear force in the post-bomber phase.

The ban-the-bomb movement, marginal though it was to party politics, brought the issue of Britain's nuclear deterrent right to the centre of the political scene. The Labour Party was split between the anti-bomb Left, with neutralist and pacifist sympathies, and the centre and right committed to the NATO alliance and the nuclear deterrent. The centre and right held, though there were some empty gestures in opposition to placate the Left, such as a call for the delaying of tests until an East–West summit meeting, and opposition to the establishment of a U.S. Polaris submarine anchorage at Holy Loch, Scotland.

After the cancellation of Blue Streak, the Labour Party swung around to opposition to the prolongation of an independent nuclear force. They derided it as 'nuclear vainglory', in Patrick Gordon Walker's terms, a great-power pretension, immoral and, since it depended on American help, fraudulent. After Nassau, the opposition rose to a clamour. At its 1963 annual conference, the Labour Party passed a resolution saying: 'Britain should cease the attempt to remain an independent nuclear power, since this neither strengthens the alliance nor is now a sensible use of our own resources.' Harold Wilson quoted this approvingly in Parliament, and said, 'That was our position. Was and will be our position.'

Labour often argued that the independent deterrent was

even harmful to the Western alliance, because Britain should be spending the money it cost on bringing forces in Germany up to strength. The Labour Party at this stage combined emotional opposition to nuclear weapons with intellectual fidelity to the Atlantic Alliance. It managed to be both pro-American and anti-bomb.

During the 1964 election campaign, the ageing Lord Attlee was brought before the television cameras to refute Conservative arguments on the usefulness of Britain's bomb. In a brief appearance in a party political broadcast, he said: 'I see Sir Alec Douglas-Home says he wouldn't feel confident in meeting leading politicians from other countries unless he had an independent deterrent. Now it's odd, you know, I never felt like that. ... If a man had any personality, he could put across British policy without a nuclear bomb in his hand.'

This is not what he said some years earlier, when the days when he was Prime Minister of a nation possessing nuclear bombs were closer and fresher in his mind. In the parliamentary debate on 2 March 1955, he said: 'I think we have influence in the world. This influence does not depend solely upon the possession of nuclear weapons, although I have found in practical conversations that the fact that we do possess these weapons does have an effect upon the rulers of other countries. It is quite an illusion to think that it does not have an effect.'

Labour went into the 1964 election pledged to maintain the V-bombers for the rest of their useful life, to convert the Polaris submarines into non-nuclear weapons or else cancel the programme, and to 're-negotiate the Nassau agreement', Wilson was never explicit about what he meant by this last. As it turned out, it did not matter. When he returned from his first visit to Washington shortly after becoming Prime Minister, he was asked whether the Nassau agreement was discussed. He said it was not, and little more was heard of it.

There was a curious lack of surprise when the Labour Government came to power and ignored what was probably the only Labour defence policy ever to have the support of all factions of the party. This does not reflect total cynicism about election promises. Most likely, it reflects a disbelief that anyone can give up nuclear weapons, whatever they may say when they don't have to make the decision, as if there would be something unnatural about such a renunciation, a reversal of the order of things. It almost seemed sometimes that the H-bomb had a growth and development of its own, the 'apparently compulsory trend' that Einstein saw in the original super decision.

The Government turned over the V-bombers to NATO, abandoning their independent nuclear war role, but retained operational control. It continued the Polaris submarine programme, first of all with the intention of turning the vessels over to some kind of NATO nuclear force. While such a force was under discussion, a potential British contribution could give Britain some influence over its composition. When the idea of a NATO nuclear force was finally killed, the Government went ahead with the programme anyway, reducing the number of submarines from five to four. Mrs Denis Healey, the wife of the Minister of Defence, launched the first one in early 1967. In mid 1969, the last of the V-bombers were phased out, rendered obsolete by the advances in anti-aircraft missilery, and the submarine fleet took over the role of Britain's deterrent force.

The Government does not see this new weapons system as an independent nuclear weapon in a military sense. They do not envisage its ever being used independently of the alliance. They will not consider any international move that could lead to its use, such as a defence guarantee, along the lines of the U.S. guarantee to Western Europe, to some country with which Britain has particularly close ties, like India. If nuclear weapons represent power to Britain, it is political power. They are a status symbol, a token that might be traded; they are for political-psychological rather than military use.

But the weakness in Britain's position as a nuclear power has always been political and psychological rather than technical. It was not the means to destroy that was lacking, but the will to do so. In so far as a country can have communal feelings, Britain does not *feel* like a nuclear power.

Britons underrate the destructive power of their country's nuclear weapons, as if they shrink from accepting responsibility for this kind of power. Many less well-informed people think vaguely that it is tied to some kind of American button; like many people abroad, they know very well that France and China have their own nuclear weapons, but are not sure about Britain. Yet in 1966, the Hudson Institute, a research organization in Harmon, New York, that does studies on nuclear strategy, calculated that Britain had 1,000 times as much nuclear bomb power, measured in kilotons, as China. The Hudson Institute calculated also that in purely military terms, until 1958, Britain could have inflicted more nuclear damage on Russia than Russia could have on the United States. Hardly anyone in Britain at the time would have believed that.

There was stiff resistance in British official circles, and in the services, to modern American thinking about nuclear strategy, a mocking rejection of any subtleties, any complexities, any calculations that would make the problem either broader than a narrow, specialized military one – 'In the end, it's a common-sense military problem, old boy' – or smaller than apocalyptic – 'Once those buttons are pushed, that's it, and I don't care what your computers say.' This resistance has been overcome partly by years of contact with the strategic debate, assisted by the presence in the Defence Minister's post of Denis Healey, who believes at least in thinking things through. Even so, there has never been a public study made of the overall effects of a nuclear bombing attack on Britain; evidently, that does not bear thinking about.

There is a comfortable finality about this. Nothing can be done. There is no need to look for ways to limit the war, or the damage. No prospect of struggle, bereavement, or agonizing problems of survival. There is no need now to worry about civil defence, or compulsory military service either, for that matter.

The simple, fatalistic view of nuclear war was put for many by Jimmy Edwards, the John Bull of British television comedy, when he was, on one slightly eccentric occasion, a Conservative candidate for Parliament: 'I'm interested in human stuff, you know, rents, traffic, housing and all that. Defence? Not really. I think there's an inevitability about it: one day, somebody's going to let one off, and that'll be that, won't it?'*

There is a significant dissonance in the answers to two questions put to Britons by the National Opinion Polls in May 1963.

One question was: 'If there was an atomic attack on Britain, how many people do you think would be killed on the first day?' The replies revealed a picture that is surprisingly far from total annihilation. Only 3 per cent thought that more than half the 60 million population would be killed. Twenty-nine per cent gave figures under 10 million, and 20 per cent under 2 million. In this picture, most people would have a fairly good percentage chance of surviving. But when the question was asked, 'In such an attack, how would you rate your *own* chances of survival?' 70 per cent of those questioned said 'poor' or 'no chance'.

To most people, the idea of anyone in Britain having the power to initiate this obliterating, once-and-for-all war is pure fantasy. The button just does not seem to be British. But the weapons exist, and some men in Britain do have the power to use them.

Several men who know what it is to share in this power were asked by the author, 'Can you imagine ever giving the order to go to nuclear war?' Here are some of the replies:

Sir Alec Douglas-Home, former Prime Minister: 'If we were the victims of a nuclear attack, the response would be ordered; the Polaris are second-strike weapons, and therefore never used first. Even after the attack, there would be remnants of the community on which to build.'

Peter (now Lord) Thorneycroft, former Minister of Defence: 'If the deterrent has to be used, it's failed. I think it's

* In an interview with Peter Black in the *Daily Mail*, 12 March 1963.

wiser to spend more time thinking of safety catches than of what you would do if war came.'

Denis Healey, Minister of Defence: 'If you asked me whether any possible gain is an adequate cause for initiating a nuclear war, I'd have difficulty in replying. But if you asked me whether it is justifiable to prevent war by threatening to initiate nuclear war, then I think it is. I won't answer more directly than that.'

And two others, who at one time would have participated in such a decision: 'Yes, I would do it. If you're in this business, you must be willing to ask a few people to lay their lives on the line. And if you're prepared to sacrifice some lives, then you can be prepared to sacrifice many more. I don't see any difference morally.'

'I've been a soldier. You have to make choices like that as a soldier, and you sometimes choose death, for yourself and others. The Poles knew they could only lose in 1939, but they fought. The Jews of Warsaw fought, though they knew they were going to die. The military virtue means that: being willing to choose death instead of life, to say that life under certain circumstances is unacceptable. People do choose death in certain situations; that's what makes human beings dangerous.'

Others in Britain live close to the button in a different sense. They are the men who man Britain's four Polaris-carrying submarines. Each of them spends two months at a stretch under the sea, playing his part in maintaining Britain's deterrent, along with about 150 other officers and men and sixteen missiles with H-bomb warheads. The power to kill more people than in any war in history is in each one of these submarines. The nuclear trigger here really is a trigger, the butt of a pistol without the barrel, connected to the wall by a wire flex. Gripping this butt and squeezing this trigger launches a missile. There are two triggers, and one finger on each of them, one belonging to the Captain, one to the Polaris Systems Officer, though others' help is needed in carrying out the entire launching process.

When one of these submarines is on its mission, it is in a state of something like war. The point of a deterrent is that it must be ready for use at any time. Besides, the world can change a great deal during the two months that a submarine is at sea, and it is not for a naval officer to decide whether the international situation has become tense or relaxed. At every moment, one of these British submarines, and often two, is within striking distance of the Soviet Union, its weapons at the ready, maintaining radio silence so that its location remains undetected.

But life on board is not tense, or strained in any way. There are the normal problems of isolation, familiar to navy crews. But life is much more comfortable than in most submarines because these are much bigger, 425 feet long. There is at least some privacy. Each man has his own bunk with a curtain and locker, instead of sharing one with a man working a different watch. Officers and men each have a small wardroom. With an effort, one can lead something like a civilized life. The men in these submarines, as well as being above average in their technical skills, are chosen also for their stability of temperament. 'A man's got to have a sense of humour,' senior officers say, in a very British sort of way. The atmosphere in the officers' wardroom is one of cheery informality, braced by a stiffening of service tradition and manners, the officers genial, very agreeable, middle-brow professional men. A coffee percolator is always on the stove, a sign of the American background of the weapons and American training of many of the officers, which has had its influence on their life-style and terminology.

Until recent years, all submariners were volunteers. But now that the Navy is much smaller, men are assigned to submarine duty. Few of these want to go into the Polaris submarines, but, when they have the option of leaving, more than 80 per cent of them, officers and men, elect to stay in.

There is no one overriding reason. For many, the closeness of life in a submarine seems to have a womb-like attraction. With this, in the Polaris submarine, there goes the sense of being a cog in a very complex and finely-tuned mechanism. There is also the technical appeal of working on a part of the most sophisticated and complex weapons system in the world.

As with any nuclear war mission in any service, operations are too tightly programmed to suit some adventurous spirits. As one slightly discontented Polaris man said, 'I'm used to going around looking for ships to sink, even on an exercise. On one of these boats, you aim at a quiet life; if you see any other ship, you get out of the way.'

In their skills, their attitudes, and their life-style, Polaris submarines represent, probably more than anyone else, what is often termed 'the new Navy'.

The old Navy was the White Ensign fluttering in the breeze in ports on every continent. The new Navy is courses in abstruse technologies, and merit awards for refinements in computer techniques. The old Navy was tea on senior officers' lawns, and silence before the opinion of the Admiral's wife. The new Navy is family life in an executive-style estate bungalow with an officers' dining-in night once a month. The old Navy was a 90-per-cent intake of officers with public school backgrounds; in the new Navy, it's 30 per cent. The old Navy was the barking of orders. In the new Navy, it's 'I say, Smith, I think it would be an idea to check over the spare parts inventory.' The old Navy was waiting for a war so that you could do the job you'd been trained to do. The new Navy is meeting a technical challenge, in the hope and expectation that there won't be a war.

There are two crews for each Polaris submarine, called the port and starboard crew, and there is also one additional full crew from which specialized replacements for any of the others are taken. Each crew takes the boat (in the Navy, a submarine is always a 'boat', not a 'ship') for two two-month missions a year, so that each is ashore for eight months of the year. While they are ashore, they have training and administrative duties.

The base of the Polaris fleet is Faslane, on Gare Loch, a few miles away from Holy Loch where the American Polaris submarines have an anchorage. A sizeable support base and submarine school have grown up at Faslane, where the brown-heathered hillsides glow picturesquely in the sun when they have a chance, but more often lie dank and sodden under the battering rain. Polaris submarine crewmen have administrative duties there; they help maintain shore equipment and they help run the Polaris weapons school. The living quarters are landscaped handsomely into the hillsides, and the facilities are excellent, from the ratings' newly-equipped gymnasium and heated swimming pool to the panelled officers' mess with its picture-window view of the loch and its basement night club that is available for private parties. But Faslane is not a popular base with Navy men: it is a bit isolated, and there is little local life for them. Some leave their families in the South and commute.

Wives have mixed feelings about Polaris submarine duty. The husband is at home more than most men on seagoing Navy duty. And his life has a schedule, so that, unlike most Navy men, he can plan a social engagement or a holiday months ahead, and know that he will or will not be home for Christmas. But most wives find the lack of communication from their husbands nerve-wracking. As one put it, 'I keep thinking of him sitting at the bottom of the ocean in that metal hulk, and know I'll have to wait until the end of two months to know whether he's alive, whether the submarine comes back. I'd rather he was living it up in foreign ports. At least I'd get postcards from him. Still, you get more used to it.'

The wives do not generally think of their husbands' roles as potential agents of annihilation, nor do the men themselves. For the issue of firing the weapon hardly ever arises. For one thing, it is easier not to think much about it. As one said, 'If you spent two months in a submarine *thinking* about that, you'd go crazy!' For another, they believe, when they do think about it, that the deterrent works. 'I don't think a nuclear war will ever happen,' said one officer. 'The deterrent makes sure of that.' This was a hesitant answer to a question, not the snappy confident response that would have come from a well indoctrinated S A C man.

It takes a wilful act of imagination for a submariner to connect his work with fiery slaughter and destruction. A bomber pilot must at least know where his target is, and fly towards it. Not even the captain of a submarine knows where the targets of his missiles are. Most of the crew never know where *they* are.

In the officers' wardroom, the politics are mainly Conservative, but mildly so, and rarely passionately anti-Communist or passionately anything. Belligerency would be out of tone. It is difficult to imagine one of these men saying, as one R.A.F. V-bomber station commander said, jabbing his forefinger aggressively into the air: 'If a few million of our people are going to get slaughtered, then I want to make jolly sure that a few million of theirs are going to get slaughtered too!'

At sea, work occupies most of the day. Equipment has to be maintained in working order: the computers that operate the navigation system, the ones that operate the missile guidance, the devices that measure the temperature, density and flow of the water outside the submarine, the ones that monitor life inside it. There is a constant monitoring of all the parts and the links between them, and frequently minor repairs have to be made.

The missile section, just behind the conning tower, is a forest of great vertical tubes bisecting the boat. At its entrance, a chain slung across the aisle supports a red-bordered sign that says 'Entrance to unauthorized personnel is forbidden'. Near the entrance, dials and indicators carry intriguing names: Systems Logic and Control; Elapsed Time; Underwater Launch Current.

When the term 'nuclear' is used on one of these boats, it does not refer to the explosive power of the warheads, but to the engine. A whole staff maintains the atomic reactor behind its lead shielding, in the stern. Everyone wears a disk containing a piece of photographic film that is checked at the end of each voyage for radioactivity. No submariner has ever received a dangerous dose.

Navigation is the biggest technical trick in the Polaris submarine, locating one's position under the sea precisely enough to fire a missile accurately. The submarine's position changes, the change is programmed into the missiles' guidance systems.

Contact with the outside world is constant one-way communication. The stream of incoming radio messages contains orders and weather reports; enough news to make up a one-page mimeographed daily news sheet; and messages from home, in the form of one twenty-word 'familygram' per week per man. Every man fills out a form when he joins a crew saying when he wants to be told if there is a disaster in his family: immediately, forty-eight hours before landing, or upon landing. It is a strain if he is told immediately, since he cannot do anything about it, or even send a message back.

Men read, usually light novels, and practise their hobbies. Model-making is a favourite one. On a recent cruise on the *Resolution*, a model contest was held, and crewmen entered ships, a bone knife, a plaque, a matchstick galleon, and a tapestry. Sex and women are constant topics of conversation, of course, and there are as many pin-ups as on other ships. Among the ratings if not the officers there are the jokes about masturbation that are a part of boarding-school lore.

Each crew of Britain's Polaris submarines has launched one missile, minus the warhead, on a Caribbean firing range, in the course of its shakedown cruise. But Polaris missiles are very expensive, and after this one, there are no more test firings. Frequently there is a readiness test, in which a simulated firing procedure is ordered from home base, and the crew go through the entire firing procedure as an exercise.

The Captain of the port crew of the *Resolution*, the first of Britain's Polaris submarines, is Commander Howard Mann. He first went to sea in 1945 in a cruiser, and has been in submarines for some nineteen years. He is patently decent and painstaking, sensitive to the needs of the men under his command, but reticent about his own feelings. He does not believe there will ever be a nuclear war. 'It would be insane to start one, and nobody would do it,' he says. But then he adds, with some emphasis, 'If it was ever required of me, I would not hesitate to carry out my duty. Any decision on the moral aspect has to be made before joining the Polaris programme.'

He is a religious man, and when they are at sea, he takes a Church of England service every Sunday. At every service, he reads the same short prayer, which he wrote himself shortly after taking over his *Resolution* command: 'God bless this ship, and her true purpose. May the fact of her being and the reality of her presence ensure that the awesome weapons she carries are never used, and guide the leaders of nations to this end. Through Jesus Christ's sake. Amen.'

At sea, a Polaris submarine Captain carries on him at all times the key to the firing control system. The Polaris Systems Officer, or P.S.O., carries another, similar key. Only when these two keys are inserted in their locks and turned can the missiles be launched. But the co-operation of other officers and men is needed to carry out the launch.

The location of the places from which orders are sent to the submarines is one of the most closely guarded secrets in Britain, since eliminating these would in effect eliminate Britain's nuclear deterrent. The procedure for sending a message to fire, and for the actions to be taken upon its receipt, are laid down rigidly, and a similar procedure is followed in a firing exercise.

An exercise message is received on a teleprinter in the submarine's radio room, and the wireless operator deciphers it. When he sees what it is, he sends out an alert to all senior officers. One officer comes to the wireless room, and confirms the interpretation. Then they take the teleprinter message together to the Captain.

By this time, the Captain has gone to the control room along with his executive officer. This is located just where the control room is in a conventional submarine, beneath the conning tower, looking up into its cylinder. It is more of a foyer than a room, since it looks out along the main corridor of the submarine in both directions. Here, he is surrounded on all sides and above by dials, indicators and switches, the rococo of the age of technology. On one side of the control room are two seats facing two three-quarter-circumference steering wheels and a set of controls, looking like the cockpit of an airplane. Two ratings sit in these seats manning the controls, and the Captain gives them orders.

The Captain speaks into a microphone: 'Set condition 1SQ.' Everyone on the boat goes to his action station; clerks become missile men and cooks become engineers. There is a crisp tautness in the air now. This is what it is all about – a perfectly-executed exercise, that is, not anything to do with nuclear war. Commander Mann gives orders to the two ratings at the steering wheels to manoeuvre the ship into a suitable position for firing. He inserts his key into the missile launch lock, and turns it.

The key man on the ship now is the Polaris Systems Officer. In the port crew of the *Resolution*, this is Lieutenant-Commander Brian Marshall, a characteristic product of the new Navy. He has a creased but boyish face, clear blue eyes, and large, stubby, strong hands, with which he likes to make things. He made crystal radio sets when he was nine, and now he makes tape recorders and hi-fi equipment in his hobby-room at home.

Lt-Commander Marshall did well at Oundle, but was more interested in mechanics than the classical education he was getting, and decided early on to join the Navy. He signed on for twelve years when he was seventeen. He was assured at the recruiting office in Charing Cross Road in London that he would get a commission within three months, but he was still a rating six years later. This was the only time he had doubts about his choice of career, but the commission came before they became too serious. He rapidly acquired specialized skills in radio and radar, and enjoyed some of the last days of the Old Navy life in Malta and the Persian Gulf.

He married a schoolteacher he met on a ski-ing holiday in Austria, and during a recent cruise, received a message from the Commander of the Polaris Squadron that read: 'mrs marshall wife of lt cdr marshall delivered daughter mother and baby well'.

Lt-Commander Marshall spent a year at school at Faslane learning about the Polaris weapons system. Almost all the time was devoted to the maintenance and launching of the missiles, very little to the consequences at the other end of the trajectory. He found the course fascinating, and enjoys the job that followed it. 'I like machinery, and this involves working with some of the most advanced machinery in the world,' he explains.

He has gone up to look at the teleprinter message with the Captain, then gone straight down to the missile control room. There are seven men at their action stations in there, all checking or monitoring the missile system. One wall contains 120 lights flashing on and off at different times, each one to announce that one particular part of one missile is functioning properly.

The count-down is a tense time for Marshall. Occasionally he has to report a delay, and then he feels it as a personal blow. 'The launch configuration is slow in coming to an action state,' he might have to say. He reports that all missiles are ready to fire, then he opens a safe for which only he has the key, and takes out a black pistol butt. There is also a red pistol butt for a real firing.

The Captain says, again over a loudspeaker system so that everyone hears: 'You have the Captain's permission to fire for an exercise.' Marshall grips the pistol butt in that strong hand and squeezes the trigger, and a sequence of lights shows that the missile would have left the firing tube and would be on its way upwards. If it were a real launch, he would then squeeze the trigger again to launch his second missile. The submarine would lurch a little as each one left its tube, through the operation of a compensating weight system. Water pours into the empty tube, and an amount of water equivalent in weight to the difference between the water and the missile is ejected from the ballast tanks. Marshall would squeeze the trigger sixteen times, and people a long way away would not know where the disaster and the pain were coming from. Then the *Resolution*'s mission would be over.

No, Marshall does not believe that moment, with its little lurch, will ever come on one of his regular operational cruises. But he has no doubt that if the order came, he would carry it out, any more than any of the others involved in the process. They all tend to think that the order would only be given in circumstances of appalling holocaust in which most of Britain would already be wiped out anyway, including their own families. 'It would mean that our world up there was already gone. It wouldn't make any difference' is the kind of remark one hears. Marshall does not make much of his moment with the trigger, but he does have some sense of his part in his country's military posture. 'Britain may not be a world power any more, but she does have this enormous potential power,' he says. 'Do you realize that the explosive power in those sixteen rockets is more than all the bombs dropped during the Second World War, including the atomic bombs at Hiroshima and Nagasaki? The Polaris submarine is the battleship of today, the Navy's main striking arm. Once you've been on one of these, anything else in the Navy seems less important.'

But deterrence is the reason why the *Resolution* is here, not the reason why he is here. It gives him a job to do. As far as he is concerned, it is a useful, honourable and challenging job, and he does it well. So for four months of the year he is under the sea, honing the equipment in his care, on the alert, ready to squeeze the trigger that is for him the trigger of a fascinating and complex machine.

7. 'Ban the Bomb'

The million-fold increase in destructive power during the first half of this century, and the vastly greater rapidity with which destruction could be inflicted, combined to produce the nervous world of the late 1950s, in which the megatons mounted and the hair-trigger response grew more delicate.

There were more bombers on both sides, more bombs, tighter alerts. H-bombs were delivered to more planes in S A C and to U.S. Navy planes on aircraft carriers, then, as they were refined and made smaller, to one-man fighter-bombers as well as the big planes, and, in the big ones, two to a plane. At Offutt, the target list grew longer, and priority ceased to have the same importance, since it seemed that there were going to be enough bombs for everything. One A.E.C. official said of this period, 'More targets were constantly being dreamed up. There were times when I thought *individuals* would be named as targets.' *

The danger was frightening, but of such a new kind that it was difficult to believe in it. But, like the twinge in the heart that is a coronary warning, there were the tests, in Nevada, in the Pacific, in Siberia, already shedding their radioactive fallout into the atmosphere, and putting strontium-90 into the world's milk supply.

By the middle of the decade, quite ordinary people were accustomed to seeing maps of their own towns with concentric circles showing radius of blast and fire effects, and they became familiar with terms like fallout and strontium-90. As more people realized the situation they were in, there was a movement to reverse this increase in megaton power, and to banish

* Quoted by Daniel Lang in *An Enquiry Into Enoughness.*

167

from the scene the weapons so laboriously acquired. It was an attempt to turn back the clock a few years, and annul the decisions in several capitals to build thermonuclear weapons.

A new viewpoint came into being, not directed against any particular group of people or any idea, but against a thing, the nuclear bomb. It went something like this: 'The hydrogen bomb is an evil so immense that it dwarfs any good purpose to which it could ever be applied. Its effects are too awful to be a factor in international power politics. As a means, it overwhelms any conceivable end. It is like the symbol of infinity in algebra: feed it into an equation and the equation is unbalanced, whatever you have on the other side. We don't want to be defended by the H-bomb. We're against all H-bombs, everywhere, whoever they belong to, whatever cause they are supposed to serve.'

This was not a pacifist viewpoint, but it drew a line in international violence this side of nuclear bombs; in America, this came to be known as 'nuclear pacifism'. People who espoused it wanted, like the members of the G.A.C. who recommended against a super programme, 'some limit to the totality of war'.

Initially, this feeling found its outlet in a campaign against tests. In America, the National Committee for a Sane Nuclear Policy (SANE, for short) was formed, with Norman Cousins, editor of the *Saturday Review* and author of *Modern Man is Obsolete*, as its Chairman. This sprang out of the wide response to a newspaper advertisement signed by several prominent figures, saying: 'We must stop this contamination of the air, the milk people drink, the food we eat.' In Britain, the Golders Green Committee for the Abolition of Nuclear Weapons Tests expanded to become the National Council for the Abolition etc., but it still seemed like a small, special-interest philanthropic group.

More eminent voices raised the test issue in the 1956 presidential election campaign. Adlai Stevenson called for an agreement to stop testing, a proposal that was denounced by President Eisenhower as 'a theatrical gesture' and by Vice-President Nixon as 'catastrophic nonsense'. Linus Pauling, the Nobel

Prize-winning chemist (he was also to win the Nobel Peace Prize in 1962), circulated a petition calling for a test ban among scientists; 11,021 scientists in forty-eight countries signed it.

In March 1958, following a series of nine test explosions, the Supreme Soviet announced that the Soviet Government would test no more nuclear bombs, and it expressed the hope that other governments would observe the same restraints. The U.S. Government declined to follow suit, but Washington was mindful of the goodwill that was accruing to Russia from this move. The following month, as part of the continuing pressure for arms control measures, Eisenhower suggested an East–West meeting of experts to discuss technical arrangements for a possible agreement to ban tests. The meetings started in Geneva in July; Ernest Lawrence was a member of the American delegation, Sir John Cockcroft and Sir William Penney were on the British one.

On 2 October the Soviet Union announced that it was resuming tests; it said it was forced to take this step because America had tested its weapons in the interim and gained a military advantage. But at the end of that month, after a long series of tests in Nevada, the United States and Britain announced that they were stopping all testing for a year. A few days later, the Soviet Union followed suit. When the year was over, the moratorium was extended by all three countries.

But by now, the anti-bomb movement had gathered momentum, and was not likely to be satisfied with this temporary, quarter-way measure. It became a movement to ban bombs as well as tests.

The biggest anti-bomb movement of all, the one that made the most impact and set off the biggest debate, was in Britain. It was here that the difficulties, contradictions and dilemmas of the position were manifested most sharply. The growth of this movement was a reflection of the world's thermonuclear predicament: its senescence is a reflection of another situation. This movement, as well as a home-grown hydrogen bomb, was Britain's special contribution to the thermonuclear age.

The anti-bomb sentiment must have been growing, as people learned what happened at Bikini and heard the arguments about genetic damage. In November 1957, a few months after Britain exploded its own H-bomb, the author J. B. Priestley wrote an article in the *New Statesman* arguing that Britain should give up its nuclear weapons as a contribution to ending the world's peril, in shrill, urgent tones ('Three glasses too many of vodka, or of bourbon on the rocks, and the wrong button may be pushed'). This was a fairly new idea then. The article had a surprisingly wide response; the *New Statesman* received more than 1,000 letters in support. Some came from well-known figures, not all of them the usual celebrities of liberal protest.

Kingsley Martin, who was then the editor, believes that another voice at about this time contributed to the flood of approval of Priestley's idea, one that contains an echo of the original H-bomb debate in Washington. Each year, the British Broadcasting Corporation commissions and broadcasts a series of lectures by one person, named, after the Corporation's first head, the Reith Lectures. This is a prestigious cultural event with a wide audience, and the lectures are usually published. The Reith Lectures in that year were given by George F. Kennan. In these lectures, he depicted the acquisition of more and more nuclear weapons as dangerously unrealistic, and the pursuit of a chimerical idea of national security.

Martin sent all the letters in support of Priestley's article to the National Council for the Abolition of Nuclear Weapons Tests (testing was still going on at this time) suggesting that this was a list of sympathizers if they wanted to get a broader movement going. The Council wrote to Canon John Collins, the Canon of St Paul's Cathedral, who had already spoken out against the bomb, and asked him if he would call a meeting of interested people. The Campaign for Nuclear Disarmament was born in Canon Collins's flat at a private meeting in January 1958. A number of people who were there became sponsors, including Professor Josef Rotblat, who solved the Bikini bomb mystery, Priestley, Martin, Bertrand Russell,

Ritchie Calder and the author Doris Lessing. The National Council representatives turned over to the C.N.D. the Council's membership list and funds. The C.N.D., with Canon Collins as its chairman, presented itself to the public at a meeting in Central Hall, Westminster, in February. More than 2,000 people attended.

Curiously, it was not this high-powered body that created the real outlet for public feeling, but a much smaller and more obscure body. This had its origins in a sort of nuclear-age *satyagraha* against Britain's H-bomb test by Harold Steele, an English chicken farmer and pacifist. Steele flew to the Pacific with the announced intention of sailing a boat into the Christmas Island testing area just before the British H-bomb test was due, so that if the British Government wanted to atomize a section of the Pacific Ocean, it would have to atomize him along with it. He arrived too late, but British support for his gesture coagulated into the Direct Action Committee Against Nuclear War. The leaders of this were pacifists, and were not public figures. The Chairman was Hugh Brock, the Quaker editor of *Peace News*, the pacifist weekly, a gangling, large-boned, gentle man.

They decided to stage a fifty-mile protest march, over four days of Easter, from London to the Atomic Energy Authority's weapons production plant at Aldermaston. If fifty or sixty people could be found to march, they decided, this would surely get into the newspapers. They laid plans and posted bills. A few left-wing Labour members of parliament said they would march; at a meeting, 250 people promised to come.

As the project grew, Pat Arrowsmith, an intelligent, high-voltage social worker who had volunteered to sail with Steele, was hired to organize it. Two weeks before Easter, she told Hugh Brock that several hundred people might march.

'The revolution always takes the revolutionaries by surprise', wrote Auguste Blanqui, the French prophet of insurrection and Communard. The Aldermaston March took its organizers by surprise. Their frail but passionate voice crying in the wilderness met with a thunderous response.

Five thousand people gathered in Trafalgar Square, in the centre of London, on that Good Friday morning in 1958. Four thousand of them filed through the streets leading westward out of the city in a two-mile column. On the wettest, coldest, windiest of those four days, there were never less than 900 people in the rain-lashed column that marched along the highway. A crowd of 10,000 shivered in the field opposite the Aldermaston plant with its barbed wire perimeter, and listened to Canon Collins, Michael Foot, the left-wing member of Parliament, Pastor Martin Niemoeller from Germany, and others tell of the terrible weapons that were being manufactured there, and the love of humanity that was being murdered.

One of the marchers was an American visitor, Bayard Rustin, the Negro civil rights leader. He was enormously impressed with the emotional power of this kind of demonstration, and it became the inspiration for the 1963 Civil Rights March on Washington, that high-water mark of the pre-Black Power civil rights movement.

'Ban the bomb' said all the banners on the road to Aldermaston, and this was the theme of the march. The enemy was not a country or a person or a party, but a thing. From the first day, Canon Collins marched ahead of the column, and the C.N.D. took over. The Aldermaston March became an annual Easter event, a mass pilgrimage of protest all over the world against nuclear bombs. Marchers in other countries even borrowed the Aldermaston marchers' symbol: the semaphore sign for N and D (for 'nuclear disarmament') in a circle, white upon black.

Why now? And why Britain? Why did the bomb move masses of people to protest at this particular time and place in the world's unease? Apart from world-wide nuclear fears now maturing, there were several local factors that can be isolated.

1. The 1957 Defence White Paper, which offered the British people no hope of survival in a nuclear war, but merely of a

posthumous victory by Bomber Command, presumably on points. Some people criticized the ban-the-bomb marchers for lack of hard-headed realism, but the marchers found Sandys' idea of defence practically metaphysical.

2. The recent disclosure that U.S. planes armed with H-bombs were flying patrols from British bases. This was intended to reassure the American public about America's readiness, but it certainly did not reassure the British. Many felt about SAC much as the Duke of Wellington once said about a particularly rough-looking bunch of his soldiers after he had reviewed them: 'I don't know whether they scare the enemy, but by God they scare me!'

3. The unique power position of Britain in the world. Britain had the nuclear bomb. Therefore, her moral problem was a real one, and she could act out a solution that she chose. It was not a theoretical problem about what *other* people should do. However, Britain was a second-class nuclear power, and not primarily responsible for deciding the fate of the world. She had some room to manoeuvre, and could afford the luxury of moral evaluation.

Also, the Russians now had nuclear weapons and the power to annihilate Britain. The possibility of annihilation is a sharp spur to rethinking one's moral position.

4. The spread of nuclear weapons. Britain had just joined the thermonuclear nations, and France intended to join. If Britain pulled out immediately, this might induce others to draw back. It seemed to some that the world had reached a crossroads.

5. The Anglo-Saxon Protestant conscience, which is rooted in the soil of England, and of which this movement is a typical product. This involved an attitude which insists on the right and the obligation of the individual to make up his own mind about moral issues, and to act on his decision. It is a melodramatic, rather than a tragic, view of life, which believes it is possible and even obligatory to separate good from evil, and to condemn evil. It has produced Victorian missionaries, *John Brown's Body*, and that admirable illogicality, the right of conscientious objection.

173

6. The climate of Britain at the time. This was post-Suez Britain, a time of confusion, scepticism and disillusion, and of emigration. It was a time when the first postwar generation came of age, a generation with no sense of fulfilment stemming from the Battle of Britain and V-E Day. It was the time of *Look Back in Anger*. 'There aren't any good, brave causes left', complained John Osborne's Jimmy Porter, looking back on the Spanish Civil War.

Well, here was a cause, and it seemed good and brave. And here were some leading lights of the British theatre's new wave, and also undergraduate and postgraduate Jimmy Porters from universities up and down the country, and their duffel-coated girl friends too, marching under banners like 'Cambridge University Students Against the Bomb' and 'Southampton University Says Ban the Bomb'. The students were very much in a minority, outnumbered by young parents wheeling children in push-chairs as proud proof of their concern with the bomb's threat; stolid, middle-aged couples forcing back grins of British embarrassment at their public display of feeling; some homely old Socialists, and a few gaudy eccentrics. Volunteers with cars provided logistic support, and collected droppers-out with blisters or sore feet.

Here and there in the column were walking jazz bands, wearing bowler hats and garish waistcoats, bringing marching tunes and cheerful frivolity, and they beat out with gusto the new Aldermaston March songs. The favourite began:

> Can't you hear the H-bomb's thunder,
> Echo like the crack of doom? ...

There was an attractive cameraderie there, an infectious moral enthusiasm, a certainty of the rightness of their cause, that was to pull more people into these hikes, and that many people today look back on nostalgically. It was easy to feel that the marchers represented all that was healthy in a world ruled increasingly by fiendishly destructive machinations. Or at least to feel as the wife of a political journalist did after watching them file by with their songs and their banners. 'I think I'm for them,' she said thoughtfully. 'Their answer is a negative one, but all the other answers are negative too, and in a much nastier way.'

On this first Aldermaston March, one found all the elements that were to make up the unilateralist movement, as those who favoured unilateral nuclear disarmament came to be called.

There were fellow-travellers on all these marches and demonstrations, and a fellow-travelling tone crept into a lot of the speeches, through wishful thinking. If you are arguing, in effect, that it is better to be Red than dead, it is easy to slide over into saying that whereas being dead is awful, being Red is not really all that bad.

There was the mixed dislike of being mass murderers and fear of being murdered. Some of the speakers at the nightly meetings along the march demanded, 'Do you want to threaten millions of men, women and children on the other side of the globe?' More often, they reminded their audiences how few thermonuclear bombs it would take to exterminate the population of this crowded island.

There was the left-wing philistinism, with its scornful talk of 'these politicians', its huge oversimplifying of the problem of means and ends, its rejection of subtleties and necessary abstractions in favour of 'common sense'. The marchers applauded platform statements like: 'The politicians have mismanaged things until the world is on the edge of disaster! Let the ordinary people have a say.' C.N.D.'s oversimplification of issues was to be aptly parodied in the stage revue *Beyond the Fringe*, with a caricature of a unilateralist union leader saying, 'We polled the members of my union, and asked them, "Do you want your wife and children to go up in smoke?" Ninety-eight point two per cent said "No." If that isn't an overwhelming vote for the unilateralist position, then I don't know what is!'

One also heard ordinary people questioning, sometimes semi-articulately, the whole meaning of international politics and action in the thermonuclear age. They were taking a fresh, worried look at the standard tokens of political intercourse – country, freedom, victory, defeat – to see what they represented now in the hard currency of human life and happiness and dignity. 'I fought for my country in the war, but that sort of thing doesn't seem to make sense any more.' 'What are these H-bombs supposed to be defending?' A lot of remarks like this were heard along the march.

The number of Aldermaston marchers increased after that first year. The C.N.D. organized all the subsequent ones, and expanded its influence. All over the country, people marched against the bomb in smaller demonstrations. There were marches to American Air Force bases, a march by seventy teenagers across England, a march led by a vicar's wife riding a white horse.

The Aldermaston March was an inspiration to people in other countries, and the white-on-black C.N.D. sign was adopted widely as an anti-bomb symbol. In Japan, the Council Against A and H Bombs quickly acquired widespread support and an anti-American tinge, and came under Communist influence. It spawned a radical, non-Communist anti-bomb body with a wide student following, the Zengakuren. In West Germany, the anti-bomb movement also had a large youthful following, and came under the dominance of the Social Democratic Party, then in seemingly permanent opposition. For these and other national movements, Easter became a time of protest. At Easter-time, 1960, there were ban-the-bomb marches in twenty countries including America, all carrying C.N.D. signs.

In Britain, the C.N.D. had some influence also at the upper levels of society. A number of supporters had close links with the Establishment, people like Commander Stephen King-Hall, the writer and former member of Parliament, Professor P. M. S. Blackett, and Ritchie Calder, a science writer, and these saw that the C.N.D. view was at least heard and discussed in high places.

The movement began by being a-political. But there were questions that seemed to demand answers, and the activists found they had to take sides. It was not enough just to be against the bomb; it was not *quite* that simple. Were they only against the British bomb? Did they want to be protected by the American bomb?

The first national C.N.D. conference, shortly before the second march, adopted a platform that called for unilateral nuclear disarmament by Britain *and* withdrawal from NATO. This did not immediately affect the character of the demonstrations, though some of the sponsors quit. But later, the C.N.D. came to be identified with the left wing of the Labour Party. For a while, it seemed that they aimed at converting, not the whole country, but the Labour Party, then in opposition. They thought briefly that they had succeeded. At its 1960 annual conference at Scarborough, the party came out for unilateralism, over the fierce opposition of Hugh Gaitskell, the leader. But the vote was a fluke; the parliamentary party did not follow this policy, and it was reversed at the next party conference.

The C.N.D. still retained its vigour, and its moral enthusiasm. A right-wing Labour M.P. threw a familiar argument at them when he offered to pay their fare to Moscow if they would demonstrate in Red Square. Shortly afterwards, they did just that, taking advantage of an invitation to a Moscow peace congress to carry Russian 'Ban the Bomb' banners in Red Square, until they were torn down by some Muscovites. They did not dun the M.P. for the fare.

The C.N.D. grew in numbers, too. Sixty thousand took part in the 1961 Easter March, which was *from* Aldermaston, where the bombs are, *to* London, the centre of national power, an army of banners that stretched for four miles. But it was already becoming something of an all-purpose, left-wing ritual. Slogans denouncing Gaitskell, the Conservative Government, race prejudice and Moise Tshombe mingled with the white-on-black C.N.D. symbols and ban-the-bomb signs. Its make-up became younger; duffel-coated, folk-singing youngsters played more of a role.

The dominant mood of the first Aldermaston March was

outraged parenthood. By the fourth, it was adolescent revolt.

The C.N.D. was only one part of the ban-the-bomb movement in Britain. Most of this time, there was a parallel movement with the same aims and overlapping membership. This was the anti-bomb civil disobedience movement. People who took part in civil disobedience believed that the world's peril was so great that it transcended any obligations to the laws of governments. Some cited as precedents the early Christian martyrs, and Thoreau and Gandhi.

Again, Hugh Brock's Direct Action Committee showed the way for less humble men to follow. They organized non-violent invasions of the Thor rocket bases that were then being set up in England under joint U.S.–British control. Demonstrators marched into bases and blocked construction work. They were sprayed with cold water and dragged through icy mud. Some were arrested and, when they said their consciences would not allow them to promise not to repeat the offence, were sent to prison for two weeks.

After a number of these demonstrations, police went over to the offensive. They arrested the five leaders of the D.A.C. who had called for a demonstration at the rocket base at Harrington, and charged them with incitement to commit an offence. Sentencing them to prison for three months, the magistrate, Sir Lawrence Dunne, said in court: 'I am sorry that I have to deal in this way with people who are, in other respects, estimable citizens.' This was the general opinion of the demonstrators: estimable people, with a bee in their bonnets about nuclear bombs.

The Thor rocket sites were deep in the countryside. It was for a new organization, the Committee of 100, to bring civil disobedience into the heart of the capital, and make it a national issue for the first time since the suffragette movement in the 1900s. This new body was largely the creation of Ralph Schoenmann, a Californian student at the London School of Economics, then twenty-five. He decided that anti-bomb civil disobedience could become a mass movement to shake the Government, providing it had two things: a list of nationally-known celebrities at the head, and a mass following.

He wrote to Bertrand Russell. Lord Russell saw him and liked him, and called together several people from the D.A.C. to discuss the idea. They decided to form a committee of 100 people with a body of followers – they aimed at 2,000 – pledged to take part in a civil disobedience campaign. The idea of the executive committee of 100 people was shared responsibility before the law. They thought the police could not single out anyone as being more culpable than the others (though the police did later on). They wrote letters to prominent people asking for their support in breaking the law.

The refusals are as interesting as the acceptances, reflecting the atmosphere of Britain at the time. Most were apologetic, and contained the underlying assumption that the cause was good. A well-known artist wrote, 'I hope you will not file my refusal among the mental dodgers and physical cowards.' A clergyman: 'I dislike holding back from so good an adventure, but ...' A retired Field-Marshal wrote to say that he was 'utterly opposed to nuclear war', but that as a reserve officer on half-pay, it would hardly be proper for him to take part in a campaign of civil disobedience. He went on, 'But apart from this consideration, I am not convinced that civil disobedience is the best or the right way to achieve your object, with which I am in entire agreement.' (Most people are opposed to nuclear war. It is doubtful that the Field-Marshal was really in agreement with *unilateral* nuclear disarmament.)

Others decided that the time was ripe for such a movement and gave their support: three leading playwrights, John Osborne, Robert Bolt and Arnold Wesker; Vanessa Redgrave; Penelope Gilliatt, the critic; Christopher Logue, the poet. A working committee was set up, and one of the less urgent topics it discussed was how to have the sciences better represented on the Committee as well as the arts.

The twelve-man working committee met in a room at Friends' House, the Quaker headquarters, to discuss what they would do with the civil disobedience troops they had acquired. Some bizarre suggestions were considered: disrupting Royal processions, jamming the B.B.C., kidnapping the Chancellor of the Exchequer on the annual budget day. What they decided upon was a demonstration at the Ministry of Defence which was then working out with the U.S. Government the agreement for the use of an anchorage at Holy Loch, Scotland, by Polaris-carrying submarines. They wanted 2,000 supporters to sit down and illegally block the pavement for three hours, while the leaders nailed a protest against the Holy Loch agreement on the door of the Ministry. Some of the more fanciful on the Committee compared this in its significance with Martin Luther nailing his Theses on Indulgences on the door of Wittenberg Cathedral.

This was the Committee's début, and it was a resounding success. Well over 2,000 people answered the call on that Saturday afternoon. It turned into an occasion which had a quintessentially English character: in the crowd's well-mannered orderliness, the authorities' pragmatic attitude; the leaders' punctiliousness about principles.

The crowd that squatted on the pavement behaved politely. The demonstration stretched from the steps of the Defence Ministry around the corner, and fifty yards down Whitehall. In legal terms, the demonstrators were all committing an obstruction, and the police could have arrested them. But no passer-by was being obstructed in fact, so the police looked on benignly. Lord Russell and the Rev. Michael Scott rose from their places at the head of the column, and marched over to the door. Lord Russell, his leonine features stern and set, his white mane bristling in the wind, carried the manifesto of protests, Scott a hammer and nails.

The Ministry door was large, shiny, and gleaming with golden polish in the cold March sunlight. The uniformed doorkeeper reacted with alarm at the sight of this tall and powerfully-built man advancing on it with a hammer and nails. He appealed to the senior police officers present for protection for his door. The officers told the pair that the door was

Government property, and they could not hammer nails into it. Lord Russell was adamant, and refused to leave the Ministry steps until he either nailed up his manifesto or was carried away.

The doorman seemed upset at the trouble he had caused. He came up with a suggestion. If his Lordship wanted to fix his sheet of paper to the door, couldn't he do it with transparent tape? He had a roll inside. (He clearly did not grasp the point of this demonstration.) Russell and Scott conferred on the steps on whether taping the protest rather than nailing it would be a compromise of principle or only of tactics. They decided that it would leave the principle inviolate, so they accepted the doorman's offer, and taped their document to the door. Then they strode back down the column to applause.

The 2,000-plus demonstrators stayed on the pavement until six o'clock, and no one was arrested. Clearly, Ralph Schoenmann had achieved his aim. The committee had big names, and it had mass support.

The Committee called other demonstrations, and people came to break the law in the middle of London. Thousands sat down in Trafalgar Square; police arrested and carried away 826 people, including Michael Scott, Osborne, Wesker and Logue. Four hundred and twenty-two fines were meted out. Much of Britain watched all this on television. There were sit-downs, picketings, peaceful invasions of nuclear bomber bases, and a spectacular attempt to board an American Polaris submarine tender in Holy Loch. There were pirate radio propaganda broadcasts.

Fifty demonstrators were arrested under a 600-year-old statute for refusing to call off a demonstration in Whitehall, during the autumn 1961 Berlin crisis. Forty-five of them, including Lord Russell, were sent to prison for a week, along with Lady Russell, Wesker and Logue. Scotland Yard invoked a little-used Public Order Act to ban Committee of 100 activities in central London during that weekend. Twelve thousand people thumbed their noses at the law and turned up in

Trafalgar Square. Barred by a massive cordon of police from marching down Whitehall, they sat down in the square and stayed all afternoon and some of the evening. Police arrested 1,140, an all-time record for arrests on a single day.

Most of the demonstrators were law-abiding, bourgeois citizens, who would rarely if ever demonstrate against anything else, let alone break the law, but were compelled by what they saw as the unique urgency of this situation. This is easily forgotten in a later period, when conspicuous protest is the characteristic gesture of the youthful and the rebellious. (In Scotland, where the unions are more politically active, the demonstrations had a more working-class character.)

Their mood responded to the widely-distributed leaflet signed by Lord Russell headed: 'Act Now Or Perish!' which began: 'Every day, and at every moment of every day, a trivial accident, a failure to distinguish a meteor from a bomber, a fit of temporary insanity in one single man, may cause a nuclear war which, in all likelihood, will put an end to Man and to all higher forms of animal life.' This was the characteristic ban-the-bomb voice, urgent, human, simple, direct.

The voice is heard in Wendy Butlin, a Committee member, writing from prison to President Kennedy: 'A friend of mine told me, "I am a Catholic. I am not so much concerned with what others do to me, as with what I may do to others." You, Mr President, are a Catholic, and you have it in your power to do great good or great harm to others.'

It is heard when some of the more boisterous demonstrators sing a song to the tune of *John Brown's Body*:

To hell with all the humbug and to hell with all the lies,
To hell with all the Charlies with their gift for compromise,
To hell with all the strontium continuing to rise,
If they don't ban the H-bomb now!
Ban, ban, ban the bloody H-bomb,
Ban, ban, ban the bloody H-bomb,
Ban, ban, ban the bloody H-bomb,
If you want to stay alive next year.*

* Words by the author Alex Comfort.

The voices had some impact, though more conventional views of armaments prevailed. A National Opinion Polls survey showed that in March 1959 the proportion of those who would approve of Britain giving up her nuclear weapons unilaterally rose to 30 per cent, with 50 per cent opposed.

With the Committee and its followers saying that the life of humanity was at stake, and the authorities talking about the need for law and order, no meeting of minds seemed possible. But once, the issues as both sides saw them were presented for all to see, in a court room. This was when the authorities staged a show trial of Committee of 100 members. As this was British justice, each side was able to stage its own show.

The ostensible subject of the trial was a non-violent invasion by several thousand people of the U.S. Air Force's fighter-bomber base at Wethersfield, Essex, in December 1961; the F-100s stationed there carried nuclear bombs. This time the police staged a counter-attack. They raided the offices of the Committee and the homes of its members, and arrested six of them. They were charged with conspiring to enter the Wethersfield base for purposes prejudicial to the interests of the state.

The state brought up star performers for the trial. The Attorney-General himself, Sir Reginald Manningham-Buller, was the prosecutor. The authorities wanted to make examples of these leaders of civil agitation. The six defendants pleaded not guilty, and proceeded to turn the trial into a political debate by arguing the last phrase of the charge: 'prejudicial to the interests of the state'. They said that they did indeed conspire to break into the Wethersfield base, but that the unobstructed operation of this base was prejudicial to the interests of the nation.

Trevor Hatton, a young accountant and unpaid treasurer of the Committee of 100, denied categorically that his own action was prejudicial to the interests of the state, and then added tendentiously, 'I ignore the question of the safety or interests of the United States of America.'

Terry Chandler, a full-time pacifist protester since student days, said, 'I did this in order to prevent the operation of a base which is in itself prejudicial to the wider interests of humanity.'

The Committee brought up big guns that it was not permitted to fire. Linus Pauling flew from California to give evidence for the defence on the ethics of civil disobedience. Sir Robert Watson-Watt, the inventor of radar, came from America to testify on the dangers of the hair-trigger deterrent situation. The Judge ruled that these questions were irrelevant, and would not allow them to give evidence.

It was Pat Pottle, a stocky, tweedy-looking twenty-three-year-old, who elicited the most dramatic piece of testimony in the trial, arguably the most significant words ever spoken in an English courtroom. Pottle was conducting his own case, and he cross-examined a key witness for the prosecution, Air Commodore Magill, the Director of Operations at the Air Ministry. The prosecution had brought in the Air Commodore to tell the court that the occupation of the Wethersfield runways by demonstrators would impede planes ready for instant takeoff.

After he had given his evidence, Pat Pottle asked him what he would have done if a state-of-war emergency had occurred when the demonstrators were blocking the runway. Would he have given the pilots the order to run over the demonstrators and take off? Would *he* if he were ordered to do so? Air Commodore Magill said, 'It is my duty to carry out any order that is given to me.'

Then Pottle asked suddenly, 'Would you press the button that you know is going to annihilate millions of people?'

Some people in the courtroom drew their breaths. This was an awful question to put to a man. The button was the great folk image of the second half of the century. Yet it existed, and this boyish-looking man in the witness box had access to it. Air Commodore Magill hesitated. Then he said, 'If the circumstances demanded it, I would.'

The five men on the Committee of 100 were sent to prison for eighteen months, the woman for twelve.

The Committee's style took on something of the knockabout

nihilism that was fashionable in Britain in the early 1960s, seen in the new destructive 'satire'. The Committee turned to stunts like publishing military secrets, blocking some M.I.5 telephone lines, and, the most successful of all, the 'spies for peace' stunt during the 1963 Aldermaston March. Following up some rumours, a few Committee members found an underground bunker built by the Government to serve as an administrative centre in the holocaust following a nuclear war, and inside it, details of some others and the names of those who were to occupy them. A group calling themselves 'Spies for Peace' mimeographed a seven-page pamphlet giving these details, and distributed 14,000 copies along the march, as well as sending them to newspapers. Then, defying the entreaties of the marshals of the march, they led a breakaway group in a detour to demonstrate at a bunker nearby. They scuffled with police at the entrance, and the Committee's Peter Cadogan told reporters, 'We're sitting on this place because we want to satirize the whole effort that's going into the preparation for nuclear war', using the vogue word of the year. For a brief time, the Spies for Peace were a national sensation. Coming after several security scandals, the circulation of nuclear war secrets as freely as trading stamps put the authorities in a ridiculous light.

Law-breaking has its own momentum. In time, the means came to overshadow the aims. There was a new bitterness in the Committee of 100 against the police and the courts, which lost them some of their support among respectable middle-class demonstrators. These were willing to defy the law for a moral principle, but not to become cop-haters.

They were replaced by younger elements, the folk-singing, mildly rebellious youngsters who gave the Aldermaston marches their characteristic appearance. Lacking an artistic *rationale* for their bohemian instincts, these found it in a political one. The movement also acquired its own *lumpen proletariat*. Shaggy-haired, rowdy youths fringing on the underworld, they used demonstrations as occasions to snarl, jeer and shout obscenities at the police. When the Committee of

185

100 staged a demonstration during the week of the Cuba crisis at the U.S. Embassy, Committee officials formed a cordon to throw back some of these who wanted to smash the Embassy windows, in co-operation with the police.

Support fell off, and big names dropped away, though few took the step of formally renouncing their connexion (no one wants to seem *pro*-bomb). Bertrand Russell left to start his Peace Foundation. The politics of the Committee came to be guided more and more by the activists who spent much of their time in the dingy offices above a printing works in North London rather than by the 100 or so people who gave it its name. There were more young intellectuals down from the universities taking a hand.

The passage of time and the continued existence of the human race have taken some of the drive out of the ban-the-bomb movement. Their deadlines have passed, and we are still here. 'Act Now or Perish!' is not a warning that can be repeated convincingly over many years. A C.N.D. member, Nicholas Walter, faced the position squarely when he wrote in a letter to the C.N.D. journal *Sanity*: 'The chief single cause of the decline [in support] is surely that most people are bored with it, and have learned to stop worrying and, if not actually love, at least live with the bomb.'

The difficulties of saying something simple about the bomb have multiplied since those first brave days at Aldermaston. The longer you live with the bomb, the more questions come crowding in. The C.N.D. and the Committee of 100 took stands on the NATO nuclear force and Vietnam, and some spread their net wider still.

Richard Boston, a young pacifist on the Committee of 100, expressed the dilemma in a pained and personal article in *Peace News*: 'You start with the slogan "Ban the bomb", and you very quickly find that you cannot take a stand on this one isolated issue without taking a stand on many other issues as well. You begin to look for the causes of war, and you try to think of ways of eliminating these causes, and you find that you have to make up your mind about race relations, the Common Market, industrial conditions, housing schemes, and everything else that concerns the individual and the state.'

This made it more difficult to go on feeling that the bomb was something qualitatively different from any other social evil. Yet it was this very feeling that drove and inspired the movement. The line they had tried to draw in international violence became blurred, and more difficult to define.

Some in the movement came to think more like politicians, to accept the world that has the bomb and try to manipulate it for the better. They devoted their moral energies to politics, the art of the possible, even though this meant joining the 'Charlies with their gifts for compromise'. Former C.N.D. supporters became members of the Labour Government.

Some who could no longer draw the line clearly at the bomb moved it in the other direction, and extrapolated their anti-bomb stand into an extremist world view. The Committee of 100 has contributed new vigour and new blood to two radical ideologies: pacifism and anarchism. Some Committee followers thought their way into a modern kind of pacifism, a tough-minded, knowledgeable rejection of war as a method of conflict. The leadership of the pacifist movement in Britain has passed largely into the hands of these young intellectuals, who tend to find the older, mostly Quaker pacifists fustian and woolly-minded. This development has its parallel in other countries. Many of the Committee of 100 have become anarchists, who see the hydrogen bomb as the *reductio ad absurdum* of government. Some became perennial demonstrators, and were sent to prison for storming the Greek Embassy in protest against the military dictatorship.

Participants in the C.N.D.'s annual Easter marches, greatly diminished in number, are more concerned with the international gamut of left-wing causes than with the bomb. In the United States, other causes drew the moral energies of young enthusiasts: civil rights, Vietnam. SANE became involved principally with agitation over Vietnam, and as a clash of values erupted in American society, protest became almost a social movement on its own with the C.N.D. white-on-black semaphore sign in a circle appearing at many of the points of confrontation. Protest demonstrations against some public action – marches, sitdowns, fights – became a part of the social scene; the ban-the-bomb movement began it.

For a little while, when the bomb was new, a great many people felt that there was something simple that they could say about it, something positive and right that they could do. Now, again, it seemed too big, and too complicated.

In its first great evangelical phase, the ban-the-bomb movement posed the question of the bomb, not in terms of politics, but in terms of conscience. Its questions were sometimes oversimplified, or distorted. But its voice will remain a nagging reminder of what is being talked about when nuclear strategy or nuclear politics are discussed: the trafficking in pain and death, or the threat of it, on a new order of magnitude. Others may find it easier to regard these things abstractedly, or remote from the imagination; not the ban-the-bomb people. They are a pressure group for the consequences.

8. The Protester: the Conscience of Pat O'Connell

If Mrs Pat O'Connell goes into a telephone booth, she puts the toe of her shoe into the door, holding it open just a crack. It is a little trick, nearly unconscious, to offset the fear she has always felt, since a child, at being in an enclosed space. She is so law-abiding that her husband laughs at her for it, and says she must have unconscious guilt feelings. She was very proud of her son, Sean, when he was eleven, and was commended in court by a magistrate: a man had robbed a shop and was running away followed by cries of 'Stop thief!' when Sean grabbed him and clung on until a policeman came.

Mrs O'Connell is the head teacher at a centre for delinquent girls, the mother of five children, and a young-looking grandmother. She has often left home in the morning and warned her husband that she might be under arrest instead of at home in the evening. Twice, she was sent to prison and locked in a small cell, once for a month. She was arrested because of her protests, beyond the bounds of the law, against nuclear weapons. The hydrogen bomb occupies a central part in Mrs O'Connell's life. Its existence has changed it beyond her imagining. Her society's possession of hydrogen bombs is something that she takes on her own conscience .

She is a tall, chunky woman with a warm, engaging, homely face, and burnished brown hair flecked with grey. When she relaxes, the separate parts of her face collapse into a soft smile, which is her natural expression. Her home is eight rooms of a brick-and-wood semi-detached house, in Norwood, a South London suburb, which they rent. A lodger, an old friend of her husband's family, lives in one of their rooms, a tall, spare, elderly man who is a wood polisher in a computer factory; he is friendly with the family and eats his meals with them. They also have a garden, which consists of a lawn and some casually planted flower beds, where nature is kept polite but not servile. The main room in her home is the kitchen-cum-dining-room, which has a separate larder and scullery, and is warmed by a large coal stove. Here members of the family spend most of their waking time, eating, drinking cups of tea, washing, ironing, reading, talking, playing with the cat.

Mrs O'Connell was born in Ireland, and though she came to England more than thirty years ago, her voice still has more than a touch of the brogue, and that characteristically Irish softness of tone that makes every statement seem like a confidential whisper.

The atmosphere in her home has always been one of warmth, gentleness and harmony. The family seem to take it for granted, and not to know how rare it is. Unlike most families where the ages of the children span eleven years, everybody has always been interested in what everybody else is doing, sister's boy friends and brother's exams. Everyone knows the people that everyone else knows. Even as children they would address one another in the gentle, courteous tones of their mother: 'Care to come into the garden and play a game of chess?' or 'Would you mind getting something for me while you're out?'

All the children support to some degree their parents' political views: anti-Establishment, anti-nuclear weapons, sentimentally left-wing, in their different manners. When Edmund, known always as Sonny, was ten, he told his mother he had persuaded five boys in his class that 'atom bombs are all wrong'. In these matters, as in most things, there is harmony, and this helps pull them through the difficult periods when Mother or, in one case, Father is in prison.

When she took her job at the remand home, she promised that she would stay out of prison and pay a fine as an alternative if she was arrested, so long as her conscience permitted it. She has always worried that a prison sentence would separate her from the children she was teaching, usually difficult or disturbed children. But, as she once explained, 'If the world doesn't get rid of its hydrogen bombs, then there won't be any children left for teachers to teach or for mothers to love.'

Mrs O'Connell was born Margaret Williams in a mining town in Kilkenny, a few score miles south of Dublin, where her family were members of the small Protestant community. She was one of six children of a stonemason who was often out of work for several months at a time. The family was poor, and there were weeks in which meal after meal consisted only of potatoes, or sometimes only of bread.

Pat went to England when she was sixteen, to get away from both the narrowness and the poverty of her life at home. She went first to stay with an ageing aunt in Bournemouth, who turned out to be a religious fanatic convinced that no girl should be seen in public except on her way to or from church, and also so parsimonious that Pat was even hungrier than she had been at home. Pat stuck this for two months, then took a train to London and got a job as a chambermaid and waitress in a small, good-class hotel. Her wages were just under a pound a week, plus her room and board and tips, but she refused all offers of tips. She laughs at this now. 'It was a kind of pride,' she says. 'I thought it was wrong to accept money as a gratuity. I wish I had my time there over again. Those other girls were *pulling* in money.' War was threatening then, and Pat took a Red Cross evening course in first-aid, because she wanted to be of some use.

She met her husband, Phil, during the Blitz. Phil O'Connell was small, sandy-haired, beefy, tough and politically-minded. A one-time regular in the Royal Air Force with nine years' service, he had been for a short time one of the mass of industrial unemployed, and he says today, 'I learned my politics on the dole queue.' He was a member of the Labour Party and marched in 'Arms for Spain' demonstrations. Phil came from Liverpool, and had joined the R.A.F. as an aircraft fitter at fourteen. He was assigned to the R.A.F. planes then carried aboard aircraft carriers, and he served in the Far East. In an accident in 1937, one hand was chopped off by a whirling propeller blade, and he was discharged.

When war broke out, Phil became a clerk in the Air Ministry, then, after he married Pat and took a refresher course in ordnance, an inspector in aircraft factories. He was sent from one factory to another all over the country, and she followed, living in furnished rooms, and had her first two children.

They made a good couple, complementing each other, and they do now. He is tougher-minded than she, realistic where she is tender, using his intellect where she would rely on her feelings, assertive where she would be retiring. When they are out driving and another driver commits some blunder, Phil will bawl a reprimand, but Pat will urge softly, 'Let it go, Phil. It was just a mistake.'

The O'Connells used to talk a lot about politics. Pat, with sympathies for the underdog and a strong feeling for social justice, decided that she was a Socialist; this was what Socialism meant to her. Like many humanitarian leftists, she talks about politics leaving out the factor of power. She sees Communism only as the spread of an idea. In the Cold War, she is usually quicker to blame the United States than the Communists, but she is no fellow-traveller, and she can be just as critical of the Soviet Government as of any other, and just as cynical about its motives.

They moved back to London in 1944 and took a small flat. Pat offered her services to the local Labour Party during the 1945 General Election, and did door-to-door canvassing. The party, recognizing her sincerity and intelligence, asked her to stand as a candidate for the Lambeth Borough Council in the local elections a few months later, and she was elected.

Her disillusionment with orthodox politics came quickly, and inevitably, 'I was disgusted with all the jockeying for position,' she explains. 'They were all worrying about who was going to be chairman of this committee and chairman of that one. That wasn't what they were elected for.' They persuaded her to serve her three-year term on the Council, but she did not run again. She shunned the pettiness of local political strategy as she was later to shun the moral ambiguities of nuclear strategy. She has a tendency to will the end and scorn the means.

Also in 1945, when Phil was thirty-two, he took up a new career, teaching. Though his formal education ended when he was fourteen, he was well read, and full of ideas about social needs. He applied for teacher-training, passed the interview, and took an emergency one-year teaching course. After teaching for some years, he became an Education Guidance master. Soon after, Pat also took a teacher-training course.

As a teacher, she became worried about the number of children who could not even read and write. So she took a three-month course in teaching educationally backward children, and taught special classes for these. It was gruelling work, but, she felt, worth while.

They worried about the Cold War in those years, and got angry at Senator Joseph McCarthy and John Foster Dulles, but they were not politically active. Their two eldest daughters, Wendy and Leni, went on the first march to Aldermaston when they were a spirited fourteen and sixteen years old, and Pat waved them off approvingly.

The first step towards involvement was taken by Phil. The action was straightforward, the motivation subtle. But he does not accept anything unthinkingly, and he has analysed this motivation. 'It was,' he explains now, 'one of those times when thoughts and feelings come together, so that they are the mainsprings of action. Like when you know something, but only after a long time does it suddenly click with you and become real, so that it influences the way you behave.' At that time, he was attending evening classes in abnormal psychology; social ills and possible remedies were coming to interest him more and more. One evening, the class was discussing morality, and how it can change from one social situation to another. Quite casually, as if the fact were axiomatic, Phil cited the accepted immorality of atomic weapons. And when he said it, the thought occurred to him, 'They *are* immoral, they *are* accepted, and I'm accepting them too. My God, I've got to do something about this. I can't go on accepting them.'

They joined the Croydon branch of the C.N.D., which was the nearest one to their home. The branch secretary, a solicitor, realized that he had a catch in Pat O'Connell's energy and dedication, and she was immediately co-opted on to the committee. She helped to organize three successful jumble sales, which raised money needed for meetings and propaganda but did little to express her own strong feelings. Like almost everyone in the C.N.D. at the time, she discussed with others the moral question of the civil disobedience resisters who were then beginning their campaign, and was not sure how she felt.

What decided her was the jailing of five Direct Action Committee members for calling an unlawful demonstration at the Harrington missile site. She was indignant at this. As she was making supper that night, she said to Phil, 'I don't know about you, but this is more than I can take. When they start arresting people for even *calling* a demonstration!' 'Let's talk about it later,' said her husband.

They waited until the children had all been put to bed, and then they talked about it, sitting in the two padded armchairs in front of the stove in the kitchen where they have all their talks. 'One of us has got to do something,' Pat declared, still angry. 'We can't both go because someone's got to look after the kids. I think it ought to be me. You're the chief wage-earner of the family. You earn nearly twice as much money as I do.'

So Pat wrote to the Direct Action Committee and said she was ready to take the place at the Harrington demonstration of one of the people arrested. She went along to their offices, was interviewed, and accepted.

The R.A.F. station at Harrington, which was being made to accommodate Thor rockets zeroed in on targets in Russia, is in Northamptonshire, some 160 miles north of London. Pat drove up there, in the four-seater car they had just bought, taking with her Wendy and Leni, who were to see her start the demonstration and return home that night. Pat packed as if for a picnic: thermos flask, sandwiches, warm clothes, change of sweater, and Sean's boy-scout tent. It was early January, when the schools were still out on Christmas holiday, so she was not working then.

She tried not to show Wendy and Leni, but she was frightened. She had seen photographs in the newspapers of other demonstrators being dragged through the mud by their feet, and flung aside. She is, and always has been, afraid of physical violence. When she talks now about seeing personal violence, her body tenses and her voice becomes a little more shrill. She was also afraid of the idea of breaking the law; she could not imagine not doing what a policeman told her to.

It was chilly and damp up at Harrington. It had been raining, and there was soft, squelching mud. When the demonstration got organized, with everyone in place, there was a row of ninety-two composed, conscientious law-breakers, blocking the entrance to the still uncompleted rocket site, and in front of them the police, a thin blue line. Everyone kept to his post like a sentry on duty. Pat stood, the icy mud seeping over the top of her boots, all through a wet and cold Saturday afternoon.

After the C.N.D. branch meetings and the jumble sales, she felt like a soldier who has passed through the rear areas and finally arrived at the front line. Here, she was confronting the nuclear weapons themselves, here she joined battle at last with the men who made decisions and had fingers on buttons. For a few unopposed hours, she helped to bar the way into a site where nuclear-warhead missiles were being erected and readied for firing. It was a good feeling.

At five o'clock, when darkness was coming on, the leader passed the word along that they were to pitch their tents and settle down for the night. There was a flapping and rippling of canvas down the line, and a police officer called out, through a megaphone, 'Please take your tents down. If you persist, I shall have to arrest you.' The demonstrators ignored the polite threat. Pat started to struggle with Sean's tent, and even with the help of a neighbour, she was having difficulty getting it up; she had never pitched a tent before. She was saved the trouble. A constable put his hand on her shoulder and told her she was under arrest. Stiff with cold, and dreading a night in the open, her only feeling, she found to her surprise, was one of relief.

The men and women under arrest were all shepherded into waiting police vans, the police helping them with their tents and carrying suitcases for some of the women. The vans drove to the little police station, where the ninety-two law-breakers milled around the desk while a sergeant wrote their names on a charge sheet and constables gave them all hot cups of tea. The hearing was set for the Wednesday, and they were remanded in custody.

So far, it was all rather cheery. Then the women in the party were loaded into two other police vans to be driven to a women's prison. Pat had an idea that from here on, it was going to be grim, and she was right.

The nearest women's prison was in Birmingham, forty miles away, the Winston Green Prison. It was midnight when they arrived. Here Pat entered a different world, where she was treated as she had never expected to be treated in her life. She was taken before a woman prison official and ordered to strip off her clothes. Then she waited, naked, while a doctor gave her a cursory examination, and asked her a routine series of blunt, personal questions about her age, personal history and medical background. Her stomach muscles tightened in rebellion as she answered.

Pat was handed two blankets, a sheet, a mug of cocoa and a bun. A wardress took her along to her cell, and locked her in. She was frightened and wretched as the door closed behind her, and she came near to panic when she looked ahead to three months or more in a cell. By now it was five o'clock in the morning, and she threw her sheet on her bed, pulled the blanket around her, and fell asleep in her clothes. She was woken an hour later by the morning alarm bell.

She washed in icy water, and was told to collect her breakfast, which was tea and coarse bread and margarine. She found all the food cold and hard. After three days, she was suffering from constipation and bad headaches. Phil, meanwhile, had made contact with the wife of a man who had been arrested with Pat, and they drove up to Winston Green together in her car, sharing the costs. He was shocked when he saw Pat. Her face was drawn, and almost yellow in complexion; she was unkempt, with her hair uncombed, and was listless and lethargic. She perked up just a little when he told her the children were well but missed her.

The next day, the Winston Green women's contingent of the Harrington demonstrators were all taken to Northampton Magistrates' Court for the hearing, and the demonstrators all met again.

The three lay magistrates decided to give the defendants a conditional discharge, the only condition being that they should not repeat the offence. To the magistrates' surprise, the defendants said they wanted time to retire, to consider whether they would accept the condition.

In the room they were given for this discussion, Pat argued, in effect, for going back to Winston Green prison, to the cold cell and dirty blanket and hard food. 'If we really feel that it's our moral duty as individuals to block the entrance to Harrington, then we shouldn't promise not to do it again,' she reasoned doggedly. The lawyer defending them had a professional disinclination to see his clients go to prison, so he produced a point calculated to influence them in favour of accepting the discharge. He said that new local circumstances had arisen. There had been a particularly brutal murder in Birmingham, a girl beheaded in a Y.W.C.A. hostel, and local police were looking for the killer before he committed another murder. To demonstrate again and tie down a hundred or so police would pull them off this desperately important hunt. Pat argued that the military could protect the camp, but a majority voted to accept the conditional discharge, and she went along with the majority decision.

She drove back to London with Phil. It seemed strange, for she had expected to be away in prison for much longer. It took her two or three days to get used to the idea that she was home again. She did not want to leave the house; she just rested, did

197

the housework, and felt the closeness of her children around her.

From now on, Pat was a full-fledged member of the D.A.C., and then of the Committee of 100 when that succeeded it. She marched to Aldermaston, sat down in Trafalgar Square, demonstrated and even spoke in Whitehall. She squatted outside the Ministry of Defence and cheered when Bertrand Russell taped his protest on the door. She attended committee meetings, put forward suggestions for more and more militant actions, and argued with others when she thought their tactics were wrong, or their motives shallow.

The others came to respect her and, most of them, to like her. They found a strength in her that they did not at first see, which came out in what she did and how she behaved. It is not something that is immediately apparent. In those blue-grey eyes, there is no glint of steel, no fierce, dogmatic note in her voice, nor even in what she says. She is certainly not without fear; no one has ever compared Pat O'Connell to a tiger.

But when she decides in her own mind that a certain course of action is the right one, then this becomes the only conceivable thing for her to do. It does not occur to her to turn aside for prudent self-interest. Nothing can make her do so, not fear of what she hates, like being separated from her family and locked up in prison, nor fear of losing her job, nor, it is quite clear now, the disapproval of others, nor hell or high water.

Pat used to speak sometimes at public ban-the-bomb meetings, and she was most effective with a small audience, not rousing but moving. What comes across when she speaks is a personal concern, a feeling that she is speaking to you and about you. She sees world affairs simply in terms of human beings. When she talks about international affairs, she sees a problem only of human consciences and human consequences. She has scant regard for the labyrinth of means that human beings enter to achieve human ends. She says to people, with genuine puzzlement, 'How *can* you be willing to drop a hydrogen bomb?' If somebody starts to talk about 'the Chinese' or 'the Americans' or the Cold War or national self-interest, she brings it back to you, and what *you* want and will accept, for yourself and your children, and children on the other side.

When she writes to a statesman – she has written to American and Soviet leaders about their governments' nuclear bombs – she is one person writing to another, about what the one might or might not do. She expects him to read the letter, or at least, if he is too busy for that, to be informed of its contents. If she asks a serviceman to pause and think about whether he is doing the right thing, she expects him to do so. *She* would stop and think if he asked *her*.

After Winston Green, the next to go to prison was Phil. The O'Connells were both arrested after a hastily-called sitdown to block the driveway at the Soviet Embassy, to protest at Russia's announcement that she was ending the test moratorium. The O'Connells appeared in court the next day, and were fined a pound. To pay would have been to admit that they were wrong, and would be against their principles. They stuck to the policy that only one of them should go to prison at a time, so that the other could take care of the children. She was facing a sensitive period at school, with a difficult class coming up for exams. They discussed it quickly; she paid the fine, and Phil went to prison for fourteen days. Partly as a result of this experience, Phil is now a member of the Prison Reform Council, and spends much of his spare time helping and counselling ex-prisoners, many of whom regard him as a sympathetic friend.

Pat O'Connell and six other women went to the Soviet Embassy again when Russia exploded a fifty-eight-megaton bomb. They sat down in the lobby and demanded to see the ambassador. After some delay, they were ushered into a reception room where an Embassy officer heard them out. He explained that Russia had to test nuclear bombs because of the threat of America's nuclear arsenal. Pat told him, 'You're all waiting for somebody else to take the first step towards peace. Why don't you take it? You say the same things that the others say. It's six of one and half a dozen of the other, so far as I can see.'

When the United States resumed testing shortly afterwards,

Pat and some other women wrote a letter to the American ambassador asking to see him. They received no reply, so they marched into the cool, spacious foyer, and refused to leave until they were carried out by policemen.

Some of the Committee of 100 people were committed pacifists, and gradually they persuaded Pat that her dislike of war could be unqualified, that her gentleness could become an ideology. Now she holds that even violence used in self-defence is wrong, that turning the other cheek is a viable way of life. Phil does not go all the way with her in this.

Pat was in on the early planning of one of the Committee's biggest demonstrations of all: a 500-mile march from London to Holy Loch, the newly-created anchorage of the U.S. Polaris-carrying submarines in the spring of 1961. The idea was to take a canoe up there, and then use it in an attempt to board the U.S.S. *Proteus*, the submarine tender which stores the missiles and their warheads. The hike was to start at Easter, immediately after the Aldermaston March, and finish on Whit Monday, seven weeks later.

A few weeks before Easter, the march leader dropped out after a sharp difference with the volatile Pat Arrowsmith. Pat O'Connell was at this meeting, and she went afterwards to a coffee-bar with Pat Arrowsmith. They discussed the problem of an alternative leader. Pat O'Connell made several suggestions, but they were turned down as unsuitable for one reason or another. Then Pat Arrowsmith said, 'You know who could lead this march?'

'No. Everyone I suggest, you turn down.'

'You could,' said Pat Arrowsmith. 'You'd make an excellent leader. And there's really no one else.'

At home, Pat told Phil about the suggestion, and gave all the reasons why she could not accept: the difficulty of being away from school for six weeks, of leaving the children, and so on, and she told him, too, about the Committee's difficulty in finding anyone else. Phil listened, then said, 'Of course, you know you'll have to go.'

There were sixteen on the march, pulling a kayak on the wheels of a baby carriage, accompanied by a car carrying their baggage. Having agreed to lead it, Pat was going to act as leader and set standards. She insisted that the march be sober, common-sensible, even respectable. (Her revolt against the H-bomb is not accompanied by any general bohemian revolt against convention.) One of the marchers had a beard, and she made him shave it off. She would not let any of the women wear slacks, except for the seaborne part. 'We're going to be talking to ordinary people on this march, to housewives and factory workers, and you're not going to convince them of anything if they think we're a bunch of bearded weirdies,' she told them.

They did not walk to Holy Loch the shortest way, but by a planned route that took them through a lot of towns, particularly in the Midlands. They held a public meeting in each town. Pat or one of the others spoke, and they handed out leaflets. Accommodation was planned in advance; local sympathizers put them up, or arranged for them to bed down in their sleeping-bags in public buildings.

As the miles of England rolled by and the days became sunnier, and the smoky industrial towns gave way to the open stretches and farming villages, there were times when Pat really felt that the hearts of all decent people in the world must be with them as they marched for sanity and against the bomb. She will remember all her life the sunny spring morning when they crossed the border into Scotland after an early breakfast in Berwick-on-Tweed, and found a Scottish miners' bagpipe band waiting to greet them, and to pipe them into their first Scottish village with the stirring 'Scotland the Brave'.

Near Holy Loch, Pat telephoned the commander of the *Proteus*, Captain Richard Laning. Surprisingly, she got to speak to him (*she* was not surprised). She told him that they were going to try to board the *Proteus*, but assured him that they would be strictly non-violent. He listened to her, but refused to receive a deputation to explain their viewpoint. He said cautiously, 'I've heard there are a lot of Communists among you, Mrs O'Connell.'

'No, that's not true,' she replied. 'There was only one Communist on the march, and he joined half-way, at Peterborough. And he's not taking part in the demonstration tomorrow. He doesn't believe in non-violent resistance, like we do. There are a lot of Quakers, though.'

Captain Laning shifted his ground. 'You should appeal to the British Government,' he told her. 'We're only here by courtesy of the British Government. I'm just carrying out orders.'

'It's not enough to say you're only carrying out orders,' Pat admonished him. 'You can still refuse to do something if you think it's wrong. Remember the Nuremberg trials? Defendants there were told they shouldn't have carried out orders if they were committing crimes against humanity!'

Captain Laning was adamant in his refusal, but he did say, 'I believe you're sincere, Pat.' (He had started by calling her 'Mrs O'Connell'.)

When Pat O'Connell recalled this episode some time later, in her home, she explained, 'I wanted to talk to Captain Laning just as one human being to another.' A characteristic, good-natured argument broke out, with her husband, Phil, laughingly tossing aside her insistence.

Phil said, 'You *couldn't* talk to him just as a human being!'

Pat: 'Why not?'

Phil: 'Because he's a naval officer.'

Pat: 'But he doesn't *stop* being a human being just because he's a naval officer.'

Phil: 'He does while he's got his uniform on!'

Pat: 'I don't see that. I just don't see it! He's still a human being underneath.'

Phil: 'Naw. You'd have to see him when he's off duty and in civilian clothes.'

Pat: 'But whatever clothes he's wearing, he's still ...'

Glasgow, some thirty miles from Holy Loch, was the jumping-off point for the operation. The plan was to stage a non-violent assault on the *Proteus*, in as many boats as could be found, and also, a sitdown on Ardnadam Pier, the pier used by the *Proteus* crew, to block access to the ship. Pat O'Connell found a man with a motor launch, and negotiated the hire of the boat with his own services as captain for one day, for fifty pounds. Then she picked her boarding party of fourteen, from among the demonstrators who had gathered. All had to be able to swim. Two were former Royal Marines, and these had constructed rope scaling ladders with bamboo rungs, to be flung up on to the deck of the *Proteus*.

It is difficult for the outsider, who is not committed to the demonstrators' cause and emotionally tied to their movement, to grasp the earnestness with which this mission was planned and carried out; difficult, once this is grasped, not to find it a little absurd. It is true that, for Pat O'Connell and some of the others, this kind of demonstration does take on some features of a game; admittedly, a game with risks, and risks that she accepted. There was up here an element of pretence that there is in a game, like in 'Capture the Castle' when the castle is only a sand castle. But the nuclear bombs were real, more real to Pat O'Connell and her friends than to most people, because she had thought often about their effects, and they outraged her whole sense of human decency. It did not seem likely that they could actually remove or disarm the bombs, but the attempt must be made, not symbolically but actually, and it must be seen to be made.

On the Sunday morning, Pat and her party took sandwich lunches, boarded their motor launch near the Glasgow docks, and sailed for two hours down the River Clyde, watching the shipyards fade into the blue-green heathered countryside.

As Pat expected, Holy Loch was teeming with boats. The *Proteus* was anchored in the middle. Other boats were swarming around it like flies around a horse, with police boats fending them off, Pat Arrowsmith's large, lumbering motor launch with twenty-four ban-the-bombers on board yelling and waving banners, five small ban-the-bomb canoes, and Press and TV boats.

Pat calculated that in that confusion, they would be able to get in close if they did not identify themselves. The plan worked. No one tried to stop them as they eased in nearer to the *Proteus*. Fifty yards away from the American ship, they suddenly ran the black and white C.N.D. flag up the mast like the Jolly Roger and headed straight for her, the two ex-marines ready on deck with their ladders, Pat crouched beside them. She intended to be first up the ladder herself, as there was some risk attached to this. Then a canoeist with a C.N.D. sign suddenly crossed in front of them, and the skipper had to sheer off to avoid running him down. They lost the element of surprise.

For an hour they motored around the *Proteus*, dodging police boats, and circling the ship five times, getting soaked by hosepipes from the ship's deck. Then some seamen found sport in hurling bolts and screws at them, and one crashed through the window of the cabin. The owner-captain became alarmed at the damage to his boat, and he pulled away, and they landed at Ardnadam Pier.

They stepped down to join the 1,000 sitdown demonstrators. Weary, wet and cold as they were, Pat and her crew were among the 100 who sat across the pier all through the night and until noon the next day, to block the way to the *Proteus*, cheering themselves by singing C.N.D. songs.

On the Monday morning, when *Proteus* sailors arriving by taxi at the pier found their way barred, the police were called, and they waded in and dragged the sitdowners aside, more and more roughly as the morning went on. Each time a policeman bent over Pat to lift her out of the way, she looked him directly in the eye. This was her new pacifist training. 'I always believe in looking someone in the face if they're doing something to you,' she explained to some of the others afterwards. 'It establishes some contact as one human being to another, however briefly.'

One policeman, who evidently recognized her from newspaper photographs taken of the leaders that weekend, said as he took hold of her arm, 'I'm sorry, Mrs O'Connell.' But another dropped her on the heads of other sitdowners, and her back was bruised. Others were dragged and bumped across the pier. Each time they took up their positions again, and resumed singing. Later, a group of reporters protested to Glasgow police at the treatment of the demonstrators.

At twelve noon it ended, and Pat, after her 500-mile walk, her sea fight, and her all-night demonstration got to her feet with the others and limped over to a bus. As they boarded it, they saw the nuclear submarine *Patrick Henry* sailing into Holy Loch. 'It stayed away while we were here,' Pat told the others. 'We did something at least. We immobilized the base for one day.'

The next time Pat was arrested, it was an an instigator of Committee of 100 activities. This was in September 1961, during that year's Berlin crisis, when tanks faced each other across Checkpoint Charlie. The Committee of 100 called for a mass meeting in Trafalgar Square, behind the slogan 'No War Over Berlin'. The Ministry of Works refused to allow it; the Committee went ahead with their plans anyway. The police summoned fifty leading members, and two detectives gave Pat her summons as she left a Committee meeting. 'They've nicked me,' she told Phil when she got home. She was already using a quasi-underworld jargon.

She did not realize until then how much she had forgotten, or repressed, about her five days at Winston Green Prison, and now it came back to her with a horrible thump: the terrible fear when the cell door locked, the loneliness, the humiliation of being treated, as she put it, 'like a naughty child'. In the days before her appearance at Bow Street Police Court, she spent as much time as possible with her children.

In court, the fifty were all asked whether they would be bound over to keep the peace. Forty-five of them refused, including many of the star names of the movement, Bertrand Russell, Lady Russell, Robert Bolt and Arnold Wesker, and, of course, Pat. Her sentence was a month.

She was sent to Holloway Prison, in North London. This time, she had to wear prison clothes: thin cotton dresses, rayon stockings drawn together with thread around the holes, and ill-fitting shoes that had been worn by other prisoners before, and bent out of shape, and still smelled of their feet. She never knew before how fastidious she was about shoes. She had a cell to herself, with dirty, cream-coloured brick walls. They were covered with graffiti, many of them obscenities.

The month passed slowly, particularly the first fortnight. The nights were the worst. She used to get into bed early in the evening because it was so cold, and try to read. It was an uncomfortable bed, with a hard mattress and a horsehair pillow, and she never slept through the night. Sometimes, she would hear a woman in another cell screaming out for drugs half the night until she was put to sleep with tranquillizers. After this, Pat would tremble uncontrollably. Sometimes, she would have nightmares about nuclear war, in which her children were dying of burns, or radiation sickness, and writhing in pain, and she was trapped behind prison walls.

A Committee of 100 clique in the prison shared the magazines they got from outside, *Peace News* and the *New Statesman*. But Pat is not a person to restrict her sympathies to a clique. She came to know the woman in the next cell, a lesbian who had murdered another woman, and to feel sorry for her. Even in the month, others came to know her too, and to ask her for advice.

There were more demonstrations for Pat after Holloway. She has been arrested twice for blocking the entrance to nuclear bomber bases. During the Cuba crisis, she was arrested trying to get a letter to Macmillan at 10 Downing Street. She accepted fines instead of imprisonment on these occasions, because her new job would suffer if she went to prison, which would mean people would not get help they needed. She says this is not a compromise of principle, and anyway she has not promised to do so in all circumstances.

After taking a year-long course that the University of London offered to teachers, she became Head of Education at Cumberlow Lodge, a detention and classifying centre for girl juvenile delinquents. It is a wearing job, and it can be a harrowing one: the girls are usually undisciplined, often abusive and sometimes violent. 'It's not difficult to love them once you know their backgrounds,' she says. 'They've had very little love.' Coming from somebody else, this might sound soupy. But there is nothing flabby about Pat's gentleness. Sex, drugs and viciousness come into most of these girls' stories. Pat takes them in her stride, and gives help. When she talks about an individual girl, it is as often as not in the terminology of modern psychology, but her learning informs her feelings, rather than limiting them.

Nor is there anything monastic about her dedication to the anti-bomb cause. It has not separated her from the things of this world, nor the varied interests of her family (one daughter is married to a naturopath, the other to a newspaper writer). She looked distraught and near to tears recently when someone dropped a bottle of whisky after pouring her a drink, and it smashed on a tile floor. 'That's a terrible sight!' she moaned, as the amber liquid spread around the broken glass. 'It's almost sacrilege.'

Through their naturopath son-in-law, the O'Connells became interested in nature cure, the treating of illnesses without using drugs, and so became dedicated to another unorthodoxy. Now Pat is a member of the committee of a charitable nature cure clinic, and Phil has given up teaching to become its full-time secretary.

As the Committee of 100 broadened its view and changed its style, Pat stayed on, so that a core of originals should remain. Anyway, she joined with a will in the demonstrations against the American war in Vietnam. On her own account, she staged a week-long fast outside the Greek Embassy in London, as a protest against the military dictatorship in Greece. But she has not joined in any of the mass protests for left-wing causes that have become part of the scene in London and other Western capitals. It is not her generation that is protesting, and it is not her style. Politically, Pat describes herself as an anarchist, as Phil does, saying she believes in complete personal responsibility without governmental control. 'It's something that's got to be acquired in time, through education, and knowledge of oneself,' she says.

But it was the bomb that first alienated her from her own government, and made her cease to be a law-abiding member of society. 'The hydrogen bomb,' she explains, 'is the ultimate in violence and cruelty. How can I be responsible for that?'

9. Two-and-a-half Beaches

The invention of the hydrogen bomb was not only a revolution in weaponry; it also made possible another, the intercontinental missile.

In the late 1940s, there was some far-fetched talk of rockets with a range of several thousand miles, that could be fired from one continent to another, but this was ruled out as a military weapon. The power might be there one day, but never the accuracy. It could not be relied upon to land closer than three or four miles from a target.

The compact H-bomb changed this. In 1953, after the Mike test at Eniwetok, when the 'dry' H-bomb was being developed, the Air Force set up a panel to see whether long-range bombing with rockets had a future. It was headed by Professor John Von Neumann of the Institute for Advanced Study, the mathematician and physicist who created the fast computers for the H-bomb programme, and it included several scientists who were by now accustomed to giving advice on strategic matters. Among them were Wiesner, Kistiakowsky and Lauritsen from the M.I.T. group. The panel reported that an H-bomb could be fitted into a rocket warhead, and that its area of destruction would be so great that the intercontinental rocket would be a feasible weapon even with its limited accuracy. More than feasible: obliterating and unstoppable, it would be the ultimate weapon. The panel urged a high-priority programme to develop one.

In May 1955 President Eisenhower announced a space rocket programme. He said the United States planned to use a rocket to hurl a small metal object out of the earth's gravity so that it would go into orbit, an announcement that caused

209

enormous excitement. A rocket built for space exploration would have military uses. It soon became clear that Russia was working to this end also, and articles appeared forecasting the appearance of the intercontinental ballistic missile, or I C B M. They usually said that the race to build an I C B M was vital for survival, that if Russia achieved it first, the West would be at her mercy.

Russia won the race. On 26 August 1957, Tass, the official Soviet news agency, announced the successful flight of an I C B M. Questioned about this, the Secretary of State, John Foster Dulles, said, 'We have no particular reason to doubt the veracity of the announcement.' Actually, he knew it was true. In one of the most important intelligence-gathering developments of the Cold War, American scientists had built a very long-range radar system in Turkey near the Soviet border, which was monitoring rocket flights inside Russia. This had a record of the I C B M flight.

Five weeks later, on 4 October, a Soviet rocket put the sputnik into orbit around the earth. The rocket that carried it was potentially the I C B M, at least in a crude version. This time, the Russians proclaimed the importance of their lead. Chou En-Lai, whose government was then a staunch friend and ally of the Soviet Union, hailed it in a speech as 'a new turning-point in the world situation'. Khrushchev, with characteristically exuberant overstatement, said at a reception in Moscow, 'Fighter and bomber planes can now be put into museums.' The sputnik triumph was a staggering blow to American conceptions of the world. Russia was seen until then as a backward country, though coming along fast. Very few Americans could imagine her leading the United States in any field of technology.

In a sense, the sputnik marked the end of the Eisenhower era in America. Eisenhower's term of office was to last for three years more, but its characteristic atmosphere of intellectually slothful paternalism was finished, to be followed by national self-doubting and breast-beating, in which the frivolous productions of Detroit, Hollywood and Madison

Avenue were contrasted with the serious purposes to which intelligence was applied in the Communist world. Studies and reports pointed to the shortcomings of American education, and to its incentives to conformity rather than excellence. America was pictured by its editorial-writers as an over-ripe, over-indulged Babylon. In the anti-philistine reaction, intellectuals were deemed to be valuable citizens, and their views were sought by congressional committees and television panels.

Immediately after sputnik, the U.S. rocket programme was speeded up. This meant that phases that were to be in sequence, one component being tested before parts for it were ordered, were carried out concurrently, making a certain amount of waste inevitable. The first American satellite was put into orbit a year after sputnik by an Atlas rocket, which was soon to be the first American ICBM.

U.S. intelligence estimates gave the Russians a serious lead in missile production, and the 'missile gap' alarm was sounded. A few weeks after the sputnik, official estimates said that Russia could have 500 ICBMs by the end of 1960, far more than the United States could build in the time. The next year the Defense Secretary, Neil McElroy, said this turned out to have been exaggerated, that they would not reach this number until 1961. Some thought this downgrading of the estimates was an attempt to gloss over a dangerous situation, and avoid pressure to spend more money on missiles. General Power, the commander of SAC, warned in a speech that Russia would have enough missiles to devote three to each American one, and wipe out the entire American force on their launching pads. With a Republican Administration in office, the Democrats made great play with this situation.

The missile gap never materialized. The intelligence estimates were based on the number of ICBMs Russia could produce in an all-out effort. After all, Khrushchev had thrown out a remark about Russia 'turning out long-range rockets like sausages'. But in long-range missiles as in long-range bombers, Russia did not make an all-out effort. Contrary to most Western fears, the capability of landing H-bombs on the United States was not given a high priority.

Russia did not have 500 ICBMs by either 1960, as the alarmists said, or 1961, as more conservative estimates had it. She reached that figure in 1968. The United States caught up with Russia in 1961, when each had about 30 ICBMs in place. After that, the United States pulled far ahead in numbers, and stayed ahead.

Missiles were clearly replacing bombers as the primary means for delivering hydrogen bombs, though Air Force generals argued for the role of the manned bomber. Even the economics of missiles would be incomprehensible to an earlier age of air warfare. Who could have thought of building the most complicated and expensive bomber imaginable in order to carry out one mission? The Atlas, the first American ICBM, contains 300,000 parts, making up 23,000 components. Each of these components was tested separately before the first rocket was launched. During a test flight, 250 instrument points radio back information on the behaviour of parts, and this is recorded on ten miles of magnetic tape.

The production of hydrogen bombs is an expensive industrial operation, but small in scale. The production of missiles entailed the creation of a whole new industry. Most aircraft companies formed separate divisions to handle missile systems, and these grew so big that they in turn spawned separate divisions to handle different operations. The aircraft industry became the much larger aero-space industry. This was not just weaponry. It was also space exploration, the moon race, and the placing into orbit of reconnaissance satellites of extraordinary variety and ingenuity – from 1960 onwards, it was these reconnaissance satellites that enabled the U.S. Government to check the U.S.–Soviet missile ratio. But missiles were the only product of this industry that were turned out in quantity.

Hundreds of thousands of industrial workers flocked to work on missiles in Southern California, where the wages were rising to a level well above the national average, and where there was a healthy outdoor climate for the kids. California, the home of the greatest concentration of aero-space plants, became even wealthier, more powerful and more populous.

Lives were changed, careers opened up, minds enlarged. The corporations sought out more brains and technical skills, in other industries, in the colleges, in Europe. Thousands of scientists and engineers were fascinated by absorbing, challenging new problems in hundreds of different fields: solid-state physics, high-temperature metallurgy, data processing. They built things such as an autopilot that steers a missile rocket by regulating the engines far more accurately than a human pilot ever could, computers and radar that operate under a pull sixty times that of gravity, and metal coating that insulates against a heat of thousands of degrees.

On the executive side, vice-presidents of aero-space corporations with $1,000-a-week salaries and bathrooms in their offices and private planes with pilots spent lunches, dinners and golfing weekends on country estates with generals and admirals, many of whom would soon become vice-presidents of aero-space corporations with $1,000-a-week salaries and bathrooms in their offices and private planes with pilots. Public-relations teams produced glossy pamphlets and colour charts, wrote speeches for corporation presidents on the defence of the free world, and thought up new and more rousing descriptions of their corporations' products, like 'Titan: Nuclear Tipped Sentinel in the Earth' (Martin Company). This became the biggest part of the 'military-industrial complex', which President Eisenhower warned against in an unexpected passage in his farewell address.

Administration proliferated in Washington, until there were several dozen service, departmental or interdepartmental committees dealing with missiles and space, all with their chairmen and vice-chairmen, their reports and secretaries. Everyone worked hard at his or her job, all to the one distant end of creating potential violence of mind-numbing ingenuity.

The process worked, perhaps expensively, but producing remarkable results. The improvements in all the technologies of

213

missile development surpassed the expectations of the specialists in any one field; it was geometric rather than arithmetic. Every major new step was years ahead of the predictions for it.

The Atlas rocket had its shortcomings as a weapon in the age of instant strategic warfare. Standing high on a launching pad, it was a sitting target. Its fuel required liquid oxygen to ignite which was kept in a special compartment, and it took two hours to ready it for firing, so that it was slow and cumbersome compared with the alert bombers which can take off in minutes.

The next type of long-range rocket to be built was the Titan, and this was emplaced underground in a concrete silo, for protection. The Titan was fired from 160 feet down, and roared up out of a vertical tube sunk into the earth. It became an operational weapon in the middle of 1961. Even as the Atlas and Titan rockets were being hastened through the development stages and put into production, another, newer kind of missile was being developed. This was a rocket propelled by a solid fuel that needed no preparation, and could be fired in a matter of minutes, and it replaced the Atlases, even though its warhead was smaller. The name for this rocket was the Minuteman, after the farmer-soldier of the American War of Independence, always ready to take up his rifle and fight at a minute's notice.

A few people in the Navy had an idea for a missile that was less vulnerable still; a solid-fuelled missile hidden under the world's oceans in a submarine, perhaps even one of the new nuclear-powered submarines that could stay underwater almost indefinitely. The first nuclear-powered submarine, the *Nautilus*, put to sea in January 1955. Soon after this, the missile men got hold of one, the *Scorpion,* when it was still unfinished. It was bisected, a rocket-launching mid-section was inserted, and it was renamed the *George Washington*.

A new solid-fuelled rocket was developed, the Polaris, fired from under the sea. Propelled upwards, it continues to rise after it breaks the surface, and then its guidance systems steer it to a target. The *George Washington* fired two Polaris rockets from under the water off the Florida coast on to a target 1,000 miles away, on 20 July 1960. Combining as it did new developments in many different fields, the Polaris-carrying submarine was a virtuoso accomplishment of modern technology.

At first, the solid-fuelled rocket was not as accurate as the liquid-fuelled one, nor did it carry as large a warhead. But the motors were given more power so that the rocket could carry more weight, and the guidance system was made more accurate. Finally, the land-based long-range missiles that were made feasible by the development of the H-bomb became so accurate, contrary to expectations, that they would be effective weapons if the warheads were only fission bombs.

The development of H-bombs proceeded apace. Bombs were made more efficient, that is, producing a more powerful explosion in relation to the size. As the size of the warhead that a rocket can carry is a limiting factor, this became more important in the missile years.

H-bombs were also made 'cleaner', in the terminology of nuclear weaponry, that is, giving off less fallout. Since only fission produces fallout, the proportion of the explosive power that comes from atomic fusion is increased, so that in a Bikini-type fission-fusion-fission bomb, the third stage, the natural uranium envelope that fissions and produces most of the fallout, can be made smaller or eliminated.

In the Bikini test, 80 per cent of the explosive power came from fission. In the years that followed, A.E.C. scientists produced H-bombs that were just as powerful, and in which only 5 per cent of the power came from fission. But there was a case for continuing to make 'dirty' bombs. Though some fallout is spread throughout the world, most of it remains locally, and kills a great many people in the area around the explosion. A military man might want to have these available.

Military men learned to make the distinctions between one kind of bomb and another, and between their different effects. They plotted air-bursts and ground-bursts. An air-burst of a nuclear bomb, high enough in the air so that the fireball does not touch the ground (about a mile for a one-megaton bomb, and increasing after as the cube root of the power) maximizes

215

the area burned and blasted; one on the ground increases the intensity of the blast at the expense of area covered. Also, because the fireball irradiates directly a lot of matter and hurls it into the air, it creates much more fallout than an airburst. Paradoxically, an attack aimed at an underground missile site could kill more people than one aimed at a city, for the explosion would be a ground-burst to penetrate the protective shielding and reach down to the missile site, and so would spread fallout.

The Russians ended the test moratorium and staged a spectacular series of tests in October 1961. This included the largest H-bomb explosion ever, before or since, a fifty-eight-megaton explosion high in the stratosphere, where the bomb was carried by a rocket. There was widespread dismay at the resumption of testing, and angry objections from some whose denunciations were more often aimed at the United States. Bertrand Russell said in a public statement: 'Russia's willingness to risk the health of mankind should be held in contempt.' Sixty-two Labour members of parliament sent a cable of protest to Khrushchev. The Soviet leader replied, linking the resumption of testing to the Berlin crisis of that summer and the consequent American forces build-up in Europe, and said: 'We are compelled to answer military threats by strengthening our country's defence capacity. We have no alternative.'

President Eisenhower appointed a panel of scientists headed by Hans Bethe to analyse the radioactive debris from the Soviet explosions, and determine whether and how they had improved their bombs. By doing the kind of scientific detective work that was by now becoming common, the panel decided that the new bombs were more efficient than previous Soviet bombs, and much cleaner; only 3 to 5 per cent of the explosive force came from fission.

When they were first produced, it was thought that nuclear bombs would have a scarcity that somehow related to their destructive power, but it turned out that there were to be lots available. Uranium, once thought to be very scarce, proved to be plentiful. There were postwar discoveries in South Africa and Australia, as well as in Eastern Europe. The uranium finds in Canada and the United States made some people rich and ended America's reliance on overseas supplies, so that now almost all uranium for American weapons is domestically mined. Refinements in engineering techniques and production methods made bombs cheaper and easier to produce.

Nuclear bombs were made smaller as well as bigger. Fission bombs of less than a kiloton were tested; the size of the uranium ball was the same, but the explosion was deliberately made less efficient. Nuclear warheads were devised for battle-field use, and put into bombs for light planes and warheads for artillery rockets. The smallest of these has the explosive power of a massive air raid with high explosives. In the new scale of measurements, a bomb with the power of the one dropped on Hiroshima is a tactical size weapon.

Bombs were refined in other ways. An H-bomb is much more than a nuclear explosion, if it is to be used as a weapon; it is a machine that must work precisely and reliably under rigorous, specified conditions. There are men to whom the hydrogen bomb is a problem in engineering. If it is to be an aerial bomb, it must be impervious to storage for long periods at airfields in tropical heat or Arctic cold, and to the vibrations and tempera-ture and pressure changes of high-altitude flight. If it is to be a warhead for a missile, it will be stored in one place at even temperature, and must survive only one brief flight, albeit a jarring one. Clearly, the requirements for a nuclear artillery shell or a Polaris warhead are different still.

These problems are handled at the Sandia Corporation. Sandia is owned by the Western Electric Corporation, but it exists solely to do nuclear weapons engineering work for the A.E.C. It is located on the outskirts of Albuquerque, in the middle of a military site where servicemen are instructed in the handling of nuclear weapons. Sandia engineers designed the arming mechanism for the bombs. With an engineer's zeal to improve design and performance, they refined these over the years, to make them proof against either accident or un-authorized use.

M.P.G. – 10

The fission-bomb core of a hydrogen bomb consists of pieces of fissile material kept apart from one another. The triggering mechanism brings them together sharply, so that the mass is of critical size. The arming process puts the trigger into a position where it can work. As it was designed at Sandia, the arming process consists of a series of electrical impulses, which must reach the triggering mechanism in a certain order, with split-second timing. Two people are required to set off these electrical impulses, and they must go through a number of motions simultaneously at switches at opposite ends of the weapon.

The A.E.C. gave out contracts for the production of bombs to outside contractors, usually large firms working in technically advanced fields, and these operated factories owned by the A.E.C. The fissile materials were sent to these factories, along with the plans and designs from Los Alamos, Livermore and the Sandia Corporation. The ultimate deterrent, the ultimate evil of government, the instrument of man playing God, whatever the thermonuclear bomb was, it rolled off assembly lines in quantity. Assembly lines for producing nuclear weapons were set up at an A.E.C. plant in Albuquerque operated by the Monsanto Chemical Company; in one operated by the Dow Chemical Company in Rocky Flats, Colorado; the Bendix Corporation factory in Kansas City, Missouri; the Pantex Plant in Amarillo, Texas; and the Mason and Hangar-Silas Company factory in Burlingham, Iowa. To the men who work in these factories, it is an industrial product to be turned out to the customer's requirements like any other they make, refrigerators, fertilizers or nylon fabrics. To the companies concerned, H-bomb production is a routine business operation and a fairly small one. 'Who would build a hydrogen bomb?' was no longer a question to put to a few scientists. The answer seems to be, 'Just about anyone.'

Radiation and fallout were matters of such concern that the Joint Committee on Atomic Energy established a special Radiation Subcommittee. Under the chairmanship of Representative Chet Holifield of California, who had pressed hard for Truman's decision on a super programme, it became as vigorous and enterprising as the Committee itself.

The Radiation Subcommittee set out to determine just what a nuclear bombing attack on the United States would be like, and made its findings known in a series of public hearings in June 1959. Experts gave testimony during five days, and there were panel discussions. With the help of specialists on their staff and the A.E.C., they devised a plausible, quite specific attack on the United States, and, because fallout patterns vary with the weather, they gave it a particular date, and assumed the weather for that day. As a public and realistic appraisal of nuclear attack on any country, this is unique.

They assumed that bombs totalling 1,500 megatons landed on the United States, admitting that this was not the maximum that Russia could do. The targets were cities, Air Force bases and nuclear weapons installations; the ratio of fusion to fission explosive was 50-50; the time was 12 noon on 17 October 1958.

In this attack, they found that approximately 20 million Americans would be killed on the first day, and 22 million would die in the following sixty days, most of them from radiation illnesses. This totalled 28 per cent of the population.

The estimation of genetic damage was uncertain to a factor of more than 100. In the thirty generations following the attack, genetic mutations resulting in obviously defective births would total between 240,000 and 38 million; mutations resulting in fatal deformities or deaths at birth would total between 5 and 384 million. (The outside figure is unrealistically high; it leaves out, because this cannot be calculated, the elimination of some defective genetic strains through the deaths of those carrying them.) Statistics in this field are deceptive. This amount of genetic damage would mean an increase of somewhere between 2 and 110 per cent of genetic defects or deaths.

Some grisly details were spelled out. On a clear day, the heat flash from a twenty-megaton explosion would cause fatal third-degree burns to someone standing in the open twenty miles away, and would blister the skin of anyone twenty-five miles away. One of the facts that emerged to surprise the Committee members was that Negroes are one-third more susceptible to flash burns than white people because of their skin pigmentation. Any kind of shelter would reduce burns, but, even so, lungs would be damaged six miles from that twenty-megaton explosion, and ear drums ruptured ten miles away. The strongest skyscraper two and a half miles away would be smashed to pieces, and brick-built apartment houses four miles away would crumble.

Man lives in an environment of living things, and is dependent upon their health for his own. A study of the effects of the nuclear attack on this environment indicated that deaths in the long run might be far more than the 28 per cent of the population killed directly by the bombs, and that effects would extend into new dimensions of destruction. Dr John N. Wolfe, Chief of the Environmental Sciences Branch, Division of Biology and Medicine, A.E.C., testified before the subcommittee on the effects of fire and erosion from this particular attack.

In the Eastern United States [he said], the dry oak and pine forests of the Blue Ridge and Appalachians from New England to Virginia, adjacent to multiple detonations, would undergo a like fate [that is, they would be destroyed by fire, like the great forests of California], as well as the pine on the Southern Atlantic and Gulf Coastal plains. In the agricultural land of the Mississippi valley, with the crops harvested, fire is likely to be more local, less severe and widespread. Add to this the denuding effects of radiation and/or chemically toxic materials. ...

I visualize those people unsheltered in heavy fallout areas after three months to be dead, dying, sick or helpless; those sheltered, if they can psychologically withstand confinement for that period, would emerge to a strange landscape.

The sun will shine through a dust-laden atmosphere; the landscape in mid-January would be snow-covered or blackened by fire in a mosaic. I do not mean it would be snow or black. There would be a mosaic of burned areas. At higher latitudes, blizzards and sub-zero temperatures would add death and discomfort; both food and shelter would be inadequate and production incapacitated.

At Holifield's suggestion, Colonel Richard Lunger, a staff consultant, interrupted to confirm Wolfe's picture of the sun shining 'through a dust-laden atmosphere', with a recollection of the Bikini explosion.

We shot early in the morning [he recalled], and the entire task force was steaming north and south trying to keep out from under the local fallout. Later in the evening of shot day, I remember, we were in the wardroom getting our first hot meal, and they came down and told us there was a phenomenon on deck we should see. It was just about sundown. We got on deck, and there was an amber glow along the entire horizon. It was the most *artificial* thing I have ever seen and sensed in my life. . . .

So the picture Dr Wolfe has presented is very real. When you multiply this phenomenon I have described by approximately 200 weapons in this hypothetical attack, it would be a psychologically unreal world for quite a period after the attack.

The destructive power of the nuclear nations continued to increase as more and more bombs were produced, and even the congressional subcommittee's estimation of possible casualties were soon left behind.

Donald Brennan, a specialist in arms control, encompassed the new situation in a joke, perhaps the most mordant sick joke of all time. At a summer study on arms control, he invented a new unit of measurement, the 'beach', derived from the film *On The Beach*. A 'beach' is a quantity of nuclear bombs sufficient to wipe out half the world's population with fallout.

This was taken up by others in the field. Professor Freeman Dyson, a physicist concerned also with strategic problems, calculated a 'beach' as an amount of fissionable material with an explosive power of 3 million megatons (since only the fission process causes fallout): this was a very rough estimate, accurate only within a factor of three, which is to say that it could be three times the correct figure or one third of it. By taking the announced figure of uranium purchases by the A.E.C., and estimating the amount for Russia, he arrived at an estimate of

221

the world's stockpile of nuclear bombs at the end of 1960. It was two-and-a-half beaches.

This goes beyond the arithmetic of even the advanced military thinker, who can calculate in proportions of a country to be lost. For most people, a concept like the 'beach' is the end of a line of thought. But a scientist, used to calculating in trillions of light years and microseconds, measurements totally abstracted from human experience, can go on from there and *use* this as a measure. This is what Professor Dyson did.

He worked out the amount of fissionable material that would wipe out just about the entire population of the United States or Russia with local fallout, and, showing the same whimsical humour as Dr Brennan, he called this unit of measurement a 'Kahn', after Herman Kahn, who was frequently making calculations involving large-scale loss of life. He estimated this figure at 10,000 megatons, again accurate only to a factor of three. In an article in the *Bulletin of the Atomic Scientists* in March 1962, he manipulated these two units to make out a case for *not* building nuclear bomb shelters.

Working out that a beach is some 300 times greater than a Kahn, he said that this ratio of 300 is 'the safety factor which prevents the bulk of the human race from being annihilated as a consequence of local quarrels'. However, he pointed out that an effective shelter programme would raise the Kahn, the amount required to wipe out the American or Soviet populations, and so reduce the safety factor. If the populations were exposed, the war would be likely to end in a few days or less, with the annihilation of one or both; but if they were protected by shelters, the two sides might go on firing off nuclear weapons until their stockpiles were exhausted, and the beach might be exploded.

He concluded:

Our present policy of peace through deterrence, so long as we have no bomb shelters, is a policy of finite risk. At the very worst, if deterrence fails, the populations of the nuclear powers may die, but the rest of the world will survive to carry on the aspirations of the human race. Only if we plunge into the vicious circle of building more and more massive bomb shelters do we risk the whole future of humanity itself.

There is no certainty in this area. Most scientists now think that a beach is higher than was supposed; that to create this kind of havoc, the weapons would have to be exploded at optimal points throughout the world instead of in two warring countries. This is a disagreement about quantities; it is certain that there is the capacity to inflict great injury outside the target country, and beyond any military intention.

It is small wonder that, to most people, measurements and calculations like this do not seem to apply to the world they live in, any more than a light year seems a real measurement or curved space a real entity. Underlying most talk of nuclear war is the phenomenon that Raymond Aron calls 'nuclear incredulity'. To most people, nuclear war does not seem to belong to the world of things that can really happen, like business troubles or school exams or next summer's holiday. More and more facts and more and more figures do not make it seem real, any more than, to use a Zen parable, more polishing can make a stone into a mirror.

This was seen in the general lack of interest in civil defence, despite the widespread preoccupation with the possibility of nuclear war. There was much to be done; the U.S. Air Force assigned the Rand Corporation to make a study of the subject, and this took more than eighteen months. There were two major programmes that could be carried out: one was evacuation of cities, another was the building of blast shelters or at least fallout shelters. Either could save millions of lives in a nuclear attack, but it was difficult to work up public or even congressional interest. When someone from a government department talked at Rand about the need for public education, one member said, 'Look, the twenty men in this study have been making calculations in this area for more than a year. They are literally the best educated people in the country on civil defense. And *not one* of them has a fallout shelter for his family.'

223

In the Soviet Union, escapism took a different form. The Soviet Government carried out a vigorous programme of education in civil defence. It distributed millions of pamphlets, and organized lectures and film shows for city-dwellers on the use of basements as shelters and other measures. But until 1957, these were all based on the explosion of nuclear bombs of the power of the Hiroshima bomb.

It is not only the immensity of the horror of nuclear war that makes it difficult to accept it as a real possibility; it is also its contrast with the world in which we live.

Usually, a dangerous situation is an unpleasant one. If you are dangerously ill, you are probably *feeling* pretty ill. If you are in a frail boat in a turbulent sea, it is not difficult to believe that you are in danger; the lurching and rocking of the craft, the cold waves splashing against your face are themselves uncomfortable, and constant signals of the worse fate that may come. If you live in an area ridden by banditry, the danger is one with which you are familiar; you have seen the corpses, and the bereaved families, and the sobbing, violated girl, you have heard the shots and been afraid. It requires no feat of imagination to believe that one day you could be a victim.

But those countries that have been longest threatened by hydrogen bombs, the largest and most powerful of the modern, industrial countries, have constructed what are incomparably the most comfortable societies that have ever been known in history. Sickness and death have been banished to peripheral areas. Ailments, discomforts and perils which afflicted the most powerful and the wealthiest even a century ago have now been eliminated from the lives of all but the poorest. Even compared with the period between the two world wars, existence in most of the countries of Europe, at any rate, has been remarkably tranquil. The four horsemen wait over the calm horizon, and they were put there, ironically, by the same industry, technology and organization that created the comfort and security. If the disaster should ever come, it will produce, in the survivors, the same kind of shock of incongruity that the iceberg brought to the passengers of the *Titanic*.

If, beset by the moral questions raised by the world of two-and-a-half beaches, and the arguments around them, people turned for guidance to the Western world's traditional source of moral direction, the Christian churches, they found no authoritative answer. This was not to say that no churchman spoke out on the subject. But within the churches as without, there was an array of viewpoints from which to choose.

In the Vatican, there have always been voices of condemnation, but none that laid down any rules for action or prohibition. After Bikini *L'Osservatore Romano*, the Vatican newspaper, said in an editorial about the H-bomb, 'It is disproportionate, enormous heresy in both the technical and the moral fields of war ... [the Church] protests against it and denounces it vigorously.' But the Church never denounced as heresy the acquisition of nuclear weapons, nor would it do so. In private, some Catholic churchmen have said that this would create, as one of them put it, 'an impossible dilemma for millions of Catholics'.

A number of Catholic clergymen have argued that any war waged with nuclear weapons is an unjust war according to the Church's traditional criteria, in that the killing of civilians would be an intended aim and not an unavoidable secondary one. A majority of French bishops have issued several statements denouncing mass bombing, nuclear and otherwise. But they came up against temporal considerations. When de Gaulle came to power and made a French nuclear deterrent a prominent part of his programme, the bishops were warned by their superiors that outright opposition to this policy, in the liberal years of Pope John, would be seized upon by the French Communists as political ammunition. They were asked to tone down their opposition and they did.

The most sustained and consensual attack on the problem was made by a committee of the World Council of Churches, the Protestant body, in August 1958, in a document called *Christians and the Prevention of War in an Atomic Age*. The document makes no drastic or radical recommendations, but even so, in the interval between its completion and its publication, the World Council of Churches said several times that this was only a study document and not a statement of Council policy.

The churchmen on the committee found no simple answer to the moral questions posed by nuclear weapons, accepting as they did, for they were not pacifists, the tragic dilemma that sometimes seems to call for violence to men's bodies and minds in order to prevent some greater evil. A minority on the committee said the use of H-bombs is never morally permissible, not even if an enemy uses them. The majority arrived at a more complicated and almost contradictory conclusion.

On the circumstances in which the weapons might be used, they had this to say:

We are all agreed on one point, Christians should openly declare that the all-out use of these weapons should never be resorted to. Moreover, that Christians must oppose all policies which show evidence of leading to all-out war. Finally, if all-out war should occur, Christians should urge a cease-fire, if necessary on the enemy's terms, and resort to non-violent resistance. We purposely refrain from defining the stage at which all-out war may be reached. ...

It is not necessary for a nation, or group of nations, to announce in advance the precise point at which they will stop. This might tempt a hard-pressed enemy to test that point. It is necessary for them to possess a plan whereby they can stop, and to have the will to carry it through.

This prescription envisages a degree of cool control that is rarely found in the conduct of war. It envisages a government waging war with mounting violence, but with a secret plan to reverse its course and surrender if a certain point of violence is reached. It also runs the risk that the enemy might wage pre-emptive all-out nuclear war. Nevertheless, this approximates many people's thinking on the subject.

The second session of the Vatican Council discussed nuclear weapons in its deliberations on 'The Church Today'. It condemned total war and the nuclear arms race, and appealed to the nations of the world to reach agreement to end the arms race and war. But it reaffirmed the right of armed national self-defence.

There was much lobbying on the wording of this text. Some of the delegates, including most of the Americans, wanted the condemnation of total war watered down, since they felt it would give aid and comfort to the enemies of Christianity. Others wanted a more unequivocal condemnation of nuclear war, perhaps in terms that would make its prosecution and therefore its preparation a sin.

One priest who argued for outright condemnation said privately: 'I'm sure this would mean a massive bolt from the Church. Catholics would ignore the proscription and just back their governments. If they were in the armed forces, they'd stay in. But I felt that, as prophetic witnesses, we should take this stand anyway, whatever the consequences.'

The final agreed statement showed a sensitivity, not only to the horrors of nuclear war, but also to the moral atmosphere in which decisions in this area are taken. It said in part:

Any act of war aimed indiscriminately at the destruction of entire cities or of extensive areas along with their populations is a crime against God and man himself. It merits unequivocal and unhesitating condemnation.

The unique hazard of modern warfare consists in this: it provides those who possess modern scientific weapons with a kind of occasion for perpetrating just such abominations. Moreover, through a certain inexorable chain of events, it can urge man on to the most atrocious decisions.

This still leaves room for Catholics to argue that the use of thermonuclear weapons would not be indiscriminate since civilians would be secondary targets, and also that these weapons are intended to deter war. These arguments were put forward when some Catholics in Britain cited the Vatican II document in objecting to the participation of a Catholic chaplain in the commissioning of the first British Polaris submarine.

The churches have provided food for thought for those who wanted to question the morality of nuclear weapons, but have made few demands on those who do not.

In the Soviet Union, the important debate on the H-bomb was not conducted in moral terms, but it contained profound implications for the Soviet view of the world. There as elsewhere, the hydrogen bomb posed a fundamental challenge to orthodox assumptions, as men grappled with what they had built, and tried to fit it into the scheme of things.

When matters such as war and peace are discussed in Soviet writings, it is in a conceptual framework that is alien to most Western ways of thought, a framework that seems metaphysical. Since 'metaphysical' is one of the harshest rebukes that a Soviet Marxist can give to 'Western, bourgeois thought', this sounds tendentious, but it is difficult not to see it in this way.

To the orthodox Soviet Marxist, social and political events take place according to certain laws, which are as inviolable as those governing the physical universe. The system of these laws is dialectical materialism. Understanding social phenomena means seeing them in relation to these laws; this is called the 'scientific' way. It is a process of discovery and interpretation analogous to that of the physical scientist. A purely pragmatic consideration of a major political or social event would be regarded by an orthodox Soviet thinker as shallow and frivolous. To achieve anything in the social or political sphere, one must act in accordance with these laws.

Here, for instance, is a statement on war by a Soviet military man, quoted by H. S. Dinerstein in his book *War and the Soviet Union*. It is from an article by Colonel V. Petrov in *Soviet Aviation*, 20 May 1958:

Soviet military science, based on the theoretical foundations of Marxism–Leninism, assumes that the phenomenon of war, as of other spheres of the life of society, are completely knowable, and that our knowledge of the laws of war, based on experience, is trustworthy knowledge which has the importance of objective truths. A knowledge of the laws of war is a necessary condition for the scientific prediction of the events of war and the successful leadership of troops on the field of battle.

If Colonel Petrov were to put this to, say, an instructor at a

Western military staff college, he probably would not even find enough meeting ground for rational argument.

According to the doctrine promulgated by Stalin, war is a clash between two societies; the decisive factors are not found in manoeuvres on the battlefield, military equipment or strategies, though these are important, but in the nature of the societies in conflict, the 'permanently operating factors', as Stalin called them. It is a test of these societies. This in itself is a familiar viewpoint in the West, though it is rarely expressed in these terms. Most of us are imbued to some degree with the idea that moral virtues have a strength of their own that tells in conflict, that right contains an element of might.

Stalin said specifically that surprise is a local and transient military factor that cannot be decisive. There was good reason for emphasizing this: Stalin was writing in 1942, when the Germans had broken the Russian front with the surprise of their assault, and were deep inside the country. In the postwar years, the Stalinist view had the political advantage of putting the military in their place. If it was the nature of the societies in conflict that determined the outcome of the Second World War, then the true victor and the saviour of the fatherland was Stalin, the architect and leader of Soviet society, along with the Communist Party, which provided the political direction.

Stalin died in March 1953 and fundamental changes were initiated by his successors almost immediately, beginning with the halting of the last Stalinist purge, the so-called 'doctors' plot', and the unprecedented admission that the charges against the accused had been faked.

The following year, an article appeared in *Military Thought*, a monthly journal published by the Ministry of Defence, which suggested a change in the Stalinist view of war. It was written by the editor of the journal, Major-General Nikolai Talensky. The tenor of his argument was that nuclear bombs could overpower the permanently operating factors. A war of the future might consist, not of a testing by fire of the social fabric, but of a sudden, swift, annihilating blow. One might be able to formulate 'a new basic law', which improves upon Stalin's doctrine. This would provide for 'the possibility of a decisive defeat within a limited time ... given the existence of certain conditions'.

General Talensky is a former infantry officer who has been a military writer and editor since the Second World War. He has said in conversation that he wrote this article on his own initiative, without consulting the Ministry, intending to start a discussion. It certainly did; the debate that followed, with letters and articles in reply, and extensions in other publications, constituted a public clash of opinion that would have been unthinkable when Stalin was still alive. The radical implications of Talensky's thesis became clearer as the argument developed. For he went on to say that a war was not decided in the social sphere, but in the sphere of 'armed conflict'. In a conflict of arms, the same factors apply to both sides equally, and the superiority or otherwise of the social system does not count.

There was support for him in the *Military Thought* debate, though some hedged their opinions with an acknowledgement of the importance of social systems. Marshal P. A. Romistrov, a Second World War tank commander of some intellectual abilities, wrote:

When atomic and hydrogen weapons are employed, surprise is one of the decisive conditions for the attainment of success not only in battles and operations, but also in war as a whole. ... Surprise attack with the massive employment of new weapons can cause the rapid collapse of a government whose capacity to resist is low as a consequence of radical faults in its social and economic structure.

There was also heated contradiction. Colonel A. Kapralov wrote:

The law of victory formulated by General Talensky differs very little in principle from the well-known theories of bourgeois military theoreticians such as Douhet, who asserted in his time that victory in modern war could be attained by crushing aerial blows.

In March 1955, the editors of *Military Thought* terminated for a while the argument in its columns, and summed up with:

'The editors suggest that it is not yet possible to propound any final and definite formulation of the basic law.' But this was itself a radical conclusion, because it left the question open. In Stalin's day, the basic law was accepted as final and the question was closed.

This argument was about much more than Soviet military theory. The inevitable outcome, the view imposed by the power of the hydrogen bomb, reduced human beings in stature. Though it is expressed in iron-clad dogma, the Stalinist view of war contains something of all humanist aspirations. It contains the belief that men are more powerful than the things they build, that people's feelings and ideas can decide the outcome of events. But now, after the conclusion of this argument, attitudes such as these seemed as empty and futile as an adolescent's idealism beside the power of megatonnage, or the decision to press first the fateful button. The hydrogen bomb was becoming like the grape:

> ... that can with logic absolute
> The two and seventy jarring sects confute.

One purely military aspect of the argument begun by Talensky contained worrying implications for the West: the emphasis on surprise and the possibility of victory through a single surprise blow. This reasoning led to a call to be ready to launch a pre-emptive attack, if necessary, to forestall a surprise attack on Russia by the West. Romistrov warned in his article that a pre-emptive attack might be necessary. The editorial in *Military Thought* which terminated the argument said: 'We cannot ignore the lessons of history, and we must always be ready for pre-emptive actions against the perfidy of the aggressors.'

The distinction was made between a pre-emptive attack, which would be launched in the absolute certainty that the enemy was just about to strike, and a preventive war, which was condemned. But the difference rested on someone's assumption about what was going to happen. This could mean an increased danger in time of crisis, when the Soviet Union might well fear a surprise attack.

Meanwhile, Soviet nuclear weapons policy was being argued out in the highest councils of the political leadership. Georgi Malenkov, as Prime Minister, produced his own modification of orthodox Stalinist lore. He indicated in several speeches that a new world war would lead to 'the destruction of world civilization', and that fear of this might prevent one. There was an opposing view. In March 1954 Khrushchev accused the West of 'preparing a new war', and Marshal Voroshilov said that despite the increases in Soviet strength, 'we live in encirclement all the same'. Some other high-ranking officers warned against 'the dangerous complacency' of those who thought that the possession of nuclear weapons ensured Russia's safety.

Western analysts saw in this a reflection of the American argument over massive retaliation. Malenkov had a programme of increasing production of consumer goods at the expense of investment in heavy industry. It seemed that, like the Eisenhower Administration, he wanted to reduce the burden of government expenditure by cutting down on military spending, relying on the capacity for nuclear retaliation for defence. Khrushchev, Bulganin and others opposed this, as they opposed the rest of his economic policy, and they won out.

In later years, however, Khrushchev was inclined to go overboard on the power of new weapons. And in January 1960 he propounded a new military policy to the Supreme Soviet. This sounded remarkably like the American 'new look' policy of a few years earlier. He said in his speech that nuclear bombs and missiles were now the principal elements in war; and that the opening phase of a war would probably be decisive. He said that Soviet retaliatory power would deter a potential aggressor. And he announced that the armed forces would be cut back by a third from their present level of 3,600,000 men. The armed forces were not cut back to this level, however. There was opposition to the policy among the military men, reflected in some guarded articles in the military Press; and the American build-up in Europe during the Berlin crisis in the summer of 1961 arrested the cuts. The more traditional Soviet attitude towards defence of their country prevailed. The Soviet masses in arms would still defend their territory.

At least the situation was being discussed, rationally. Under Stalin, incredible as it seems, not one article on nuclear weapons appeared in the Soviet military Press.

Just as the hydrogen bomb posed a moral challenge to Christians and Marxists, so from the very beginning it posed one to scientists as scientists, with their concern for dedication to truth, disinterestedness and objectivity. After the shock of the Bikini bomb, an international movement grew up among scientists to try to cope with it.

The Pugwash Movement, as it is usually called, had its origins in a moving appeal for peace that sounded far too idealistic to have any practical effect. It was drafted by Bertrand Russell (this was in the days before the ban-the-bomb movement began) and sent to several eminent scientists for their signatures. One of the first to sign was Albert Einstein, two days before he died, and it is generally known as the Russell–Einstein Manifesto. Lord Russell read it to a crowded news conference in London in July 1955.

It said, in part:

In the tragic situation which confronts humanity, we feel that scientists should assemble in conference to appraise the perils that have arisen as a result of the development of weapons of mass destruction. ... We are speaking on this occasion not as members of this or that nation, continent or creed, but as human beings, members of the species of man whose continued existence is still in doubt.

To convene this conference of scientists, Lord Russell turned to the British Atomic Scientists' Association, and in particular its Executive Vice-President, Professor Josef Rotblat. Professor Rotblat, the Polish-born physicist who left Los Alamos abruptly to work on radiation medicine, and was the first to solve the Bikini H-bomb mystery, was principally responsible for the organizing effort that got the meeting going, and is still the principal organizer of these conferences.

Rotblat and his fellow officers of the Atomic Scientists' Association wrote to several wealthy people asking for financial support for a conference. Aristotle Onassis offered to pay all the expenses providing it was held in Monte Carlo. A more acceptable offer came from Cyrus Eaton, the American millionaire who dabbled in private East–West contacts for peace. He offered to provide expenses and hospitality in the Nova Scotia fishing village where he was born, Pugwash. Later meetings were held all over the world and without Eaton's financial support, but they were known colloquially as Pugwash conferences.

The first meeting, private like all the others, was attended by the most liberal scientists from some Western countries, and a few Russians. It was regarded by many with suspicion, as a fellow-travelling affair; Khrushchev and Nehru sent telegrams of goodwill, but Macmillan and Eisenhower ignored it. But after the first few meetings – there were one or two a year – some scientists in contact with the power structure in Western countries took them up as useful avenues of approach to the Russians. From America, Wiesner, Kistiakowsky, Lauritsen and Zacharias of the M.I.T. scientist-strategists attended, and some others whose principal concern was strategy. Sir John Cockcroft and Sir William Penney, the principal figures in the A.E.A.'s weapons programme, came from Britain. The Russians talked as a bloc at first, echoing each other and their government's line. But later they began to loosen up, particularly as they saw that the Americans were speaking as individuals rather than as government spokesmen and that they often disagreed with one another, until one conference saw the spectacle of two leading Soviet scientists arguing with each other across the floor the merits of controlled disarmament by numbers or by percentage.

Arms control measures were and are the principal topics of discussion at the Pugwash conferences: underground tests, problems of inspection, new weapons possibilities, and the effects of all this on the strategic balance. When the Soviet–American argument was going on at Geneva about allowing inspectors on each other's territory to check for underground tests, a Pugwash conference came up with the idea of a 'black box', a device which could be installed in a country without any inspectors and could register any underground tests. The most important result of the conferences was the establishment of a dialogue that influenced the dialogue on arms control at Geneva and elsewhere, and that may have influenced thinking about nuclear weapons among the world's governments. The spirit of the exchanges at the Pugwash meetings was far from the moral exhortation of the Russell–Einstein Manifesto; these were professionals talking to one another on a technical level. But the movement has lasted.

In the early 1960s, the existence of the hydrogen bomb was rarely called into question any more, and scientists and statesmen were content to seek accommodation with it through intelligent management of the situation. But the stockpiles mounted, to the level of beaches, the pilots still lived three minutes from their cockpits, and the rockets with their thermonuclear warheads stood on the launching pads. The Cold War was still being prosecuted vigorously, despite summit meetings and exchange visits since Stalin's death. It was still a very frightening world.

In his 1960 State of the Union message, President Eisenhower told Congress:

With both sides of this divided world in possession of unbelievably destructive weapons, mankind approaches a state where mutual annihilation becomes a possibility. No other fact of today's world equals this in importance. It colours everything we say, plan and do.

10. Thinking Thermonuclear

The advent of the hydrogen bomb on the international scene seemed at first like the introduction into chess of a new move that consists of kicking over the chessboard. A natural first reaction to such an innovation would be to say that one could no longer play chess. However, you could play chess. You could devise strategies that would dissuade your opponent from making this move, while retaining the option yourself, and kick out without upsetting the whole board. It might take you a while to realize these possibilities, as you became accustomed to the drastically new situation.

In the late 1950s, there was developing a consciousness of how to incorporate the hydrogen bomb into the contest of power politics. Some people began to see it not as an absolute, incalculable and irreducible, but as an instrument in human affairs. For better or for worse, some people were learning to think about thermonuclear war instead of just reacting to the idea.

Most of this thinking was not being done by military men but by civilians. Even seen as a technical problem, nuclear war was so complicated that its planning required technical and calculating skills not always available within the armed forces. More fundamentally, any consideration of the hydrogen bomb as a military weapon must immediately go far beyond traditional military concerns. The problems of using it are not to make it effective but to use it for some rational purpose. The problems of deterrence are different from the problems of war.

The people who spent their time thinking about these problems constituted a new profession that grew up, mostly in America: the nuclear strategists, or, in less confining definitions defence intellectuals or strategic analysts. Because he is an intellectual, and his field is ideas rather than action, the nuclear strategist, rather than the nuclear bomber pilot or Polaris submarine commander with finger on button, provides the most significant contrast to Mrs O'Connell and the nuclear pacifists. He has an intellectual and moral position. He sees their attitude as a negative one, a moral squeamishness like fainting at the sight of blood, which may indicate a sensitivity to suffering, but is of no help or even relevance to the prevention and care of wounds.

To him, the hydrogen bomb exists, ergo, it should be thought about. It could be used, ergo, it should be made manageable, so that this use is as rational as possible. He does not see the H-bomb as transcending the issues of international affairs, but rather as an instrument to be fitted into their scheme. He is practical above all. He is not incapable of feeling awe, but he finds awe an unemployable emotion.

Some people feel strongly that thinking about nuclear war in practical terms is repellent, and a betrayal of standards of human decency. The image is conjured up of cold, calculating, soulless men, with powerful minds but no feelings, who reduce millions of men, women and children to mere factors in an equation, deliberately shutting out all awareness of their humanity. The strategic analyst would probably say that to contemplate the children in the target areas while he is trying to think rationally about nuclear war would be counter-productive, just as, for a surgeon, thinking about the life in his hands while he is performing a critical operation would not help to steady him. Usually, though, the nuclear strategist feels that his emotions are his own business. The enormous consequences of the issues he is dealing with oblige him to think as clearly as possible, and to test constantly his ideas and attitudes against those of others. Just as the bomber pilot feels he has fulfilled his obligations to humanity by risking his life, so the strategist feels he has fulfilled his by devoting his entire intelligence to the problem.

There is a more cerebral criticism of practical thinking about nuclear war that is frequently heard. It was expressed by William L. Miller, writing in the magazine *Worldview*, in a review of Herman Kahn's book *On Thermonuclear War*: 'Kahn does not enough admit the possibility that by making thermonuclear war more thinkable and more surviveable, one may make thermonuclear war more likely. The tender-mindedness he wishes to overcome may be a basic moral revulsion that should not be overcome.'

Some injustice is done to Kahn and his colleagues in the bald statement that he wants to overcome tender-mindedness, as if one of his objects was to make the human race more hard-hearted. But on the larger question, it is far from certain that people's moral revulsion is an adequate preventative to nuclear war, and reinforcing it provides no guarantee that nuclear war will not happen. At the risk of weakening slightly the inhibitions against allowing such a horror, the defence intellectuals are trying to make it more likely that, if it ever happens, there is some rational control. They are trying to reduce the consequences of nuclear war, even if this means increasing very slightly the risk. Most would argue, moreover, that it does not increase the risk: that if a government is in a nuclear war crisis, and none of its leaders has thought through the implications of using nuclear weapons, its thinking is more likely to be wild and wrong-headed.

The defence intellectuals and their studies of nuclear strategy are to be found mostly in the 'think corporations' that sprang up to study such problems in America in the past twenty years, and the centres at universities that were founded to study problems of war and peace in the nuclear age. Rand was the first and the biggest of these and the prototype for many others that were to follow. It acquired a reputation for independent, useful and stimulating work that brought credit to the Air Force, its sponsor, though the conclusions were not always to the Air Force's liking; other services wanted their own centres to provide civilian brains on tap.

The Army set up the Operations Research Office at Johns Hopkins University, which later became the Research Analysis

Corporation. Like Rand, this soon branched out from specific studies of military problems to scholarship on political and economic subjects, notably Soviet affairs. The Navy set up the Institute of Naval Analysis. The Department of Defense established the Institute for Defense Analyses in a tall, white stalagmite of a building out in the flat, green countryside a mile from the Pentagon. Several major universities established separate institutes for the study of international affairs and strategic matters. Among the shady lanes of Cambridge, Mass., the Harvard and M.I.T. centres hold regular joint seminars on arms control which have contributed ideas to Government policy. Some university centres of strategic studies do work on contract for the Government.

Such places form a midway position between the Groves of Academe and the powerhouse of government; the occupants can take the lofty view of the academic, but they are aware of the pressures and responsibilities of government, and often privy to some of its secrets as well. They can study and think about issues that are long-range or only remotely possible, as no government official can, harassed as he is by the pressures of immediate concerns, issues like the implications of a world police force, or of a world of twenty nuclear powers.

They can also provide factual reports on matters of some indirect relevance to world problems. In talk of nuclear war, the term 'unacceptable damage' is often used: Rosemary Klingberg Coffey of the Institute for Defense Analyses made a study of what in the past has been 'unacceptable damage' that has induced nations to surrender. Environmental effects of nuclear war? The Hudson Institute has made a study of the environmental effects of great natural disasters in history, such as the Krakatoa explosion and the Lisbon earthquake. Psychological effects of nuclear bombing? The Rand Corporation has made a study of the psychological effects of Second World War mass air raids.

Those who work directly for the Government also do fairly rigorous problem-solving, applying systems analysis and new mathematical tools to non-mathematical problems – 'tools' is a favourite word among them. The problem might be which of two weapons is the more efficient, given the technical data, or else one of logistics, or command and control. These institutions favour the active, muscular intellect over the contemplative, imaginative one.

The men in them are dedicated impressively to the life of reason. When Quakers picketed the Rand building in Santa Monica with posters denouncing nuclear war plans, some Rand men suggested that they come inside and put their views. This started a series of regular, unofficial meetings between Rand men and Quakers to exchange views on international and community affairs that has been going on for several years. The Rand people simply assumed that, however far apart their views, rational men must have something to say to one another.

Some people in the think corporations have devised categories of first, second and third-order agreements. The first is an agreement on points of substance. The second is an agreement by two people on what they disagree about; it can be defined as an argument in which each side can state the other's position to the other's satisfaction. It is rare in daily discourse. The third is an agreement, in the absence of any concord of views, that the discussion can usefully be continued no further. The people who devised this scheme say that professionals in the field should always be able to reach at least a second-order agreement, but they admit that they do not come up to this standard.

Some of these centres provide for the member a remarkable combination of the freedom to work on anything he chooses, a range of problems of interest and importance, and the stimulation of constant contact with lively minds. Many find these places much more convivial than campus life.

Rand is a kind of mental gymnasium, where athletes exercise their intellectual muscles constantly, spar with one another in pairs, play team sports and examine each other's development with admiration or friendly criticism. When Rand scholars write books, they usually pass around the manuscript in draft form; the published book usually has a long list of acknowledgements to people who have offered help, and these are often the same names. A thanks B, C, D and E for their friendly criticism and advice during the preparation of this manuscript; B thanks A, C, D and E, and thanks E particularly for suggesting the idea for Chapter 5; and so on, in a literary *La Ronde*.

The stimulation and companionship are attractions that draw young people from academic life; salaries, too, are higher than those paid to university staffs or civil servants during the 1950s, though university salaries have climbed since to a comparable level. There is also the attraction, for one kind of intellectual, of the association with the virility of power, the phenomenon described in the remark that has been attributed to André Malraux: *'Les intellectuels sont comme les femmes; ils s'en prennent aux militaires.'** It is the appeal of being, not one of the anxious, alienated, disaffected intelligentsia whose standards are higher than the world's behaviour will ever meet, but one of the knowing firm-eyed men who understand the way things work.

Rand thinking is done on several levels. Much of its work is problem-solving; some of it is scholarly work in science or mathematics, or else on contemporary or recent history. The two interact in a middle ground. When someone with a really active mind is given a problem to solve, he starts asking the questions that the answer to the problem raises. As the analysts solved management and operational problems for the Air Force, they started asking questions like 'What is an Air Force *for*?' The classic instance of this was Wohlstetter's study on overseas bases, cited earlier. This was a prototype Rand study in that it made sweeping strategic recommendations, but within the framework of the question asked. Wohlstetter did not say that it would be undesirable *militarily* to have most of S A C's bombers destroyed on the ground, because he had not been asked for a military opinion. He only said, as an economist, that it would be expensive.

*'Intellectuals are like women; they go for the military.'

The replacement of bombers by missiles as the principal weapon of strategic warfare permitted the employment of mathematical problem-solving techniques with even greater precision. As William Kaufmann, of Rand and M.I.T., wrote: 'Missile warfare is peculiarly tractable to numerical analysis. Decisions might still be subject to human vagaries, but actions and their immediate effects could be calculated. These calculations gave a solid underpinning and a professional style to speculations about nuclear war.

The numbers in these calculations are not simple numbers, but probabilities. They exist in the same shadowy world of quasi-reality as life insurance statistics and gambling odds.

The accuracy of a missile is expressed in a unit called the CEP, which stands for circular error of probability. This is the radius of a circle within which, on the average, *half* of the missiles of a particular type will fall. If you have the CEP and the power of a warhead, you can calculate quite easily the probability that it will do a certain amount of damage. If, to make the problem simple, a missile warhead is just powerful enough to destroy the target if it lands within the CEP, which may be five miles, then if you fire one missile at the target, there is a 50-per-cent chance that it will be destroyed; with two missiles there is a 75-per-cent chance, with three an $87\frac{1}{2}$-per-cent chance.

To the people who deal in probabilities, this kind of figure has a hard reality that others do not always appreciate. For instance, Herman Kahn, talking about the acceptance of risks in a deterrent posture, can write: 'If we deliberately accept a ·01 chance of killing 100 million people, we have in a probabilistic sense "killed" one million people, which itself raises several moral issues.' *

Nuclear attack calculations become much more complicated when a war plan is really being worked out. The planners must calculate the number of missiles or bombers that might be destroyed on the ground, which changes the percentage that can be expected to land in the target areas. They will be deal-

* *Thinking About the Unthinkable*, Chapter 4.

ing with a 'mix' of bombers and missiles of several types, each with a different degree of accuracy, power and vulnerability. Furthermore, they will be interdependent: how many bombers reach their targets will depend largely upon how many of certain missiles reach *their* targets, which are anti-aircraft missile sites. At this point, the planners bring in a computer to help with the calculations.

When the target lists for different war plans are drawn up by the Joint Strategic Target Planning Board at Offutt, each target is given a percentage figure. This is the probability that it will be destroyed in that particular war plan. It is arrived at by multiplying the probability of success of the different weapons assigned to it. They are not dealing only with missiles and aircraft, but also with bombs. They have options in the size of bombs or warheads delivered, whether they have a high or low fallout yield, and whether they are optimized to kill people or destroy installations.

Many of the strategic analysts are quantitative economists in their academic background, who have mastered the new instruments of calculation that mathematics has given to economics. Economists have created much of the style of nuclear strategies so that there is much talk of input and output, and how much deterrence you want to buy. Others are not mathematicians at all. They work with these figures because their sense of the job they are doing demands that they deal with the most precise data possible, even if this means that it must be expressed in probabilities or other mathematical terms. Rand computer men have devised a computer system so simple that, they say, anyone can learn to use it in twenty minutes, and all Rand men have access to the computers to help them with their problems. Robert Specht of Rand is fond of quoting the dictum 'The world today is changing so fast that the only two languages that can remain meaningful through the change are poetry and mathematics.'

The strategic analysts do not make war plans. They make calculations about what wars can be planned, and what kinds of nuclear wars might be best survived, or preferred, or avoided. To help them do this, they developed several kinds of models of nuclear war, cold and hot, which are characteristic of the way most think about the subject, and which engage some of their ideas. The three principal ones are games theory, war and peace games, and scenarios.

Games Theory is a branch of mathematics originated partly by the prolific John Von Neumann. It has encountered a certain amount of resistance among non-mathematicians because of the misleadingly frivolous connotations of the name. It is a serious matter, not a pastime, though in fact a world strategy game devised at Rand by Olaf Helmer of the Social Sciences Division was marketed commercially as Summit.

Games theory sets out mathematical models for contests, or 'games'. There are many kinds, with different characteristics. The practitioner of games theory constructs, as a simplified model of a game, a matrix, with A's possible sequences of moves along one side and B's down another. Each sequence of moves, or strategy, is compressed into a single square. The squares in the matrix where two rows meet show the interaction of two strategies, with a gain for one side or the other, the 'payoff' in games theory terminology.

The games theorist can look at a matrix and see a whole range of possibilities. He may reject a strategy that offers a chance of the biggest gain in favour of one that offers a favourable, or not-too-favourable, payoff in the face of a large number of his opponent's strategies. In other words, he may give up the chance of a big win in order to have a very high chance of a smaller win.

Games theory is used in studies of business conflicts as well as political power conflicts. It is no more a *representation* of war than it is of business. There is no attempt to substitute figures for flesh and blood. It is a model which indicates some useful points.

Some significant distinctions can be drawn between different types of games. For instance, games in which the entire situation is known to all the players (chess, go) and games in which some information is concealed from each player (bridge, poker, dominoes); games in which chance is a 'player' (any card or dice game) and is not (chess, go).

Attention has been paid in recent years to one particular distinction, between what are called zero sum games and non-zero sum games. The first is a game of pure conflict. A gain for one side must mean a corresponding loss for the other. It is like a straight gambling game between two players involving a fixed sum of money. What one side wins, the other side loses. On the games theory matrix, if the interaction of moves shows a plus for one side, it must show a corresponding minus for the other, so that the gain and the loss add up to zero. The non-zero sum game, sometimes called the mixed-motive game, has a wider range of possibilities. The payoff of a series of moves might mean that one side gains more than the other loses, or less, or even that both sides lose something. It is not pure conflict in that, if the payoff is the worst possible for one side, it does not follow that it is the best possible one for the other. (Because this model involves mixed motives and both shared and conflicting interests, it can be seen as a variant of a partnership, or alliance, situation as well as of a conflict one.)

Those who see the international situation in terms of pure conflict are interested in manipulating zero sum games as their models. Many of the strategic analysts, however, see a more useful model in the mixed-motive game, in which one side's loss is not necessarily another side's gain. In this picture, there are also many situations in which both sides lose – all-out nuclear war which neither side wants is the extreme case. The interaction of moves that brings this about must be clearly recognized, communicated in advance by the side that sees it first, and avoided.

War and Peace Games, or *Crisis Games*, are a model closer to reality; they deal with countries and weapons, and not mathematical symbols. It is a development of the pure war games that have been played by military officers since they were originated by the Prussian General Staff. In this, a real situation is created, and the players are assigned various roles to play – a nation, or a member of a government, or a movement (the Vietcong, or an opposition political party) – and given these interests to defend. Provision is made to ensure chance happenings from time to time that no one has intended: a fighter plane harassing an intruding airliner crashes into it, a secret communication is leaked to the Press. The moves and responses are written on slips of paper and handed to an umpire.

Again, a war game is not intended to be a representation of real events; human affairs are too fluid and unpredictable. Its purpose is to suggest possibilities and to educate. It might enlarge the player's vision, open up his eyes to a wider range of possibilities than he knew existed. It might also show him that the range of possible action is narrower than he thought, that the person who has to make the decisions is more constrained than he had imagined. Several of the centres of strategic analysis devise them for the use of the armed forces and the State Department, and, occasionally, for the analysts themselves.

While it cannot be definitive, a game can certainly provide material for discussion of real situations. For instance, during the early 1960s, there were proposals for a NATO nuclear force. The plan that was on the negotiating table for three years was for a nuclear-armed multilateral force, or MLF, consisting of mixed-manned surface ships carrying missiles. One of the objections was that since the United States would have a veto over use, any action by an MLF ship would simply be taken as an action by the United States, and rightly so. At the M.I.T. Center for International Studies, Lincoln Bloomfield organized some war games for staff and students, involving an MLF. Some unexpected things occurred.

In one, at a time of intense, brink-of-war crisis, an MLF ship was being tailed by a Soviet submarine. The captain radioed for instructions, and asked for permission to use his nuclear depth charges, an act that would undoubtedly have grave international consequences. He was told that he could use them only if the submarine manoeuvred into firing position. Under the stress of his danger (and players in a war game *do* feel the stress) he deliberately radioed a false picture, saying that the submarine was in a firing position. His crew were given permission to use the atomic depth charge, and they did. The U.S. Government players were dismayed at this, and immediately tried to convince the Soviet Union that this was accidental even if not, strictly speaking, unauthorized, and not an act of war. They found it was easier to dissociate the United States from this act than it would be had it been an American Navy ship. In the latter case, the Soviet Government would be bound to take some reprisal against the United States. While the M L F was being discussed in Washington, Lincoln Bloomfield was saying, with his tongue only partly in his cheek, that he was the only man in the world who knew what it was like to use a multilateral nuclear force operationally.

In another M.I.T. game, when rapid negotiations between the great powers looked like averting nuclear war at the last instant, some move had to be made quickly to demonstrate peaceful intentions by forces poised for action. The U.S. Government players had several Polaris submarines surface before Soviet ships, in what Bloomfield calls a high-speed arms control measure. It took imagination, and showed that imagination can usefully be applied now to thinking out ways to pull military forces back from the brink.

Sometimes, the games teach something about the players and the world in which they live. In 1954, a series of war games was played at the Air Force's Air War College at Maxwell, Alabama. The object was to seek ways to apply pressure with air power short of war. The situation kept toppling over into nuclear war. As Brigadier-General Sidney Giffin of the Institute for Defense Analyses comments (in his book *The Crisis Game*), 'This was in an innocent period when many thought war between the United States and the Soviet Union an acceptable alternative.' These days, crisis games hardly ever result in U.S.–Soviet nuclear war, even at military staff colleges.

Some of the educational effects of this kind of exercise were seen in a Vietnam war game conducted at a British university, Leeds. Eight governments were represented, with three members of each, and the United Nations. The players were mostly students. The predominant current of opinion among them was anti-American on Vietnam, and most thought the war should and could be ended quickly.

When they took up their roles, they found that, somehow, they could not pursue this simple aim. They were enmeshed in entanglements, in requirements, in pressures. Finance ministers of countries dependent on American aid argued with their foreign ministers that they could not afford to help the Vietcong, and won. A girl playing a foreign minister resigned in the agony of this particular dilemma. Others fell quickly into defending their interests with zeal, and with a Machiavellianism rarely exceeded in the real world of international politics. There were truce negotiations, but these broke down in an atmosphere of distrust. By the end, the war had escalated and tactical nuclear weapons were being used. When these particular students talked about Vietnam afterwards, the slogans came less readily, and solutions were not offered so glibly.

The *Scenario* is just what the name implies, a scenario, or story, depicting events. Its purpose is to stretch the imagination; its value does not lie in its accuracy, but in its plausibility. Among the defence intellectuals, a scenario is usually an extended form of an argument, designed to meet a rhetorical question, like: 'How could a test-ban agreement be dangerous?' or 'What difference would it make if you have twice the number of nuclear weapons that your enemy has if his force is invulnerable?'

One scenario much discussed at one time was the so-called 'Hamburg grab'. This was an argument against dispensing with large ground forces and relying on nuclear weapons for defence. To summarize it: West German Communists seize control one night of Hamburg, the closest major West German city to the East–West frontier. They call upon Soviet forces to 'liberate' the city, perhaps staging a raid on the lightly-guarded frontier to open it. Soviet tanks waiting on the frontier (for this is planned) race for the city, with little opposition from allied troops since these are so few, and have occupied it by dawn. The Russians announce that they have no intention of occupying any more West German territory. The N A T O allies now face an unpleasant choice. They can accept the situation, or else they can initiate a major war with Russia, which, since they are weak on the ground in Germany, would almost certainly extend to strategic nuclear bombardment, for a city now under Communist rule. The second alternative is unlikely to be adopted.

The conclusion that was argued from this was that the allies must have enough forces in Germany to ensure that the Russians cannot present the West with this kind of *fait accompli*, that in order to make any incursion into West Germany they will have to fight their way through allied troops, opening major hostilities. Others argued against the plausibility of the scenario. They said that whereas a minor frontier clash was possible, the Russians would never do anything as serious as trying to capture a major West German city, under whatever guise of 'liberation', unless they were opening a major offensive against Western Europe.

The defence intellectuals' influence has been wide. At a recent N A T O conference, American officials tried to work up a sense of urgency about the growing power of China. They said that by 1975 China would probably have I C B Ms with nuclear warheads, and these could reach London, Paris and Cologne over a Polar route as easily as the West coast of the United States. The Europeans generally remained unconvinced of the danger. One West German official who had visited several American centres of strategic analysis challenged one of the Americans on this by saying, 'Give us a scenario.'

As nuclear deterrence was the American military posture, some fundamental thinking was done on the idea of deterrence. Some divided it into active and passive deterrence. Passive deterrence is the deterring of an all-out attack on one's own country. It is passive in the sense that a response to an all-out attack requires no active decision, but can be presumed to be automatic. Active deterrence is the deterring of some other action, for instance, an attack on an ally. A response requires an active decision, and this is more complicated. A commitment must be made and communicated convincingly to a potential enemy.

Different forces are required for these two roles. A small but invulnerable missile force with hydrogen bomb warheads would serve for passive deterrence. No enemy is likely to try to conquer a country which, despite the best that it could do, would still be able to destroy it after the attack. This is called a minimum deterrence force. This would not serve for active deterrence, however. A threat of mutual suicide is not a convincing deterrent to an incursion against an ally, or any one of a wide range of hostile actions that might take place. For this, the capability for a wide range of response is needed.

It was found that uncertainty is a part of all deterrence. It is by no means certain that a government would wage a suicidal war, destroying an enemy in the process, rather than surrender unconditionally. Nevertheless, it is possible, and it would be unwise to force such an extreme choice. If a general commanding a powerful nuclear deterrence force, ready to go to war at a moment's notice, were told that there was a 50-percent chance that none of his weapons worked, and that the potential enemy knew it, he would immediately move heaven and earth to remedy the fault, and/or resign in disgrace. Nevertheless, the enemy would be deterred; a 50-per-cent chance of annihilation is quite adequate for this.

Sometimes, uncertainly is at the heart of a deterrent situation. The threat to meet aggression with local ground forces equipped with conventional weapons can be seen as a part of the nuclear deterrent, and not, as it generally is, its opposite. A limited war is a worrying prospect partly because it would increase the risk of nuclear war. As Thomas Schelling observed in *The Strategy of Conflict*, 'Brinkmanship' is not going to the brink where one can *decide* to jump off. 'It is the deliberate creation of a recognizable risk of war, a risk that does not imply complete control.' It is rocking the boat, endangering both parties to deter the other from some course of action.

The strategy of massive retaliation, or pure deterrence, belonged in an age when the hydrogen bomb was the overwhelming absolute, an ultimate violence, that blotted out all distinctions and all gradations. Now there was an interest in finding some distinctions, some gradations between the bad and the worst, in looking more closely at the possible forms of retaliation. Some of the defence intellectuals in particular found the irrational element in pure deterrence distasteful, summed up in the paradoxes it engendered – 'If we ever have to go to war on our mission, we've failed' – and in the phrase 'spasm war'.

The most powerful stimulus for rethinking on deterrence lay in the growing Soviet armoury of long-range weapons, which was indeed coming to make massive retaliation a two-way street. A temperamental reserve about a policy that implied massacre by spasm became an urgent search for an alternative when it implied national suicide.

A number of books appeared containing criticisms of the policy. Henry Kissinger, a young Harvard political scientist, wrote the first widely-read book on this subject, *Nuclear Weapons and Foreign Policy*, in 1957. He suggested that nuclear explosives were most useful as comparatively low-power tactical weapons, and that America should counter Soviet superiority in numbers by using these on the ground if necessary rather than by threatening to drop H-bombs. Later, for quite respectable reasons, he changed his mind and saw dangers in using even tactical nuclear weapons, a reversal that gave rise to the crack 'I wonder who's Kissinger now'. (Dr Kissinger became President Nixon's special adviser on foreign policy in 1969.)

Bernard Brodie put some of the ideas that he brought out in his first H-bomb briefings in Washington about 'getting war back to the battlefield' into *Strategy in the Missile Age*. He later changed *his* stance somewhat, and worried that American policy had moved too far away from the option of using nuclear weapons.

General Maxwell Taylor, after he resigned as Army Chief of Staff, expressed an army man's anxieties in *The Uncertain Trumpet*, in which he depicted an America muscle-bound with her H-bomb power, but deficient in men and equipment on the ground and the will and imagination to use them. Others argued along the same lines.

This was part of the search for a non-nuclear military posture. Others were seeking a nuclear posture in which the use of H-bombs would be rational, instead of a signal for a *Götterdämmerung*. At Rand, it was being considered in an informal group that had been meeting for years to discuss strategic war. This was begun in 1951 by a few people who became interested in strategic questions. They used to meet every two weeks or so to discuss a particular topic or book, or else a paper that someone had prepared.

One of the members was Andrew Marshall; like a number of strategic analysts, he is highly respected in the profession but little known outside it, because he does not write for the general reader. In 1957, Marshall spent three months in Washington sitting in on a defence advisory panel. When he returned to Rand, it was after the sputnik triumph, and he started thinking about deterrence in the years ahead, when Russia would have intercontinental missiles. He decided that if deterrence failed, the question of what to do next would be an open one. Whatever has been threatened before is not necessarily the best thing to do if war breaks out. This was not only a military question, so he invited two others at Rand to join him in making a study of this, Herbert Goldhammer, a sociologist who was studying political behaviour, and Nathan Leites, the author of two books on Soviet attitudes and policy.

Meanwhile, a new idea was raised in the Strategic Objectives Committee. Back in 1950, Bernard Brodie had wondered whether it might be plausible to restrict an atomic bomb attack to military targets, so as to spare the civilian population from disaster. He and Herman Kahn worked out a war plan, using their knowledge of the effects of atomic bombs. They concluded that it could not be done; even in an attack on military targets, 2 million people would be killed, and this was total disaster. Now Brodie raised the idea again in the Committee, and it was discussed. This was not because the casualty figures could be revised downwards; on the contrary, with H-bombs substituted for atomic bombs, they would be higher. But the thermonuclear bomb had brought new standards, and by these, 2 million dead, or even 4 or 6 million, was a long way from total disaster.

Marshall and his two colleagues worked out in great detail several alternative nuclear bombing strategies, including one that aimed primarily at military targets. In the first half of 1958, they wrote them up in a 120-page report. In games-theory style, they drew up matrices for a two-sided war, showing what would happen if one side used one of these strategies and the other side another. They circulated this among Rand colleagues for comments in the latter half of 1958, and in 1959 it was given to the Air Force as a classified document.

The Air Force itself was becoming sensitive to the criticisms of massive retaliation, and some of its senior officers were seeking a less rigid stance. Independently of the Marshall–Goldhammer–Leites report, they asked Rand for a study on different ways that strategic bombing could be used. Albert Wohlstetter headed the group that carried out what was called the Strategic Offensive Forces Study, and the ideas that emerged in the informal seminars went into this. The report contained several alternatives to the totally devastating attack, including one for attacking military targets and sparing cities. This was called, in the new terminology, a counterforce attack as opposed to a counter-city one.

Some in the Air Force were working towards the same idea themselves. S A C was still wedded to their original concept of total devastation, but men on the staff of the Chief of Staff, General Thomas White, were looking for an alternative. With General White's approval, a team under Brigadier-General Noel Parrish played out war games, programming different nuclear attack patterns into computers to learn the effects of their interaction, projecting force levels a few years into the future. They found, as they expected, that if both tried their hardest to achieve total devastation, both countries would suffer something approaching it, even though the side that struck first suffered less. If both sides restricted their attacks to military targets, the cost in death and damage would be very much lower. Their conclusions seemed to favour the counterforce strategy.

The strategy that emerged from these different studies is this: your missiles and planes strike at the enemy's missile and bomber bases, blunting his attack. They also attack other military bases connected with the immediate prosecution of the war. Avoiding the enemy's cities gives him an inducement to avoid yours. The model for this kind of war is both sides attacking each other's forces and sparing each other's cities, then negotiating a peace.

To those used to thinking of war only in terms of total conflict, in its means and its objectives, the startling new feature of this plan was the continuum between war and peace. War became, not the opposite of deterrence, but a continuation of it. Even while the fighting was going on, one tries to deter the enemy from doing his worst by refraining from doing the worst to him.

By the end of 1959, there were no longer one but several nuclear war strategies that had been worked out in detail. An outline of the spectrum of alternatives might go like this.

Total Devastation, or Cities-Plus. This was the original and abiding concept of SAC. War is deterred by the promise of total destruction to an enemy. Stockpiles are increased so that the destruction can be made more certain, by assigning several weapons to each target. Rocket sites, bomber bases, military bases, cities and industrial plants are all attacked; any civilians killed or property destroyed outside the target areas is bonus damage.

Minimum Deterrence, sometimes called Pure Cities. In this, deterrence is maintained by a force of invulnerable or near-invulnerable missiles, large enough only to ensure that most can escape destruction, and destroy all of an enemy's major cities in the case of war. (True to the pattern of interservice rivalries, the Navy favoured this strategy for some time.* The Polaris submarine is the ideal weapon for it. Its missile is not accurate enough to be fired effectively at enemy strategic forces.)

Counterforce Plus. In this, the attack is optimized to destroy an enemy's forces, particularly his strategic bombing forces. Cities are taken off the target list for the first attack, to be destroyed later only if the enemy attacks cities. Many of the enemy's civilians are killed all the same, since large bombs are dropped close to the ground to blast out underground military installations, which causes huge amounts of fallout. Also, some military targets are either in cities or on their outskirts, such as airfields and military headquarters. Nevertheless, after such an attack, most of the city-dwellers in the enemy's country are still alive, hostages to be spared so long as *his* bombing force spares cities.

Counterforce With Avoidance. The attack is directed at military forces, with great effort to minimize civilian deaths, even at some cost in effectiveness. It might mean using the smallest nuclear bombs necessary to destroy a target, and therefore taking a chance on missing it, and sparing some targets altogether if they are in cities. Again, the object is to induce the enemy to do the same.

Scenarios were written for these strategies with different outcomes. In some, the tacit agreement to limit war to counterforce actions broke down, and was followed by all-out attacks on cities – 'city-busting', in the grotesquely sporting phrase used by many of the strategists. In others, there was even controlled and measured destruction of cities, 'city exchanges' on a tit-for-tat basis; or asymmetrical city exchanges, in which

---

*For instance, the then Chief of Naval Operations, Admiral Arleigh Burke, wrote in his Personal Letter No. 5 to retired admirals on 30 July 1958: 'To avoid needless and provocative over-inflation of our strategic forces, their size should be set by an objective of general adequacy for deterrence alone, i.e. for an ability to destroy major urban areas, not by the false goal of adequacy for "winning" '—quoted in *100 Million Lives* by Richard Fryklund.

one side used its superiority in numbers to destroy or threaten to destroy two, three or five of the other side's cities for every one of its own. There were some in which, in a crisis, one side with superiority in numbers attacked and destroyed most of the other side's missile forces, then told the other to climb down on pain of a five-for-one exchange of city destruction.

The need to keep open communications with the enemy was a factor sometimes, and even the need to preserve something of the enemy's command and control system. If a bargain is to be made, there must be someone to make it with, someone who has power over his forces. This might in itself be a reason for sparing an enemy's capital.

Too often, ideas like cold-bloodedly 'trading' cities, or controlling and circumscribing thermonuclear bombardment, are shrugged off as too bizarre to have any relevance to the way in which a nuclear war might actually be fought by real men. But there is no standard of normalcy for thermonuclear war, by which one sort can be judged more bizarre or more unorthodox than another. To enter such a war would be to embark on a totally unprecedented situation. As an old saw has it:

> 'Life is peculiar,' said Jeremy.
> 'Compared with what?' asked the spider.

Very few things in this area can safely be rejected as so far removed from the realm of the possible that no situation could ever arise in which it might be a danger to worry about, or a useful strategy.

These counterforce wars are all, in games theory terms, non-zero sum, or mixed-motive contests. One side's loss is not necessarily the other's gain. Both sides have a common motive in avoiding total destruction. Communication between them is essential throughout. This need not be in the form of verbal messages: the communication may be tacit. But the import of an action must be understood by the other side. If an attack avoids cities as an inducement to an enemy government to do the same, that government must understand that cities are being avoided and why. The enemy is being offered a kind of bargain, and must understand the offer. Communication is also an essential part of deterrence, in fact, *the* essential part. No one is deterred by a threat that is not communicated.

One in particular among the academic strategists has had a great deal to say on the subjects of bargaining, communication and mixed-motive conflicts, Thomas Schelling. He is an economist, who has a background both in academic life and in the foreign aid service. It was through the contemplation of bargaining in economic life, among the donor and receiver of foreign aid, for instance, that he came to an interest in games theory, and then a study of deterrence. His first book, *The Strategy of Conflict*, appeared in 1960 after several of its sections had appeared already in academic journals, and it was largely theoretical. Its examples were drawn as much from the actions of car salesmen and stubborn children as the international behaviour of nations.

He is at this writing a professor at the Harvard Center for International Studies, and chairman of the Harvard–M.I.T. seminar on arms control. He has lectured to groups of government officials and military officers in many countries. Among the nuclear strategists, Albert Wohlstetter has had the most direct influence on government actions, and Herman Kahn has undoubtedly reached the widest audience, but Thomas Schelling has probably done the most to affect the thinking of people in positions of power.

He gives many examples of mixed-motive contests, making the point that even the total wars of modern times had an element of shared motives. Even the demand for 'unconditional surrender', he points out, implies the possibility of surrender rather than death, and implies also that there is a point at which this, rather than a continuation of the fighting, is to the advantage of both sides.

He indicates some different tactics for bargaining or deterrence (which is a negative form of bargaining), some of them paradoxical. One is to deliberately make oneself appear weak:

the union negotiator tells the employer that he has very little influence with the men, and if he asks them to accept only a small increase, they will reject him. Another is to reduce one's options, which is to make a commitment: a firm guarantee to come to the defence of an ally, so explicit that to fail to fulfil it would weaken irreparably one's international position; or, a more basic strategy, to burn one's boats. Another is the use of irrationality, pretending that one is not amenable to reason and cannot be deterred (or else actually creating a situation in which rational deterrence does not apply, like 'rocking the boat').

He also laid down guidelines for an agreed point in a bargaining situation. It should be easily distinguishable, either by being a round number, or qualitatively distinctive. As he wrote in *The Strategy of Conflict,*

When agreement must be reached with incomplete communication, the participants must be ready to allow the situation itself to exercise substantial constraint over the outcome; specifically, a solution that discriminates against one party or the other, or even involves unnecessary nuisance to both of them, may be the only one on which their expectations may be co-ordinated.

All this has powerful implications for wars in which both sides observe some restraints. The exemplary case since the Second World War is the Korean War, in which the constraints observed by both sides were qualitative, and were never the subject of explicit agreements. They involved natural or national boundaries, and kinds of weapons. The decisive Chinese move was intervention: the number of Chinese troops involved was less decisive.

Much of Schelling's world is a strange one for the military men and many others who hear him lecture, and are used to thinking in terms of pure-conflict situations. It is one in which, as in Freud's, every action is also a gesture. Its object is not only to achieve something but to communicate something.

As an example of a perfectly communicated action, Schelling cites the American air attack on navy ships and installations in five North Vietnamese ports in August 1964, following two passes by North Vietnamese torpedo boats at U.S. Navy ships in the Gulf of Tonkin. 'If the American military action was widely judged unusually fitting,' he writes, 'this was an almost aesthetic judgement. If words like "repartee" can be applied to war and diplomacy, the military action was an expressive form of repartee. It took mainly the form of deeds, not words, but the deeds were articulate.' *

In Schelling's world, enemies need a common understanding as much as allies. Enemies always have some common interests, just as allies always have some competing ones. Much of policy is aimed at reaching tacit understanding with the enemy on qualitatively distinguishable points.

Over the years, there grew up one sharp, qualitative distinction in the world very clearly recognized by all the contesting powers, not because of verbal messages, and sometimes in spite of them. This is the distinction between conventional and nuclear weapons.

As nuclear weapons were made smaller and smaller, as well as bigger and bigger, the quantitative distinction became less. The United States Army has tested atomic artillery shells with an explosive power equivalent to 250 tons of T N T. The vital distinction between these nuclear and conventional weapons is not quantitative. Many people said that, because of this, there was no real difference. John Foster Dulles once told the *New York Times* coloumnist C. L. Sulzberger 'We are operating on a basis where, more and more, we treat atomic weapons as conventional. It doesn't make any sense to use 100 shots or bombs to do the same job as one explosive weapon.'†

It is quite possible that if small tactical nuclear weapons had been in existence in quantity when the Korean War began, and had been used from the outset, they would today be regarded as 'conventional', and a distinction would have been drawn somewhere else. But now, whatever has been said, the gulf

* *Arms and Influence*, Chapter 4.

† *New York Times*, 3 June 1964. The conversation took place some years earlier: Dulles died in 1959.

between nuclear and non-nuclear explosives is a crucial one, and is crossed at great peril. Use of any nuclear weapon on a battlefield or at sea would have implications much larger than its immediate effects. This may operate illogically against one side or another at different times, but every government knows that it cannot use any nuclear weapon without the action being also a gesture, one that would constitute a major step in the direction of thermonuclear war.

The strongest opposition in America to counterforce and city-sparing strategy came from S A C. They still argued for their own strategy of the devastating blow, primitive in concept, sophisticated in execution. One S A C general was given a briefing on counterforce strategies, and shown matrices with the payoffs. He turned away and said, 'I've got the answer. I just had to look at one square to know that I'm against the counterforce idea.'

'What square was that?' he was asked.

'The one showing the number of Soviet casualties,' he replied. 'Counterforce means less Russians dead. So I'm against it.'

This argument has been put in a more reasoned manner by others at S A C. They have said that the more damage that is done to an enemy's society at the instant he goes to war, the less able he is to prosecute the war, even if it is a short, strategic bombing war. One communications system destroyed might prevent an order from reaching an enemy missile squadron, and save millions of American lives. Men who argue along these lines like to use boxing metaphors: 'stun the enemy', a 'knockout blow'.

Most S A C men saw counterforce, like the non-nuclear or limited war option, as one more attempt to downgrade the big blow with the big bomb, a lineal descendant of the 'liberalism' of the early opposition to the H-bomb programme, and the calls for a promise by the President not to use the H-bomb first, the 'defensive-mindedness' of Project Charles, and the 'timidity' of those who wanted to ward off attack with smaller weapons. All their instincts rebelled against it. Restraint of any kind in attacking the enemy's country seemed timorous, weak, unmanly. Bargaining in wartime seemed half-way to surrender. The only thing to do in a war was to win.

These reactions were not irrelevant. They sprang partly from these men's own experience of war. This told them that, whatever the planning and technological ingenuity that goes into it, war when it happens is a thing of fire and fury, of violence and terrible fear. To fight it requires courage, grim determination and animal aggression. The military life cultivates these qualities because in battle they are essential. To try to turn war into a closely-reasoned bargaining process, and to make the military see it this way, seemed to them to risk diluting the very qualities that are a soldier's pride and his mainstay. Many military people look on the civilian analysts as men who have a lot of ideas about how to fight a war, but no idea of what it feels like to fight one.

Relations between General LeMay and Rand deteriorated, despite the fact that Rand was largely supported by the Air Force and S A C was its biggest command. At least one study was dropped because S A C refused to give Rand staff members the classified information they needed to work on it.

The Left saw the defence intellectuals as Faust-figures, selling their souls to the military. Now the Right came to view them as saboteurs of the manly, patriotic character, undermining its qualities by an insidious process of intellectualizing, and with an arrogant, cock-a-hoop assurance that contained disdain for older people's experiences.

Some do have this kind of arrogance, in a quiet way. They tend to feel that the exchanges of ideas and the calculations and the crisis games add up, not only to useful experience and knowledge, but to a kind of wisdom that is denied to others, who have not yet entered the modern world; this attitude comes out from time to time. For instance, at an international conference on strategic issues, after an address by a European politician who was both distinguished and intelligent, and a veteran of an anti-Nazi resistance movement, one of the younger among the American defence intellectuals remarks to another 'What's he talking like that for? He's visited Rand, he's had some briefings, he knows what the score is.'

Others, however, and probably most, have an intense awareness of the limitations of their methods. Many have doubts about the effectiveness of all their studies and calculations, a profound and even tragic sense of the uncertainties and limitations of human reason and goodwill. Their motive is not an optimistic, Enlightenment faith in reason and progress, but the more modest sentiments that conclude Herman Kahn's book *Thinking About the Unthinkable*: 'The outcome of decisions that are well-meaning, informed and intelligent can be disastrous. However, few would argue that this is a good reason to be malevolent, ignorant or stupid. We have to do the best we can with the tools and abilities we have.'

11. The Strategist: the Intellect of Herman Kahn

Herman Kahn, the author of *On Thermonuclear War* and other books, the popularizer of terms like 'escalation' and 'nuclear chicken', is the most famous nuclear strategist and, for many people, the archetype of the species. Because he invented the term 'doomsday machine', for a nuclear weapon deliberately contrived so that it could wipe out the human race, he is sometimes thought to have been the model for Dr Strangelove, though there are few similarities between the two, and even Strangelove in the film did not invent the device. The *Observer* called him this when he arrived in England once, and it was denied strongly in a letter from the film's author, Peter George, who knew and admired Kahn.

He is the only defence intellectual who has become a public figure. His stance is something like that of a conjuror, performing outrageous and seemingly impossible tricks, like putting 30 million deaths into a handkerchief and making a rational choice and an acceptable postwar world come out of it, staring provocatively at the finish as if to challenge anyone to say that he cheated.

Herman Kahn is a man in his middle forties weighing around 240 pounds, cheerful, zestful and friendly, with the dark eyes of a bear and the dimples of Jackie Gleason. He has a brilliant and extraordinarily active mind, an inexhaustible drive to apply this mind constantly to the things going on in the world around him, and an equal drive to expound on the results. He lectures to public and private audiences all the way up to the top layers of government, in the United States and, on occasional visits, in other countries; he writes often and readably; he is interviewed on television. He has ideas on everything, but the subject on which he has spoken and written is nuclear war.

He has a moral passion to see that world affairs are conducted as rationally as possible, and an intense feeling of the importance of the issues involved. 'When I first got into this business,' he says, 'I was horrified to find how little reasoning had gone into nuclear war. American war planners were prepared to kill 50 million people frivolously. For no good reason at all! People in Communist countries and even some in neighbouring countries. If you asked them why, they'd just say "Well, that's war" or "They're the enemy."'

Kahn wants things to be done only with good reasons, and he wants the reasons worked out in advance as much as possible. He took upon himself the task of forcing people to face the truths of the thermonuclear contest rather than flinch away from difficult choices or unpleasant consequences. No, he has said over the years, thermonuclear war is not impossible, nor is it impossible to win one. It could happen, and it might be better to win it than to lose it. No, deterrence is not an absolute safeguard, and neither is anything else. Yes, a country might survive a nuclear war, but it requires hard thinking and planning in advance. He seeks constantly to stretch people's imaginations, to make them think realistically about questions that seem fantastic by pre-nuclear standards.

He says all this, not in the flaying tones of a Savonarola, but in a style that is persuasive, anecdotal, and full of enthusiasm and gusto.

His manner dismays some people. Walter Marseille, reviewing one of his books in the *Bulletin of the Atomic Scientists*, complained: 'Those who write on nuclear war will be more persuasive if they respect a certain code of conduct. Funeral directors are not supposed to gambol or frolic in public. Kahn does not violate these tabus, but his very readable prose deals so enthusiastically with the grimmest problems that the reader cannot help expecting him to do so at any time.'

Certainly he deals with the grimmest problems. Here is Kahn

tackling, with typical practicality, verve and dash, some problems of the aftermath of a nuclear war:

Most people already know, or will know in the post-attack world, that if you get a fatal dose of radiation, the sequence of events is about like this: first you become nauseated, then sick; you seem to recover, then in two or three weeks you really get sick and die.

Now just imagine yourself in the postwar situation. Everybody will have been subjected to extremes of anxiety, unfamiliar environment, strange foods, minimum toilet facilities, inadequate shelters, and the like. Under these conditions some high percentage of the population is going to become nauseated, and nausea is very catching. If one man vomits, everybody vomits. It would not be surprising if almost everybody vomits. Almost everyone is likely to think he has received too much radiation. Morale may be so affected that many survivors may refuse to participate in constructive activities, but would content themselves with sitting down and waiting to die – some may even become violent and destructive.

However, the situation would be quite different if radiation meters were distributed. Assume now that a man gets sick from causes other than radiation. Not believing this, his morale begins to drop. You look at his meter and say, 'You have only received ten roentgens, why are you vomiting? Pull yourself together and get to work.'*

Here he is using common sense breathtakingly in dealing with an agriculture contaminated by fallout in a nuclear war:

The common contaminated foods which would be the major source of strontium-90 might be classified into five grades – A, B, C, D, and E. [Then follows a table showing that this is in order of contamination, with A having the least.]

The A food would be restricted to children and to pregnant women. The B food would be a high-priced food available to everybody. The C food would be a low-priced food also available to everybody. Finally, the D food would be restricted to people over age forty or fifty. Even though this food would be unacceptable to children, it probably would be acceptable for those past middle age, partly because their bones are already formed so that they do not pick up anywhere near as much strontium as the young, and partly

* *On Thermonuclear War.*

because at these low levels of contamination, it generally takes some decades for cancer to develop. Most of the these people would die of other causes before they got cancer. Finally, there would be an E food restricted to the feeding of animals whose resulting use (meat, draft animals, leather, wool and so on) would not cause an increase in the human burden of Sr-90.*

Kahn can defend vigorously his cold-blooded way of looking at things, and does so frequently, for instance, in an essay entitled *In Defense of Thinking*:

It is quite clear that technical details are not the only important operative facts. Human and moral factors must always be considered. They must never be missing from policies and from public discussion. But emotionalism and sentimentality, as opposed to morality and concern, only confuse debates. Nor can experts be expected to repeat, 'If, heaven forbid ...' before every sentence. Responsible decision makers and researchers cannot afford the luxury of denying the existence of agonizing questions. The public, whose lives and freedom are at stake, expects them to face such questions squarely, and, where necessary, the experts should expect little less of the public.

Or, as he sometimes remarks, 'If you say that a certain kind of nuclear attack would not mean 100 million killed but 30 million, nearly everyone will imagine they heard you say "only 30 million". They'll think you're saying that 30 million dead is nothing to get excited about.'

His wife Jane, a relentless friend and critic, understands well his self-appointed task. When she first read the manuscript of *On Thermonuclear War*, she saw a table of possible American deaths in a nuclear war ranging from 2 million to 160 million, under the heading 'Tragic But Distinguishable Postwar States'. She pointed to the words 'Tragic But' and said to him 'Coward!'

He admits to being able to detach himself emotionally from a problem he is thinking about, or a situation he is in. 'It's something I've always been able to do. During the war, when

* *On Thermonuclear War.*

I was in Burma, although I was in a rear echelon area, there were still some Japanese guerrillas around, there were still a few risks. But I could detach myself completely, and not worry about it. When we started the Hudson Institute, we were in a very difficult financial position for a while, and there was a chance that I would personally go bankrupt, because I had guaranteed some of the costs. It didn't interfere with my work, though; my efficiency wasn't impaired, and I didn't sleep any the worse. But when we were out of the woods, I certainly felt that a burden had been lifted from me.'

He has a huge amount of intellectual energy, and has amassed an unusual amount of learning. He is probably unique in that, not even possessing a Ph.D. degree, he has been offered university posts teaching physics, mathematics and economics. (This is not something he has ever told about himself.) He once remarked of a colleague 'He has a work problem. He has difficulty getting work out.' He said it as if this were a curious and rare affliction, like alcoholism, or a 'drink problem'.

He enjoys working out how the world operates, as a dedicated engineer enjoys figuring out how a new machine works. He delights in watching it, eyeing his own time with the grand sweep of a historian, identifying the different parts and the functions they serve, often giving them his own names: the Charismatic Leader, the Model T Technology, the *Ancien Régime* Morale, the Global Interventionism.

His ideas on any subject may be original and provocative. Discussing Vietnam with him on a televison programme, someone derided the American commitment there on the ground that the Saigon regime was only a puppet government created by America. 'Do you think that means we have any less commitment to defend it?' demanded Kahn. 'I would have thought we had more of an obligation to support it, if we put it into power.'

The Black Muslims come into one of the wide-ranging lectures in a list of historical examples of the 'violent integration' of two cultures. 'Their precepts for behaviour are positively Calvinistic. They marry their girl friends, give up alcohol and drugs, work hard, dress neatly, save money. They've sold out almost completely to white culture! Yet no one can accuse them of selling out, because one of their doctrines is to hate whites. Do you know that among young Negroes generally, the cure rate for drug addiction is 5 per cent. The rate among white physicians is about 90 per cent. Among Black Muslims, it's also about 90 per cent. Their doctrine has given them the character structure of white physicians.'

He makes you think all the time that he must have missed some vital, fundamental factor, as he moves with such swift assurance through the problems of humanity, so fluid, intangible, unsolvable and tragic. There is an urge to put your finger on some crucial gap, to show that things are not so easily within a man's mental grasp. Usually, when you do, you find that he has seen it first, and included it somewhere in his calculations.

He says, before anyone else can say it, that you cannot analyse every situation mathematically, not even every military situation, that there are qualities of military heroism that are beyond analysis. He cites the *conquistadors*, like Pizarro, who conquered the Inca Empire with 183 men. 'At Rand,' he says, 'we would have analysed the situation, balanced the difference in firepower per soldier against the difference in numbers, and explained to Pizarro that he didn't have a chance, that even if the Incas made every possible mistake, he still couldn't win.' But he did.'

He even says, and this is less obvious to some practitioners of analytic methods, that systematic analysis is not always a good idea, that it can damage the thing being analysed. It can, for instance, erode the *mystique* upon which the fighting quality of a military force ultimately depends.

He gives a homely example of this in one lecture. Suppose, he says, a man says to his wife on their tenth wedding anniversary 'I think our marriage has been a success, and has brought a lot of happiness to us both. Let's see if this is so. Let's write down all the advantages of our having been married these ten years, and the disadvantages, and see how they balance out.'

The exercise would not enhance married bliss, Kahn points out. No matter how the balance comes out, the process will weaken the bonds that tie the two together. This is because marriage is usually regarded, not as an instrument, to be judged by its effectiveness, but as a value in itself. (He draws this distinction in other spheres, pointing out, for instance, that Americans tend to regard a treaty or a constitution as a value, but Europeans see it more as an instrument.)

Moral scruples about means to an end? He has included this too, in his scheme of things. He constructs a table* listing degrees of violence, asking in its heading 'Where Do *You* Draw the Line?' Underneath, he lists, in order:

1. Insecticides
2. Eating meat
3. Any violence
4. Police
5. Conventional warfare
6. Kiloton weapons
7. Megaton weapons
8. Begaton weapons (a begaton is 1,000 megatons)
9. Doomsday machine
10. Galaxy destroying machine

He says that just about everyone believes in some kind of unilateral restraint on moral grounds, and just about everyone countenances the use of some violence against living things; the pacifist usually draws the line at 3 or 4, the resolute militarist at 7 or 8.

The doomsday machine has the characteristics of many of Herman Kahn's creations. It was invented to demonstrate a point logically, but it is so provocative that the emotional static surrounding it obscures the message. The device was suggested first by Leo Szilard, the physicist, in a television discussion programme, to indicate the perils of thermonuclear war. Kahn and William Brown did some work on the physics at Rand, and decided that one could be built. Kahn coined the name.

*From *Thinking About the Unthinkable.*

The machine would contain a nuclear explosive device of gigantic power, rigged so as to create enough radioactive fall-out to kill everyone in the world, or very nearly, wherever it was exploded. It would be attached to sensory equipment and, if American, would be programmed to explode automatically if five nuclear bombs landed on American soil (or if anyone tried to dismantle it). Kahn worked out more subtle amplifications of this, like programming it to explode if an enemy committed any one of a whole range of actions deemed to be violently hostile, including building a doomsday machine.

Kahn was not suggesting this as a plausible national strategy, for the United States or any other country. On the contrary, it was intended to satirize, as he says, the pure deterrence posture, to refute, by a *reductio ad absurdum* argument, the attitude that you don't need to bother about fighting a nuclear war but only about deterring one. He listed the desirable characteristics for a deterrent, and pointed out that the doomsday machine was the most persuasive deterrent imaginable, since the consequence of hostile action would be both inexorable and annihilating. However, he said, no government would find the device acceptable, because the consequence of failure would be so great.

The doomsday machine has dogged Kahn, and since he believes devoutly that anything should be thought about and talked about, he is willing to discuss it. He remarked once at the Hudson Institute, the research corporation of which he is Director, that no American scientist or strategist would countenance building a doomsday machine. A member of the Institute's staff said he would favour it in certain circumstances. '*Someone* just had to prove me wrong,' Kahn says, grinning, and he thinks this was really their object. 'He says he'd be in favour of a galaxy-destroying machine also, in the same circumstances. He won't make any distinction between the two. He says he's not interested in saving bug-eyed monsters on another planet. I told him he has no sense of proportion. All that over a quarrel in the Northern hemisphere of Earth.'

The circumstances in which this man would favour a doomsday machine turn out to be so theoretical that even he is not suggesting it as a serious proposition. If, he says, it were a choice between a weapons system the failure of which would mean the complete annihilation of the American and Soviet populations, and a doomsday machine with a much lower probability of failure, an American President would be duty-bound to order the construction of a doomsday machine.

However, Kahn then says that there are fantastic circum-stances in which *he* would favour a doomsday machine. 'Say, for instance, there was a Nazi Government that looked like conquering the world, that had real good social techniques, and it really looked as if they would establish a 5,000-year Reich, and make it work, so that at the end of the 5,000 years, human beings would be genetically different from what they are today. Then I'd be in favour of a doomsday machine to prevent this. Even then, I'd draw the line at a galaxy-busting machine. This other guy wouldn't. He's got no religion.' And he chuckled.

This is typical of Kahn in another way, too. Having said that he would never favour a doomsday machine, he then found it necessary to qualify the statement, though the qualifi-cation is so far-fetched that it would not have occurred to most people to make it. He was a physicist before he became a strategist, and he tries to bring scientific standards of precision to any statements he makes, even about his own feelings. He will say 'Yes, I believe that, but not very intensely. I wouldn't want to argue it before a hostile audience.' Or 'We're friends. But we're armed friends, you know? There are some people with whom you're disarmed friends.'

Most of Kahn's colleagues among the defence intellectuals deplore arguments about a doomsday machine and a galaxy-destroying machine, because they clothe the subject of nuclear strategy in an atmosphere of science fiction, and detract atten-tion from serious issues. (In his high school days Kahn was an avid science fiction reader, like many imaginative youngsters in the late 1930s and 40s, when it was an esoteric taste.) But they have a high regard for Kahn's intelligence and his accom-plishments, tinged with the reserve and the slightly patronizing

271

tone with which members of a learned profession usually regard those who have popularized some of its learning.

Though his intellect is his dominating feature, Kahn does not have an academic personality. His friends are businessmen and military officers as well as scientists and professional intellectuals. When he is illustrating a point, he is likely to begin 'I know someone who was arrested for embezzlement ...' or 'I was talking to the ticket collector on the train the other day, and he was saying ...'

He is no philosopher. He is concerned only with the things of this world. He questions the manner of human existence, but not its purpose. He is, furthermore, a patriotic American. He believes firmly that Americans make good soldiers and fight well, and is angry when the American military get a bad Press. He tells a story of an exchange that took place when he was ten years old (he is excellent at recalling significant stories about himself). His mother came home and told him about a quarrel she had just had with the butcher. He asked her about it, and after a few questions she suddenly stood back and said 'What are you asking me all these questions for? Are you trying to decide who's right? I'm your mother!' He explains now 'I'm loyal. I'll always stick up for my mother against the butcher. But I want to *know* whether she's right or wrong. I'm loyal to my country, I'll go a long way with "My country right or wrong". Not all the way, I'll stop a good way this side of the concentration camps. I'll support my country in an unjust war, if it's not *too* unjust. But I want to know that it's an unjust war.'

This attitude does not make him ultra-nationalist. He has arrived at some internationalist positions through a reasoning process. He would like to see the surrender of some national sovereignty in the interests of international order.

Though he is willing to discuss the widest range of possibilities, from non-violent resistance to preventative war, he accepts, like almost all the defence intellectuals, the American consensus view of the world: that Communism is a bad form of government, that its spread should be resisted, that armed force works, and that this is a legitimate instrument in the pursuance of national aims. At times, his acceptance of this view seems like a commitment, and prevents him from following through critically some of his own thoughts. Here are two examples from *Thinking About the Unthinkable*:

He has an imaginative and plausible scenario in which at the end China, by exploiting and cheating on an international arms control agreement, becomes the world's only nuclear-armed nation. She adopts a threatening posture, and demands from the largely disarmed Western countries and Russia 5 per cent of their annual wealth, measured in gross national product, to right the 'unjust' imbalance between the rich and the poor nations. Kahn neglects to point out that any Western nation that was disarmed and forced to pay out 5 per cent of her gross national product would be making a profit; the United States, for instance, spends today about 12 per cent of it on armaments. (There are several possible answers to this point, ranging from Robert Harper's slogan in Congress in 1798, 'Millions for defense but not a cent for tribute', to the observation that once a nation is at the mercy of another to this extent there is no limit to the possible cost, Rudyard Kipling's Danegelt message. But Kahn does not acknowledge that there is any point to meet.)

Elsewhere in the book, discussing the 1945–55 period, he says that the main reasons why the Soviet Union did not engage in further aggression, it seems now, was probably not the threat of U.S. nuclear retaliation, but 'fear of U.S. mobilization potential, fear of revolt by a war-weary people, and a major preoccupation with Soviet reconstruction, and possibly even a feeling of indigestion with the satellites and a corresponding lack of desire to gobble up more'. It would be quite uncharacteristic of Kahn to say that N A T O was formed to ward off a Soviet attack when there was really no danger of one; the remark has the sound of left-wing unorthodoxy. But this is what the last three of his four points amount to.

Kahn is unique among the defence intellectuals as a communicator. No one has done more to bring before people the demands of reason in considering questions of nuclear war and peace, both people in government and the military, and anxious and horrified members of the reading and thinking public. At Rand, he found out how many people with sound ideas on military problems were failing to get them across to the military, so he planned briefings with care. Since then, he has been giving briefings and lectures to private and public audiences in government and academic life. He plans his presentation cunningly. If the lecture is public or semi-public, he tries to have a few pacifists and ultra-right wingers there, not only to provoke discussion at question-time, but also so that he can seem to speak from a middle-of-the-road position.

He makes little distinction between oral and written communication. His writing is readable and almost racy, his illustrations well chosen, his scenarios imaginative. But his sentences are often clumsily constructed, and read as if he spoke them rather than wrote them. *On Thermonuclear War* is basically a series of lectures. His lectures, on the other hand, are studded with reading matter, in the form of charts and tables that he displays one after the other to make the points sink home, sometimes going through them so rapidly that their effect is almost subliminal.

On the platform, he seems to draw energy from his audience as an actor does, as he pours out his exposition intermingled with anecdotes, many about himself, asides, witticisms, direct questions – 'How many think this would be a sensible policy? Hands up.' He exudes intelligent observation so lavishly, and with such evident enjoyment, that reasoning seems to be for him a Dionysian process.

The audience hang on to his every word, and have to grasp at a few. Just as he writes entertainingly with many inelegant sentences, so he talks enthrallingly with bad diction. He throws away phrases in a high-speed blur, or swallows half-sentences sometimes letting speech collapse into a little laugh, or a 'Y'know?'

His oral, and other mannerisms, his extroverted energy, and his physique as well, indicate a pattern of powerful unconscious forces fuelling his intellect.

The Strategist: the Intellect of Herman Kahn

He has a trick of coining thumbnail summaries of positions: democratic interventionism, provisional catastrophism. Sometimes his summaries can be caustic, e.g., 'The liberal doubt: do we have a right to intervene in the Congo when there's a Negro in Texas who's still mad?'

His humour is often directed against himself. He tells how he once wrote a letter to Admiral Hyman Rickover, the driving force behind the Polaris submarine programme, explaining why such a weapons system could not be built. 'I have a copy. I keep a black book on myself,' he says.

Another time, he explains how modern American society is coming, like ancient Rome, to include as important elements the lean, hard Stoics, who run things, the Epicureans, who retire to their gardens and friends, and the dropouts (the Christians were dropouts in ancient Rome, the hippies in America today). He expects this division to become more marked as American society becomes more leisure-orientated. Then he interrupts himself to remark 'I can just see somebody saying, "Look at him up there, a good hundred pounds overweight, and saying how everybody should be lean, hard, muscular Stoics."'

He admits that he still cannot get used to his figure, even though he has been getting fatter steadily since his early twenties, and that whenever he looks in a mirror, he is always a little surprised, and feels like saying 'Who's that, me?' The thin man who, according to Cyril Connolly, is in every fat man struggling wildly to get out, seems in Kahn to be merely staring out curiously and passively. Perhaps he is a muscular Stoic, perhaps a soldier.

Herman Kahn was born in New York City and lived there until he was ten. Then his parents were divorced and his mother went with her two children to join her sister in Los Angeles, and worked there as a clerk. The family were orthodox Jewish, but reason came into conflict with faith at an early age in Herman, and he came around to an agnostic position by the time he was eight. He had serious doubts when he was either six or seven, because he violated the Jewish law of the Sabbath by riding on a bus on a Saturday, and God did not do anything to him.

In high school, he was an outstanding student, and he used to do his brother's college homework in biology and physics for fun. (His brother, Irving, became an Air Force pilot during the war and was killed in a flying accident.) He learned very early that he liked to stand on his feet and impart knowledge. At his special request, he was allowed to present term papers as lectures, and he gave hour-long talks to his class, on Thomas Paine, and the Stock Market, among other topics.

He began his wartime army service by going to college on a technical training programme, then became a telephone lineman and a sergeant, and served in Burma. To his surprise, he liked life in the army. He did not like being ordered about in an abrupt and arbitrary manner, but he enjoyed the exercise and the obstacle courses in training, and he enjoyed the comradeship. One lasting effect of his army service was that when he went to Rand and had dealings with the military, he found it difficult not to be excessively deferential to officers. He says it took him five years before he could treat generals as equals.

He studied engineering and then physics at the California Institute of Technology, teaching himself economics on the side, graduated with honours, and looked for a job in the area that would give him some time free to do postgraduate work there. He took a job as a computer technician in Rand's Physics Division, then stayed after he finished his postgraduate work, as a laboratory physicist.

Kahn found himself enormously stimulated by the mental gymnasium that was Rand, and he excelled at every exercise. On computers, he devised a technique now widely used for solving problems by random sampling, a technique he christened 'Monte Carlo' because it is akin to playing a game of chance – he was already showing a taste for flamboyant names. He both used and developed systems analysis, and served as a consultant to the A.E.C. and Livermore. He gave a series of lectures to Rand and Air Force men that his boss in the Physics Division, Ernest Plessett, describes as 'the best lectures on systems analysis that have ever been given'.

In those days as now, Kahn was anchored firmly to practicality, and he went on to argue against the excessive use of systems analysis and other mathematical tools. He felt that some people were becoming fascinated by these and were using them in inappropriate situations, when a model had to be so idealized, with so many factors left out, that the results would be less useful than conventional judgements based on knowledge and common sense. For a while, there was a running argument at Rand between what came to be called 'the intellectuals' and the 'common-sense' men, with Kahn strong on the side of common sense. Kahn has said that much as he admired the brainpower and methodology of Rand, he would trade in the entire staff for Sir Winston Churchill at the age of sixty-five.

He became a consultant physicist and problem-solver for Los Alamos and Livermore. He worked on Wohlstetter's base study, and on other studies with him as well. He describes himself now as Wohlstetter's pupil, and says that many of his ideas on systems analysis and nuclear war he owes to Wohlstetter's inspiration.

Kahn met and married his wife, Jane, when she was a computer assistant at Rand (they now have two children). Shortly after that, her security clearance was suspended pending a hearing, because of alleged Communist associations of some members of her family. (The hearing decided that there was no security risk.) Kahn found that the preparations for this were distracting. When he worked on a physics problem, he would become absorbed in it to the exclusion of everything else, including most of his domestic and social life. He decided that while he was so involved in his wife's security problem, he would work on something less serious than physics, so he turned all his attention to nuclear strategy. By the end of three months, he decided that these problems were really the more serious ones, and deserved his full-time attention.

He came to be respected as a strategic analyst, so that in 1956, when Rand carried out its major study of strategic offensive forces for the Air Force, he was one of the three people who headed it; the others were Wohlstetter and James Digby. Kahn worked particularly on civil defence, for the Air Force had by now passed beyond the military parochialism that said the consequences of strategic air war on the American homeland were none of their concern so long as they happened on the ground.

He worked for a long time on plans for a vast fallout shelter programme. He used mathematical analysis and computers to compare their effectiveness in saving lives with active defence measures like anti-aircraft missiles. After some six months, he scrapped all these plans, and decided that evacuation of cities in the face of impending attack was the better answer.

He wrote up his conclusions in the *Report on a Study of Non-Military Defense*, which recommended civil defence planning more than civil defence construction. The main item to be purchased was 100 million dollars' worth of geiger counters, to be used in the aftermath of an attack. He also wanted the utilization of suitable buildings for fallout protection (this was done), studies of evacuation measures, and the training of cadres of volunteers.

The most striking feature of the report was not its recommendations, but its tone. Kahn stared straight into the picture of a thermonuclear attack, and refused to be stunned by it. He saw it as another problem to be handled, and set about seeing what was to be done. The report rejected specifically the idea that nuclear war would mean the end of civilization. Kahn was called to testify before the Congressional Subcommittee in 1959 that drew a picture of a nuclear attack on America, and told them, 'For the next ten or fifteen years, and perhaps for much longer, feasible combinations of military and non-military defense measures can come pretty close to preserving a reasonable semblance of our pre-war society.'

The flavour of his thinking came out in his testimony about genetic damage; he recalled a statement of his that in a nuclear war in which reasonable civil defence measures were taken, 1 per cent of babies might be born seriously defective as a result of the radiation from nuclear explosions. But this was only a 25-per-cent increase over the present number. 'In other words,' he went on, 'war is horrible. There is no doubt about it. But so is peace. To some extent, the horrors of war are only an increase or intensification of some of the familiar horrors of peace.'

In his lectures to Rand and military audiences, Kahn stressed the political value of civil defence as well as the human value in saving life. Whatever level of destruction a President might decide to risk to come to the aid of an ally, that level would be much more difficult for an enemy to attain if there were a reasonable civil defence programme. What if, in a brink-of-war crisis, America faced a Soviet Union which had already evacuated all its major cities, and America had no capacity to do the same? Wouldn't the United States almost certainly have to back down? He has always regretted the failure of the American Government to carry out the kind of civil defence measures he advocates, and sees it as one more refusal to face facts.

Kahn gave a series of lengthy lectures to high-level military groups and academic centres devoted to strategic studies, drawing on his own work, and that of others at Rand on nuclear war and war situations. One day he said to Wohlstetter, 'You know, somebody's going to write a book about this whole subject, and they'll get a lot of kudos, perhaps more than they deserve, simply because no one else has done it.'

Kahn wrote the book, based on his lectures, while he was on leave from Rand at Princeton University's Center of International Studies. He called it *On Thermonuclear War*, a deliberate play on Clausewitz's title, *On War*. It filled 668 large pages, and was published by Princeton University Press. It sold more than 30,000 copies, a phenomenal number for a book brought out by a university press, it was widely read in government and military circles, and it brought Kahn fame and just the kind of kudos he had foreseen.

It also brought him violent criticism and denigration. It was called 'thermonuclear pornography', and those briskly practical passages on what to do after the bombs fall were quoted to show that the author must lack elementary human feelings. More pertinently, many expressed the fear that contemplation of surviving a thermonuclear war was giving encouragement to those who would adopt a belligerent international attitude. A more knowing version of this argument, which was heard in the Army and Navy, was that this book was part of a Rand–Air Force manoeuvre to demonstrate that strategic nuclear war is a feasible national policy, and was intended as a counter-argument to those who worried about excessive reliance on nuclear weapons for military purposes.

Kahn provided some ammunition for this argument with his testimony before the Congressional Subcommittee, when he urged civil defence measures in order to *be able* to fight a nuclear war, and said this ability was important. He pointed out that Britain declared war on Germany in 1914 and 1939, and that if she had not been able to do so, Germany could have done as it liked.

The monthly *Scientific American*, surprisingly, summed up the emotional hostility to the book in a lengthy and very critical review, in which James R. Newman said that the analyses and distinctions it made were callous and an offence to human decency. He said thermonuclear war was unthinkable, and should remain so. Kahn wrote in reply suggesting that he write an article for the magazine to be titled *Thinking About the Unthinkable*. The offer was refused, but this became the title of Kahn's next book. The book was a more popular version of many of the ideas in the earlier book, plus some new ones, and a defence of the strategic analyst's way of looking at the world.

Kahn went back to Rand, but found himself in temperamental discord with the President, Frank Collbohm. The atmosphere became a frigid one in which he could not work, so he quit. Then he set about establishing his own non-profit research corporation, along with Max Singer, a young lawyer and student of strategic problems. He collected a group of eminent figures in science, strategy and scholarship to serve as trustees, took Max Singer as a partner, and set up the Hudson Institute in the wooded, hilly countryside at Harmon-on-Hudson, some thirty miles north of Manhattan, in buildings that used to house a mental home (and the humorous potential of this has been exhausted long ago). They started it with only 7,000 dollars in capital, and though they got government contracts right away, they operated on a shoe string for a while, asking senior staff members not to cash their salary cheques for the first few months.

He equipped the cellar at the Institute as a fallout shelter. He does not have one at home, but he lives nearby, and could always get his family over there in a hurry. Besides, he feels that he has responsibilities to the Institute's staff beyond those to his family. 'If I'm driving with my children in the car,' he says, 'I don't drive any more carefully than if I'm by myself. If I were driving a school bus, with other people's children in it, I would drive more carefully.'

The Hudson Institute is an extension of Kahn's personality. It carries out the kind of eclectic, wide-ranging studies that give his mind full rein, and it continues his mission of public education.

One contract, from the Martin Aircraft Company, was for a lengthy study on 'The National Interest and the International Order', and some of the work on this led to Kahn's third book, *On Escalation: Metaphors and Scenarios*. (This brought the word 'escalation' into general use.) Much of the book is built around an escalation 'ladder' of 44 rungs, which runs all the way from Ostensible Crisis, rung 1, through diplomatic and economic measures to Dramatic Military Confrontations, rung 9, up to the rungs of military action and past the nuclear-use threshold to Local Nuclear War Military, 23. The highest rungs are various kinds of central war – 'central war' is defined as a war against the homelands of the principal warring powers – like Slow Motion Counterforce War, 34, and Countervalue

Salvo, 40, up to the top rung, Spasm or Insensate War, 44, which Kahn sees as the abandonment of all reason.

There are the usual illuminating definitions, sometimes phrases coined by Kahn himself, sometimes obscure words that he has taken out and revivified. 'Compound escalation' he defines as escalation that brings another area or issue into the conflict: if the Russians had moved against Berlin in response to the American Cuba missiles blockade, this would have been compound escalation. He lists five types of international relations: contractual, coercive, agonistic, stylistic and familial. 'Agonistic', particularly pertinent to today's international scene, he defines as behaviour in a conflict within a set of rules which both sides have an interest in observing. (The *Oxford English Dictionary*, less imaginative, says simply 'relating to the athletic contests of Ancient Greece'.)

Always under Kahn's enthusiastic direction, the Hudson Institute staff have carried out studies for several government departments, including one on the idea of a national minimum wage. They have produced a spectacular development scheme to enlarge a lake in Columbia into a vast waterway and literally change the shape of the country. They have devised crisis games for the services. They have also made recommendations on the Vietnam War (Kahn was always a qualified supporter of America's presence in Vietnam, though one senior staff member at the Institute always argued strongly against it). These come from reading, questioning servicemen and civilians back from Vietnam, and one short group visit, and, as Kahn admits, they owe not a thing to systems analysis. One strong recommendation was for a major programme to win over the Vietcong, and this meant stopping the South Vietnamese torture of prisoners. 'I would shoot the next ten Vietnamese officers who torture prisoners,' he said at the time. His face clouded with anger, dislike of the cruelty of this practice apparently reinforcing his dislike of its stupidity.

The Hudson Institute carried out some major studies of the year A.D. 2000, some of them under government or foundation sponsorship, and these are broad enough to include ideas on just about everything. They have resulted in a book, by Kahn and Anthony J. Wiener, *The Year 2000: A Framework for Speculation on the Next 33 Years*, published in November 1967. It is a large, eclectic work, full of charts, graphs and statistics, drawing on Spengler, Toynbee, Sorokin, Goethe and the *New York Times*, among other sources, with speculation on the future of revolution, birth control, automation and spiritual *anomie*, as well as of international relations. He has developed this into a specialized interest on which he lectures and gives interviews, so that now he is occasionally called a 'futurologist' as well as a strategist.

In his conversation, he has come to sound more conservative lately, when he discusses some of the social issues and attitudes that divide the United States. He often seems to sound, once again, like one of the 'common-sense' men, supporting the common man's attitudes against the pretensions and self-doubts of the liberal intellectuals. He seems to want a more tough-minded defence of the traditional values and structure of Western society.

The principal educational effort of the Institute is a week-long seminar held three times a year at which an invited audience of people professionally interested in international problems share in the Hudson Institute's ideas and thought processes, gathered under some catch-all title such as 'National Security and International Order'. The fee is 500 dollars, but it applies mostly to wealthy corporations or government agencies which want to send people; it is waived for many individuals who might profit from the experience.

Kahn acts as a kind of master of ceremonies, and talks on a number of topics himself. The most eagerly awaited talk is on nuclear war. In this, he goes over some of the old Herman Kahn territory. He shows the audience a series of charts giving figures of American and Chinese dead in a nuclear war in 1975, under the heading 'Given the Same Peace Treaty, Which U.S. Victory Would the President Choose (or Prefer)?'

The first is always 200 million Chinese dead and 100,000 American dead. The alternatives to this include: 1 million

Chinese dead and 100,000 Americans; 100,000 Chinese and 1 million Americans; 20 million Chinese and 10 million Americans. The correct answer, he says, is always the alternative, even though this may mean sacrificing millions of Americans to save some Chinese. There are many reasons, ranging from the reaction among Western intellectuals to the massacre of Chinese with relatively slight American loss to the future ambitions of the remaining 700 million Chinese. But the overwhelming reason, and he speaks it with emphasis, is that '*It is wrong to kill 200 million Chinese if this can possibly be avoided.*'

At another point, he asks the audience what an American president should do if the Russians suddenly blow up New York with a hydrogen bomb. 'The President gets on the hot line to find out if it was a mistake. The Soviet leader says it's no mistake. He says, "You've been hearing this guy Kahn saying in lectures how the Communist bloc is losing its nerve. Well, you can forget that crap. We don't like the way you've been behaving lately, and this is our way of telling you"'

Kahn gets several answers from members of the audience. He approves of one, 'Declare war on Russia.' This leaves a whole range of options. Do nothing? 'If the Russians do this and get away with it, then Russia will rule the world!' Destroy Moscow? 'Well, Moscow is a little more to Russia than New York is to America. It's the capital. The Russians might then destroy Washington in return.'

Destroy Leningrad? 'Yes. I know, Leningrad is a city of culture, they've got the Hermitage, a great physics institute, a middle-class intelligentsia, people just like us. But – they've gotta go.' He is parodying here the author of *On Thermonuclear War*, but inside the mocking tone is the right answer as he sees it.

His office at the Institute is fitted with several kinds of gadgets; Kahn admits that he is childishly fond of gadgets. One wall is lined with books, not leather-bound sets like a lawyer's office, but contemporary books on a variety of subjects that come from bookshops and have been read.

Leaning his bulk back in his swivel chair late one afternoon, he talked about the Institute, occasionally looking out at the sun settling down into a red glow behind the fir trees. Most of the time when he talks, he is the same relaxed, provocative, persuasive Herman Kahn that stands on the lecture platform; the talk pours out as freely, the phrases are as blurred, there is the same pursuit of precision, the same high i.q. content.

He admitted that he treats the Institute as a hobby as well as a vocation, and that his studies of the future are partly a hobby. They may or may not pay their way financially. But then, as he says, if he were interested primarily in making money, he could earn anything from 200 to 500 dollars a day working as a free-lance consultant for defence industries, doing systems analysis work. He talked about Britain, the conservative mentality of British businessmen, industry and the modern worker, the problems of the cities, the military mind.

As the afternoon moved on towards a chilly evening, the talk turned to nuclear war. Kahn said that for all the hard thinking in the Defense Department about the rational control of nuclear war, things had still not been thought through. The new kinds of nuclear war plans had not been worked out in sufficient detail. The civilians in the Administration did not have the time, and, really, did not care enough.

Then he said, 'The truth is, I'm bored with nuclear war as a subject. Not repelled, you understand. Just bored. Like the people in Washington, like most people, like you, I don't really believe in it.' He paused after this, and turned to the window.

It was a grey, empty moment, with a quality of finality about it. It was like hearing a playwright explaining why his play has failed, or a middle-aged man telling you that he no longer understands his children.

But the empty moment did not last long. It was filled quickly with ideas, one after another, recharging him, as the talk spurted forward and took new turns.

'The Americans have a sense of sin. They think everybody should work hard. This is the explanation of the hippie. An American thinks it's immoral to just goof off, go lie on a beach somewhere. He has to rationalize it, to say he's against the system, that he's in rebellion. He has to be in favour of LSD. The hippie overshoots, to overcome his sense of sin. . . .

'I see a future world in which a *lex talionis* operates among nations, pretty much like today. But not the *lex talionis* of Leviticus, an eye for an eye, a tooth for a tooth. More like the code of Hammurabi. An eye for an eye if you're in the same class, two eyes if you're one class lower, and so on down to anything you like if you're in the servant class. This sort of law amounts to a kind of international order.'

Kahn goes on thinking, about the thinkable, the unthinkable, and the unimaginable. .

12. The Nuclear Cool

The Kennedy Administration was the first government anywhere in the world to bring hydrogen bombs out of the realm of awesome paradox and into that of reason, and it may well be principally for this that it will be remembered by history.

President Eisenhower and his officials had said over and over again that a thermonuclear war could never be won, and could not be a rational policy for any man or nation. Others elsewhere echoed these sentiments. Nevertheless, the nuclear forces that could not win a war were poised to fight one, and vast thought and expenditure went into providing the means for the war that could never be rational.

Not that Eisenhower was insincere. He certainly believed that no one could win a nuclear war, and he sought sincerely some kind of *détente* with Russia. His outlook was not narrowly military. Though a professional soldier for most of his career, he lacked the iron fanaticism of the true military man. The Eisenhower Administration accepted the illogicalities of nuclear deterrence only because it could find no alternative.

The Kennedy Administration's achievement in this respect was not planned in advance, for President Kennedy had few ideas on nuclear strategy before he took office, but it was a consequence of its temper and attitudes. A key concept in Kennedy's thinking was control. He wanted events always to be under the control of human reason. In matters of war and peace in particular, he had, as one of his associates put it, 'a determination that war should not make its own rules'. Like many of the defence intellectuals, about whom he knew very little, he was fascinated by the way in which events slipped out of human control in 1914 and Europe slid into a total war that was unexpected and unwanted. One of his favourite books was Barbara Tuchman's account of those weeks, *The Guns of August*.

The man in his administration who laid down the guidelines for a nuclear-armed world was Robert McNamara. He resigned as Secretary of Defense in February 1968, after serving for seven years in the post under Presidents John F. Kennedy and Lyndon Johnson, and these guidelines are his principal legacy. Kennedy did not appoint him to create such guidelines, nor to effect any particular philosophy. He had never met him before he offered him the cabinet post. This is not to say that subsequent events were a happy accident; McNamara was a consequence of the Kennedy Administration's predilections, as were his policies.

In the talent hunt in which a president-elect fills the 1,000-or-so offices that become vacant with a change of Administration, and which has no equivalent in the more confined world of British government, Kennedy heard much of McNamara, the recently-appointed President of the Ford Motor Company, as a businessman of unusual intellectual abilities. He offered him the post of Secretary of the Treasury or of Defense, and brushed aside McNamara's objections that he did not have sufficient experience for either. McNamara accepted the defence post on condition that he could choose his own staff.

This caused no rejoicing among the defence intellectuals. With the appointment of a Detroit automobile executive as Secretary of Defense, many thought they had another Charles E. Wilson. Wilson, the former Chairman of General Motors who became Eisenhower's Secretary of Defense, was for many the epitome of philistinism and conservatism, remembered best for his unfortunate remark that 'What's good for General Motors is good for the country'.

But McNamara was a different kind of automobile executive, though he does not look very different. He was one of a new breed of business executives, who earned his successes by the application of intellectual power to business and industrial problems, often through modern tools of mathematical analysis. He is an analyst by nature, who, when he looks at a situation, automatically strips it down to component parts with numerical relationships between them. When he asks questions of his subordinates, he calls for answers 'with numbers in them', which means, to him, information couched in realistic terms that one can act upon.

When the author asked him once whether a new moral issue had been introduced on the world scene with the advent of the hydrogen bomb, his answer was characteristically quantitative. 'No,' he said. 'The moral issue comes when you kill one man. We want in our foreign policy to minimize the number of casualties, whether you're talking about one, ten, a thousand, or ten million.'

McNamara taught for a while at the Harvard School of Business Administration, which gives him a distinction among high-ranking executives. During the war, he went into the Air Force as an operations analyst, and at the war's end he sold himself and the team he headed to Ford, to practise the same kind of mathematical analysis on industrial problems.

McNamara had no ideas on nuclear strategy when he accepted the post from Kennedy. He turned out to be a revolutionary, not in principle, for he had no revolutionary ideas to implement, certainly not in temperament, but in his effect. Starting from an orthodox view of the world, he examined a situation and followed it through step by step to its logical conclusion, which was one that many others found revolutionary. The techniques he employs in his thinking are brilliant, but his manner is often prosaic. He reaches each conclusion methodically, indifferent to whether it seems to most people shockingly radical or, as it often is, stunningly obvious. Thus, he announced to a House Subcommittee, as one of his conclusions: 'I do not believe we should embark on a course of action that is almost certain to destroy our nation when that course of action can be avoided without substantial penalty to us.' *

He used the few weeks between his acceptance of the post and the installation of the new cabinet to read books on defence matters, talk to people in the field, and think about his staff. He wanted to find a controller of the Defense Department's 50,000-million-dollar budget, to establish over it the broad planning and control set-up that he had at Ford, an economist rather than an accountant. One of the names mentioned to him often was that of Charles Hitch of Rand, the author, with Roland McKean, of *The Economics of Defense in the Nuclear Age*. He knew something of Rand already, and liked their approach to things. Rowan Gaither, one of the architects of Rand's independence from Douglas Aircraft, was a friend of his; when McNamara was at Ford, he had asked Rand to do a long-range study of transport problems, but they would not do work for private industry.

He was on a short ski-ing holiday in Aspen, Colorado, when he got around to contacting Hitch, who was then attending a meeting of the American Economic Society in St Louis. On the telephone, he asked Hitch whether he was interested in the job of controller of the Defense Department budget. Hitch said thanks but he was not; he had just bought a house in Los Angeles, and he liked living there. McNamara asked Hitch to at least meet him and talk about it, so Hitch agreed to stop off in Denver on his way back to the West coast. The two spent an evening talking in Brown's Hotel in Denver, and they felt a communion of minds. At the end of the evening, McNamara was certain that this was the man he wanted. Hitch liked the idea now, but said he had to consult his wife first, about moving to Washington. He telephoned from California and accepted.

McNamara wanted some brainy, analytically-minded people who were willing to think through the problems of nuclear war, and, partly at Hitch's suggestion, he turned to Santa

* Department of Defense Appropriations for 1964, House of Representatives Subcommittee, part 1.

Monica for them. He did not care particularly whether they had thought about the subject before: he wanted thinkers and analysts, not experts. From Rand, he brought into the Pentagon Fred Hoffman, who took the title of Special Assistant for Systems Analysis, Henry Rowen, who was later to return to Rand to succeed Frank Collbohm as President, Alain Enthoven and William Kaufmann. He admired particularly Wohlstetter's cast of thought, and offered him a post. Wohlstetter refused it, but he served the Defense Department as a frequent consultant, both from Rand and after he moved to the University of Chicago as professor-at-large, and his services were recognized with the presentation of a Distinguished Service Award.

Others who had been thinking hard about nuclear war and peace came to Washington from the academic centres. Jerome Wiesner came from M.I.T. to become Kennedy's Science Adviser. Morton Kaplan came from the Harvard Center of International Studies to work on arms control in the Pentagon. Others came regularly to give briefings, and exchange ideas. Some of them brought ideas about the world of the great powers, some new analytic approaches to the problems of management, some both. It was a heady time for the men of the think corporations. For a while, the Department of Defense was talked about in Washington as the most exciting branch of the government to work in.

The newcomers brought their style to the Pentagon, and it was similar to McNamara's. Blackboards were installed in executive offices, so that things could be envisaged as graphs, oscillating curves, or in figures. Issues were portrayed as matrices, with the squares showing results of interacting policies, in the games theory manner. It was all new, and rather unmilitary.

McNamara had a new approach to the job of being Secretary of Defense. Previous holders of the office saw themselves principally as administrators of a department, and as arbiters between the three services and between the services and Congress. Military policy was regarded as a technical matter, for which the military chiefs were responsible. But McNamara saw himself as an originator of policy. He insisted on re-casting military problems in his own terms, and applying to them his and Rand's analytical methods.

Not surprisingly, a Cold War broke out in the Pentagon between the military men, who felt their prerogatives were being taken away, and the new civilians, the 'pipe-smoking, tree-full-of-owls so-called defense intellectuals', as General Thomas White called them scathingly in a much-quoted magazine article written after his retirement. Military men would relate to one another happily how some brash young man with a slide rule had tried to bully an officer with thirty years' active service behind him, and had been forced to retreat. Civilian analysts would tell one another how another general or admiral had to be dragged kicking and struggling into the twentieth century. The Air Force characteristically overplayed its hand when it refused to show its war plans to Deputy Defense Secretary Roswell Gilpatrick on grounds of security, and had to give in before the resulting fury.

General LeMay expressed the wounded feelings of military men in a passage in his autobiography, *Mission with LeMay*:

We in the military, at the time I'm talking about, did not raise a blanket objection to being overruled. Sincerely, we wanted to play on McNamara's team. What we did object to was the Secretary saying 'No' to something the military wished to do, and giving a *military reason* for his action. Palpably, thus, he and his coterie were setting themselves up as military experts. ... His attitude is resented deeply by those who have spent their lives in the business of preparing for defensive warfare and/or waging defensive warfare.

By calculations of cost benefits, McNamara and his men argued against military romanticism to favour missiles over bombers and Polaris submarines over aircraft carriers. They cancelled cherished and spectacular projects besides Skybolt, notably the B-70 supersonic bomber and the nuclear-powered aircraft. They were fighting the reflex action that Eugene

Fubini, McNamara's chief of Research and Development, called 'the American syndrome: if you can do it, do it'. Charles Hitch applied to questions of the allocation of resources new cost-analysis methods that aimed at calculating the total cost and benefit of a measure to the nation as a whole. Design a still faster bomber? But would this add much to the present bombing potential, in view of the effectiveness of Soviet anti-aircraft missiles? If you want to spend that amount on the strategic offensive force, would it not give better value to buy more bombers with present speeds? Or some electronic counter-measure aircraft? Or a different kind of weapon entirely, for a different kind of war? This kind of questioning surprised a lot of Air Force men, who thought that planes became faster and more powerful every five years by a process as natural as a child growing.

McNamara's victories did not always work out as planned, notably in his biggest single clash with the military, over the F-111 plane. He ordered this as a multi-purpose plane for the Air Force and the Navy, overruling the arguments of each service for having its own aircraft; when it was produced, the F-111 did not come up to anything like the expectations. There are signs that McNamara's analytical objectivity can be distorted by the clash of opposition and argument.

Hitch's style of cost analysis – known in Washington as 'Hitchcraft' – was adopted by other U.S. Government departments (Hitch himself returned to private life as President of the University of California). It had its influence in the British Government, starting with the Ministry of Defence under Denis Healey. Healey saw the need for new costing techniques when he was opposition spokesman on defence; the advisability of remaining in Aden at a time of economic retrenchment was being debated, and he found that no one knew how much the Aden base was costing Britain.

Soon after McNamara took office, he and some of his colleagues made the most complete study yet of all-out nuclear war, in all its aspects. They came to the conclusion that even if the United States struck first against the Soviet Union, in the event, for instance, of a large-scale Soviet assault on her allies, surviving Soviet forces could still inflict on the United States what they regarded as unacceptable damage.

As McNamara told the author one day,

We came to the conclusion that thermonuclear war was unfeasible. Not impossible, in the sense that, technically, it couldn't happen. In that sense, it was all too possible. But unfeasible in the sense that you couldn't fight such a war and hope to win in any meaningful sense.

This was not a difficult problem, you know, and it wasn't difficult to reach that conclusion. The problem wasn't nearly as complicated as Vietnam, for instance. There weren't nearly as many political factors, as many uncertainties. There were uncertainties, of course, but you could isolate them, and work them into your calculations.

I took this conclusion to President Kennedy. He wasn't surprised; he'd done some thinking about this, too. And, as I say, it wasn't very difficult to arrive at this conclusion. . . .

There are several corollaries to it [he went on]. One is that having superior strategic forces had a connotation different from what it had for centuries past. You couldn't achieve victory with them. They were not even a deterrent for more than a limited number of actions, because an enemy knew perfectly well that you wouldn't dare use them, and risk destruction of your own society, in many circumstances.

Another corollary is that we need to have other kinds of forces to support our foreign policy. This, after all, is the purpose of military forces: to defend the country from attack and support your foreign policy.

Despite these corollaries, McNamara continued the planned build-up of strategic nuclear forces, and even increased the production programme for missiles in hardened silos. By August 1963 he could report to the Senate Foreign Relations Committee that the number of nuclear warheads in the strategic alert forces had been doubled, and the megatonnage more than doubled. This was because McNamara had listened to the Wohlstetter arguments on vulnerability, and he felt that America must have a large, flexible, invulnerable deterrent. He had read the books and the scenarios that indicated the wide range of actions that lay between total war and surrender.

But his main innovation was in his attitude to non-nuclear forces. The paralysis of nuclear forces meant, as he said, that one must have other kinds, and he increased the conventional forces, stressing particularly air transport to give them greater mobility, long before the Vietnam War imposed its requirements. He increased equipment more than manpower, raising the number of combat-ready divisions from eleven to sixteen. This build-up was not quite the drastic change that it is sometimes said to be. Under Eisenhower, after all, there was the draft, and never fewer than two million men under arms.

Nevertheless, the strengthening of conventional forces was the first systematic reversal of the Eisenhower 'new look'. Kennedy confirmed this reversal when he appointed as Chairman of the Joint Chiefs of Staff General Maxwell Taylor, who, in his book *The Uncertain Trumpet*, had criticized sharply the Eisenhower Administration's over-reliance on nuclear weapons. The Kennedy–McNamara policy was to enlarge the non-nuclear option – 'option' is a favourite word in McNamara's vocabulary – the option of taking military action to meet a situation without recourse to nuclear weapons.

McNamara wanted America to have, also, a *nuclear* option, the option of using nuclear weapons with some rational aim in view. This meant being able to wage a nuclear war that is less than total, a reversal of the current S A C doctrine, and one that suited the temper of the times. Just as the idea of restraint offended the martial, aggressive spirit of the Air Force, so the idea of 'spasm war' is the very negation of the rational control of events sought by the Kennedy Administration.

The policy brought in to replace massive retaliation as the official U.S. defence policy was that of the 'flexible response'. This offered the prospect of responding to anything that is considered aggression by a variety of measures, both non-nuclear and nuclear. There would be no slippery slopes; events would be controlled all the way. As McNamara explained it in a speech, 'The strategy must allow for a variety of courses of action in deterrence and war. It must give the Secretary of State a full spectrum of nuclear war threats that he can use in foreign policy negotiations.' Not being a practising politician, McNamara is often unusually frank in his anticipations.

The nuclear alternative to total and massive retaliation that was worked out most precisely was the counterforce, or no-cities strategy, introduced into the Pentagon by the Rand men. By the time McNamara ordered the Air Force to make plans for a counterforce war, the Chief of Staff was no longer General White, who was sympathetic to the idea, but LeMay, who fought against it as one more attempt to shackle the power of the big bomb. All the old arguments of total devastation strategy v. controlled response were repeated; as on every other major issue in these times, the Air Force lost.

New technical developments were making a controlled response strategy feasible. The first essential was the hardening of the strategic forces, so that they could not be wiped out quickly. With hardened and invulnerable forces, a government would not have to strike instantly or risk not being able to strike at all. Even if nuclear weapons were exploding, it could still take time to evaluate the situation, decide just where the bombs were falling, and consider its response. In a counter-force or limited exchange, the Polaris missiles in their sub-marines would be held in reserve as an ultimate threat to cities. Even the most advanced model, the Poseidon is less accurate than ground-launched rockets and cannot reach as far, so that these cannot be depended upon for bombing military targets; but they are accurate enough for the obliteration bombing of cities. Bombers would have some role in any phase of an at-tack, but they would go in after rockets destroyed some of the enemy's anti-aircraft defences.

In order to attack an enemy's strategic forces, one must know where they are, and this requirement was met in 1961 when the Samos reconnaissance satellites were put into orbit. From hundreds of miles up, these photograph Soviet and Chinese territory in great detail, and the film is parachuted back to earth in capsules. Later models were to have infra-red heat sensors that operate from orbit and can detect the launching of a rocket. Later still, sensors were developed that can detect a small electric current running through a wire from hundreds of miles up and so tell, for instance, the nature of a nuclear materials factory, or whether an underground missile is being maintained. The Russians were not far behind in satellite reconnaissance, and by 1962 they had U.S. territory under surveillance. There were important improvements also in the weapons themselves. The new missiles could be programmed for two alternative targets, then more. The Minuteman F, the latest model, can be programmed for eight. This allows for several alternative target plans employing the same missiles. McNamara instructed the Joint Strategic Target Planning Board at Offutt to draw up new target lists leaving out enemy cities for several kinds of counterforce attack, in addition to their other target lists. The combination of land and sea-based missiles and bombers, with different vulnerabilities and different capabilities, operating interdependently to different patterns, proved so complicated that a fast computer was introduced to work out the attack patterns. As one of McNamara's colleagues explained the new posture, 'We think of the different strategies as different chords of an instrument that the President can play, by pressing down different combinations of keys. He can choose the particular combination he wants when a situation arises.'

McNamara rehearsed the counterforce chords to an audience of NATO-country defence ministers at the NATO meeting in Athens in December 1961. He announced and explained it to the public in a speech at the University of Michigan at Ann Arbor in June 1962, at the commencement ceremonies. First, he gave an account of American strategic power, and said 'This strength not only minimizes the likelihood of major nuclear war, but makes possible a strategy designed to preserve the fabric of our societies if war should occur.' Then he went on to explain it.

The United States [he said] has come to the conclusion that to the extent feasible, basic military strategy in a possible general war should be approached in much the same way that more conventional military operations have been regarded in the past. That is to say, principal military objectives, in the event of a nuclear war stemming from a major attack on the Alliance, should be the destruction of the enemy's military forces, not his civilian population.

The very strength and nature of the Alliance forces makes it possible for us to retain, even in the face of a massive surprise attack, sufficient reserve striking power to destroy an enemy society if driven to it. In other words, we are giving a possible opponent the strongest imaginable incentive to refrain from striking our own cities.

McNamara and his men argued always for the retention of options, for restraint and for a response more rational than a spasm. They supported their arguments with figures rather than moral pleading. McNamara told the House Armed Services Committee that in a full-scale U.S.–Soviet nuclear exchange, 'certain elements of our Navy almost certainly would survive, and we have other elements of our forces that we believe would survive. But it exceeds the extent of my imagination to conceive of how these forces might be used, and of what benefit they would be to our nation at that point.' This was a far cry from the Navy Press statement that the Navy could win a war even if all of America were destroyed.

This was a new voice in the world, a new mentality. Its statements about nuclear war contained no rhetoric, no threats, no contemplation of an infinitude of destruction or disaster that surpassed the understanding. It declined to be awed, terrified or overwhelmed. Its tone was calm and calculating. It took a cool, appraising look at what the presence of hydrogen bombs signified, when and how they might be used, and what might happen. It recognized the magnitude of the phenomenon, not because it could imagine it, but because it could measure it.

As well as tightening their administrative and intellectual control over nuclear weapons, the Kennedy Administration established a new kind of physical control, called the permissive action link or p.a.l. This was to be put on nuclear weapons, despite the protests of many of the men handling them, to ensure that their unauthorized use was physically as well as administratively impossible. Like the ban-the-bomb movement, this reflects a special anxiety about thermonuclear weapons themselves, rather than any special enemy armed with them. The weapons themselves are to be locked.

The idea of a remote-controlled lock for nuclear weapons had been in the air for some time. The spur to develop one was provided by members of the Joint Congressional Committee on Atomic Energy who went on a tour of American military bases in Europe where nuclear weapons were kept in November and December 1960. They saw the Thor and Jupiter rockets in Britain, Italy and Turkey, that were manned jointly by the United States and the host country under a two-key arrangement. Two keys were needed to launch the missile; one was always worn around the neck of an officer of the host country, and the other around the neck of an American officer on the base. They also visited Germany, where tactical nuclear artillery and bombs were in the hands of German forces but under American control.

They came back very worried that control was inadequate. They decided that the Thor and Jupiter missiles could easily be taken over and fired; all that was necessary was to overpower the American officer and take away his key. This was conceivable in a violent and unstable situation; they had in mind the military revolt in France, which had only just failed to overthrow the Government a few months before. The problem was discussed as a theoretical one, but, as one of the members said frankly, 'We talked about the rockets in Britain, but we worried about the ones in Italy.'

One of those most concerned was a young scientist who had gone on the European trip with the committee. He was Harold Agnew, an intelligent, outspoken physicist at Los Alamos, who had become friendly with Senator Clint Anderson of New Mexico, a member of the committee. Senator Anderson visited the mesa often because it was in his home state. He had thought it would be useful to have a scientist familiar with nuclear weapons along, and picked Agnew because he had a high opinion of his judgement. Agnew encouraged their concern about control of the weapons, and wrote a report for the A.E.C. expressing some anxieties of his own. Agnew also told the members that it would be possible to build into the weapon an electronically-operated lock, which could only be released by remote control.

The Chairman of the Committee, Representative Chet Holifield of California, saw Kennedy soon after his inauguration, and urged some kind of remote control device. Work was set in motion at Los Alamos, and the designers of hydrogen bombs set out to design locks.

Los Alamos was a very different place now from the wartime desert retreat of the world's most brilliant collection of atomic scientists. A few of the old Manhattan Project crowd remained, but most of the physicists were younger men who had come because they were interested in practical applications of nuclear physics, though some basic research was done there also. Los Alamos was now a fairly ordinary small town of the American Southwest, albeit with slightly higher wage levels than most and a spectacular backdrop. It had its own traffic policeman at the shopping centre, its luxury motel, its Indian souvenir store, women's clubs, football team and chapter of Alcoholics Anonymous. True, 10 per cent of the population work for one big employer, the A.E.C., whether as scientists, typists or truck-drivers, but this is not unusual. Nor is life there as isolated as it might seem; for the scientists, there are usually several trips a year to metropolitan or academic centres for conferences, it is a forty-five-minute drive to Sante Fe, and on the narrow airstrip between the edges of the mesa, the four-seater A.E.C.-owned air taxis take off for Albuquerque several times a day.

There was a lot of coming and going connected with the electronic lock, because design work was also being done at the Sandia Corporation in Albuquerque, and at the Livermore laboratory. The scientists and engineers were seeking a compromise between a locking device so loose that it could easily be broken, and one so tight and cumbersome that the weapon could not be unlocked quickly and used.

The scientists built working models of three kinds of locks, with different degrees of protection and effectiveness. Which lock was chosen, and how much weapon-effectiveness was to be sacrificed for safety, was a political decision.

President Kennedy saw the three models in March 1962. Agnew went to the White House with John Foster, at this time Director of the Livermore laboratory, and they demonstrated all three for the President, so that he could make his choice. The lock that was chosen was not, strictly speaking, an electronic lock, opened by an electronic signal. Rather, it was a kind of combination lock. To arm the bomb for firing, one had to know the combination, and the men handling the bomb would not know it. It would be sent to them in a radio message, along with the order to fire.

By this time the electronic lock was being talked about in official circles, and there were a few mentions in the Press. The Soviet Ambassador, Anatoly Dobrynin, asked Jerome Wiesner about it, and Wiesner asked Kennedy what he should say. 'Tell him anything you feel he can be told,' Kennedy said. Prevention of the unauthorized use of nuclear weapons was, after all, in the interests of both sides, and the Russians were particularly worried about any American nuclear weapons that seemed to be within some Germans' reach.

Wiesner gave Dobrynin an outline of the locks' purpose and nature. He told him nothing about the technology, and nothing about the timetable for their installation. Dobrynin asked dubiously whether they would really work. 'It depends what you mean by that,' Wiesner said. 'Certainly they'll work in that they can prevent some unauthorized group of people from suddenly taking them over and using them. They're proof against the most expert electronic lock-breakers for a few hours. But if the weapons are captured by an enemy, then very sophisticated technologists can break the locks.'

Kennedy decided to push ahead with the locking programme faster than the inventors had intended. Agnew, who was sent as science adviser to NATO to supervise installation of the locks, wanted to see extensive training exercises before they were installed; he was worried that they might be too tight, and that weapons might not be used in the event of war. But Kennedy initiated a programme to start installing them immediately on nuclear weapons under joint control in Europe.

In a still more drastic decision, he ordered the installation of the locks on nuclear weapons in the American services.

Members of the Congressional Committee wrote to the President protesting against this. As one of them recalls their letter, 'We told him that the object of the device was to prevent the seizure of nuclear weapons, and American officers are not going to seize their own weapons.' Most of the scientists and engineers who devised the lock were similarly opposed to this, and a few blamed Wiesner, with his supposedly 'extreme' advocacy of arms control schemes. 'Wiesner's attitude', one of them said with some bitterness, 'is that if you can't get rid of nuclear weapons, the next best thing is to lock them up and throw away the key.'

The military resented the electronic lock as a slur on their reliability and their integrity. They felt that the present controls were quite tight enough. After all, they pointed out, it took three men in a Polaris submarine or two in a bomber to arm a weapon. Was it possible that these could all become psychotic in the same way at the same time? (A psychologist might say that given the isolation and closeness of life in a Polaris submarine, a shared psychosis is not impossible.) The psychotic submarine commander or bomber pilot did not worry the Administration very much, however. The picture that caused more worry was the hard-pressed battalion commander in a shooting war, with tactical nuclear weapons under his command. Civilians put this question to officers, time and time again. 'Your whole battalion looks like being wiped out. The enemy is firing tactical nuclear shells at you. Your radio communications have been cut off. You're under terrible strain, you believe that the order to use your tactical nuclear weapons has been sent, and you would have received it if your radio was working. It doesn't take much to convince yourself, anyway. Are you sure you wouldn't fire yours?'

The argument between military and civilians was a shadow one, because the real issues could never be mentioned. When the military pointed out that nuclear explosions can cause a black-out of radio communications, and prevent the weapons from being unlocked, the reply is ready: 'If a signal cannot be received with the code of the lock, then one cannot be received ordering the use of the weapon, and without such an order, nuclear weapons must not be used. This rule is absolute, and has no exceptions.' Military officers could not say that they might use the weapons without proper orders. But their military instincts tell them that civilians cannot be trusted to defend the country as vigorously as soldiers, and they saw the galling possibility of an army going down in defeat when it had weapons that were unused.

Some military men were won round to the idea because they realized that it provided greater flexibility. Tactical nuclear weapons could be stationed farther forward than would be safe without the lock. Also, single-seat fighter-bombers could take off with an H-bomb aboard in an alert, so long as the bomb was controlled from the ground. Policy before the electronic lock was that no one-man plane could take off with a nuclear bomb aboard unless a war had actually started and it was being sent on its mission.

That the Kennedy Administration was prepared, in the last resort, to use nuclear weapons was demonstrated in October 1962 during the Cuba missiles crisis. Kennedy put his strategic forces on an alert, made firm though very limited demands and refused to compromise on these – for instance, by offering to close down the missile bases in Turkey (which were deemed to be militarily obsolete anyway) in exchange for the removal of the Soviet missiles.

To most of the men of the Administration, the events of the missiles crisis were a full justification of the flexible response posture. Forces were available for all the measures that were contemplated: the selective blockade that was carried out, the bombing attack on the missile bases that was due in a few days if the rockets were not removed, the invasion that was considered and prepared, the threat of war up to any level of violence. Kennedy handled the crisis with the characteristics that go with this defence policy. He was calm, firm, applying force only in very measured quantities, in tight control, and in constant and fruitful communication with his enemy. Total war was rejected diplomatically as well as militarily. The Russians were given every assistance in their climb-down: Kennedy promised not to invade Cuba, and congratulated Khrushchev on his statesmanship.

The main events of the crisis are too well-known to need retelling here, but several aspects of the significance of thermonuclear weapons were illuminated in their course.

McNamara's reaction to the installation of Soviet missiles was surprising. In the discussions within the crisis group in Washington, he played down their military importance. He said that since Russia had ICBMs that could hit the United States, the only effect of the ones in Cuba would be to reduce the warning time by a few minutes. 'A missile is a missile. It makes no great difference whether you are killed by a missile fired from the Soviet Union or from Cuba,' he said, according to Elie Abel's authoritative book *The Missile Crisis*.

This is the sort of homely, common-sense remark that one expects from the man in the street for whom the picture of any nuclear attack is an unthinkably awful blur, and who cannot or will not see that distinctions between one kind and another are worth drawing, but not from the man who insists on precise outlines and answers with numbers in them. For in military terms, it did make a difference. At that time, Russia had only seventy-five ICBMs to America's 200, and there were strong indications, in the reports to the C.I.A. of the highly placed Oleg Penkovsky, for instance, that Russia's were of doubtful accuracy. But Russia had more than 800 lesser-range missiles with a reach of up to 2,000 miles, and apparently intended to install more than seventy of these in Cuba. She would have doubled the number of missiles that could reach the United States without building one more.

It seems just possible that for all his painstaking calculations, for all his applications of lucidity and intelligence, McNamara can keep his cool only because, deep down in his mind, he does not really believe that nuclear war can happen; that, perhaps, when the spectre appears as a real possibility, he too is blinded to any fine distinctions.

Kennedy also departed from his Administration's theory when he looked at the prospect of nuclear war that week. In the television speech in which he made the crisis public and announced the blockade, he warned, 'It shall be the policy of this nation to regard any nuclear missile launched from Cuba against any nation in the Western hemisphere as an attack by the Soviet Union on the United States of America, requiring a *full retaliatory response* on the Soviet Union.' There was no indication here of the controlled, measured response, proportionate to the attack, that seemed called for by the new American policy. Again, there was a conspicuous failure to distinguish between one kind of nuclear attack and another.

Of course, this was partly rhetoric, and the speech does not foreclose the option of a limited response. But it seemed to confirm some Western European anxieties about the replacement of the threat of massive retaliation with the more limited and less deterring one of flexible response. As Leonard Beaton wrote, 'One might observe that on imagining itself to be approaching the military position which Western Europe permanently occupies, the U.S. Administration adopted the conventional Anglo-French-German military doctrine.'*

One striking aspect of Soviet behaviour in the crisis has received curiously little attention. This is their extreme anxiety about control of their own nuclear weapons, which matches the feelings of the Kennedy Administration when it installed the electronic locks. Unlike the United States, Russia has not

---

* In his *The Western Alliance and the McNamara Doctrine*, an Adelphi paper published by the Institute for Strategic Studies, London.

stationed any nuclear weapons on the territory of her European allies, although this would put the missiles farther west. One factor determining this Soviet policy is almost certainly the possibility of seizure of the weapons. This policy was one reason why State Department Soviet affairs specialists at first discounted stories about Soviet offensive missiles in Cuba.

When Russia did station the missiles in Cuba, her fear of seizure by the Cubans was quite open. She sent 20,000 troops to Cuba, and though some of these were there to give training and technical assistance to Cuban forces, most were combat troops. There seems to have been little pretence that their role was to help the Cubans repel American invasion. They were not stationed on the shoreline but at the missile sites, obviously to defend them against the Cubans, at least long enough for the nuclear warheads to be made harmless. It is evident that the Russians placed great importance on this mission, since they ran diplomatic risks to carry it out. There was the obvious affront to the Castro Government; and also, if American planes bombed the missile sites, Soviet troops would be killed.

Talking to people in official or quasi-official positions in the aftermath of the crisis, it seemed that the higher up the ladder of responsibility one went, the more worried people were. Most people in the American think corporations, and among the scientist-strategists who make up advisory panels, slept soundly that week; they could see easily that reason would prevail. High officials were more worried, and not all slept well. To judge from the reports of the emotional tone of Khrushchev's letters to Kennedy, this was true in Moscow as well as Washington. One of the eminent pundits of American journalism told John T. McNaughton, the Assistant Secretary of Defense, soon after the crisis ended, 'I knew everything would turn out all right. I wasn't scared.' 'You weren't?' McNaughton retorted. 'Well I was!'

The different degrees of alarm were not due to different interpretations of events. It was widely felt at all levels that the two powers were a goodly distance from the brink of nuclear war, and that several thresholds had to be crossed before this brink was reached. It seems that, among men who must act and have the responsibility for the consequences, even a small risk of thermonuclear war is extraordinarily frightening. This thought holds some comfort.

To millions of people all over the world, the crisis made thermonuclear war, with giant fireballs burning up the cities, possible for the first time. It seemed suddenly that it could *really happen*. In the Pentagon, leaflets on civil defence that lay for weeks in racks at the exits were snapped up, and the racks had to be refilled every few hours. Hechinger's, Washington's largest store selling building materials, was sold out of sandbags by the end of the first day of crisis week, and was still delivering sandbags ordered that week a month later. Forty American families flew to New Zealand to escape nuclear war. The physicist Leo Szilard, one of the three who asked Einstein in 1939 to write a letter to President Roosevelt urging research on atomic explosives, now associated with Linus Pauling in a 'peace lobby', fled like the sorcerer's apprentice to Zurich. He decided that the Alps made Zurich the most protected city in the Western world from incidental fallout. He flew back to America only after the crisis was over.

Herman Kahn was worried enough to carry a transistor radio with him to listen to the news bulletins. He flew to Boston to give a lecture, and was met at the airport by a friend. As they drove away, they noticed some S A C B-52s standing near-by, dispersed to this as to other civilian airfields. 'What would you do if they took off now?' Kahn asked his friend. 'I'd keep on driving north,' was the answer.

In Britain there was a widespread sense that the end might be at hand. On the Wednesday when the first Soviet ships were due to reach the American blockade line, a teacher at a girls' school in London found that the atmosphere among her thirteen-year-olds was shrill and nearly hysterical. At lunch, when she asked some of them to quieten down and mind their table manners, one answered 'What does it matter how we eat? This may be the last meal we'll ever have!' None of the girls

307

showed any interest in the details of the crisis, or had any opinion on who was right or wrong. A telephonist at a large business house, an apparently calm, reasonably balanced woman, told a neighbour on the switchboard that she could not sleep the night before for worrying how, if nuclear war came, she would kill her small children to spare them suffering. One saw people with radios turned on for the news in unexpected places: a woman in a cigarette kiosk, a newspaper seller on the street, a ticket collector at a station. The *Sunday Telegraph* carried a cartoon showing people arriving in an office, chatting as they hung up their hats and coats, and one secretary saying to another 'If one other person says, "Well, we're still here," I'll scream.'

Pat Arrowsmith, the field secretary of the Committee of 100, decided after demonstrations outside the American and Soviet Embassies that events had gone beyond the point where public protests could make any difference, so she and Wendy Butlin, another Committee member, flew to Dublin and hitch-hiked to a village in the West of Ireland, which, they thought, might be a safe refuge. As she explained later. 'I'd have stayed if I could think of anything useful to do. I'm prepared to die for a good cause, lying in front of a bomber, for instance, if it might prevent it from taking off and killing a million people. But I couldn't see anything useful to do at this stage. I believe in trying to live. I'm an atheist, you see, I don't believe in any after-life, so I believe in living as long as possible if you can't achieve anything by dying.' She left a message for the Committee saying where she was going, but it was not passed on, so that the girls' disappearance was a mystery. As they were last seen demonstrating outside the Soviet Embassy, some newspapers carried the intriguing rumour that the pair had been kidnapped by Soviet diplomats, one of the few light touches in the Press that week.

Mrs Pat O'Connell, committed deeply to the same cause, and preoccupied with thoughts of a nuclear holocaust, kept a transistor radio by her that week. It happened to be a rare time when she was teaching but her two smaller children were home on a mid-term holiday, and she took them with her to school every day, so that, if disaster came, they would be near.

The Cuba missiles crisis was a break in the development of the U.S.-Soviet *détente*, and after the crisis was over, this was resumed. In the following year, it was formalized with three agreements on arms control and stabilizing measures. In June, the Soviet Government agreed to an American proposal to link the Kremlin and the White House with a 'hot line', a direct tele-printer line so that one government could send a message to the other in less time than it takes a rocket to travel between them.

This was followed by a milestone in *détente*, the test-ban treaty, signed in Moscow in August. After years of arguing about how many inspections per year would be needed to check for underground explosions, Russia accepted a Western sug-gestion for a ban only on tests in the atmosphere and outer space, which needed no checks since it could be verified from anywhere in the world. The world was split into those countries that signed and the few that refused to do so. A few non-nuclear countries pointed out that, as it is difficult to build bombs without testing them, this treaty would prevent other countries from developing nuclear weapons with little sacrifice by the nuclear powers. But among the major nations, only France and China refused to sign.

The treaty was very limited. Any signatory could opt out if it felt it was vitally necessary. It permitted underground test-ing; the U.S. Administration emphasized this by testing a de-vice beneath the Nevada desert while the Senate was discussing the treaty, to reassure those senators who worried that America was throwing away its safety in the world.

There were anxieties about going on from there to a treaty that would ban underground tests as well. This would place a more serious limitation on weapons development. The new weapons that were being developed were not bigger but smaller: tactical nuclear bombs and shells, and warheads for anti-aircraft missiles and anti-missile missiles, which could be tested in underground caverns. The British Government's sup-port for a total test-ban treaty involved real sacrifice for the general good, because the Atomic Energy Authority had not yet tested the thermonuclear warhead that it was developing for Britain's Polaris rockets. It was to be tested at the American underground site in Nevada. It turned out that these tests were important, for when the fission 'trigger' was tested underground in 1965, one part did not work, and this difficulty had to be ironed out.

Shortly after this, America and Russia promised mutually not to put nuclear weapons into orbit. This ended for the moment one nightmare vision created by a few writers, of a world girded by circling satellites that could launch rockets automatically at any country below, and of multi-megaton bombs in low orbit that could be exploded at the touch of a button, burning up millions of square miles. With the new accuracy of I C B Ms, it was easier to blast another country from right here on earth, so no useful military capability was sacrificed by this promise.

When the test ban was signed, the hands of the clock on the cover of the *Bulletin of the Atomic Scientists* were moved back, from three to twelve minutes before midnight. The editors explained: 'This is not a gauge to register the ups and downs of the international power struggle; it is intended to reflect basic changes in the level of continuous danger in which mankind lives and will continue living, until society adjusts its basic attitudes and institutions to meet the challenge of science.'

There was a new logic of power at work in the McNamara policy. Following this logic, since you cannot conquer a nuclear-armed enemy, you don't aim at victory; you aim at stability.

Once this is accepted, a lot of unfamiliar ideas follow. One side can win a victory, but it takes at least two to create stability. When you recommend measures aimed at stability, in defence posture, weaponry or arms control, you are not recommending them only for your own government but for others as well.

This is a world to fit Thomas Schelling's theories, a world of mixed motives and non-zero sum contests, in which one side's loss can be another side's loss as well, or both sides can gain in varying degrees, in which communications between opponents are vital, tacit agreements are reached though not acknowledged, and mutually hostile moves are co-ordinated. Much of the language in which American Government officials speak of it is Schelling's.

Some ground rules for this world were spelled out by McNamara's Assistant Secretary of Defense for Arms Control, John T. McNaughton, in an address to a conference on arms control at the University of Michigan in December 1962.

Until recently [he said], relatively little attention was paid to the possibility of mutual improvement of security through the use of non-negotiated techniques. Yet not only are decisions in this area of crucial importance to our national security, but they are being made today and every day, to a large extent by the Defense Department. ...

We must, in every decision we make, concern ourselves with the factors of stability and of the dynamic effect on the arms race. This is so whether the decision lies in the area of strategic doctrine, force structure or research and development. That is, when faced with the need to make decisions in any of those three key areas, we should have two questions in mind:

How will the action affect stability – stability against technological surprise, against accidents and unexpected or misleading events, against a tendency for every confrontation to spiral upwards in violence? And how will the decision contribute to either quickening or dampening the arms race every time? Will it lead to added destructive capability in the world, to our material impoverishment, to the distortion of our way of life?

McNamara recounted another aspect in an interview with Theodore White in *Look* magazine:

A naval commander who wants to blockade wants to blockade, period. He wants to stop all ships. That's his job. What complicates his decision is that the actions he takes during the blockade are also telegraphic messages to the Soviet Union, a way of signalling our intentions in a world where both sides have the power to destroy civilization. This situation requires that the important signals come from the highest political power in the country.*

Here are some of the messages that have been signalled out of Washington for acceptance by the nuclear-armed world.

Nuclear weapons, tactical or strategic, are different from other weapons. This is the qualitative distinction that must be preserved. A scientist from the Livermore laboratory once tried to persuade Kennedy that Livermore could produce an atomic shell that was no more powerful than the biggest conventional shell. He was surprised when no one was interested. As one of the defence intellectuals close to the Administration said, 'He doesn't understand the position. He's showing them how to carry out a seduction, bit by bit, so that it'll hardly be noticed. But they want to preserve virginity.'

Agreed arms control measures are important, as well as tacitly understood ones. The U.S. Administration was willing to try cautiously for a whole range of these.

There are good weapons and bad weapons, and the criteria are universal. This is a new idea. In the traditional value scale, two opposing nations have directly contrary views on weapons. Each nation thinks that the more powerful its weapons the better; the less efficient and the less powerful the enemy's, the better. A good weapon for him is a bad one for the enemy, and vice versa. But in the new world of the mixed-motive contest, weapons that weaken stability are bad, and weapons that contribute to stability are good, *whichever side has them.*

A first-strike-only weapon is de-stabilizing. Because it can be destroyed in the first moments of a nuclear exchange, it must be used immediately if it is to be used at all; it creates a hair-

---

*There is some significance in his choice of illustration, though it was probably subconscious. Arguments worry McNamara, and when he has one, its traces often re-emerge again and again in his conversation, like a radish. When the Cuba blockade was ordered, he had a sharp verbal clash with the Chief of Naval Operations, Admiral George Anderson, who resented his dictation on details. Admiral Anderson was not re-appointed at the end of his term eight months later, and became Ambassador to Lisbon.

trigger situation, and, in a crisis, pressures for quick use. A second-strike weapon, sufficiently shielded to survive a nuclear attack, can provide time for evaluation and judgement, and is stabilizing. McNamara favoured shielded missiles over bombers (bombers are first-strike), and dismantled the vulnerable, first-strike-only Thor and Jupiter missiles, standing high and exposed on their launching pads in Britain, Italy and Turkey.

He wanted the Russians to behave similarly. In pre-nuclear days, it might be better to have an enemy weak, worried and susceptible to intimidation. If the enemy is nuclear-armed, it is safer to have him strong and feeling secure. When Stewart Alsop, in an interview in the *Saturday Evening Post*, asked McNamara when he thought the Soviet Union would have invulnerable missiles, McNamara's answer, as Alsop summarized it, was 'the sooner the better'.

These, then, by an irony nearly as sublime as that which Sir Winston Churchill saw in the peace of terror, are the new men, who have arrived to replace the modern man who has become obsolete. They are not as anticipated. They have the global concern and the breadth of vision. Yet this does not stem from any new and wider loyalty – they are not monsters, they care about sparing the lives of Russians and Chinese as well as Americans, but this is not central to their arguments – but from a new understanding of the needs of national loyalty, from new ways to achieve the old ends of national power and survival. They arrived at their position through an extension of intelligence, not a change of moral values. They see themselves as the successors to Talleyrand and Metternich, the philosophers of statecraft, rather than to the great moralists and humanitarians. Their internationalism is the twin brother of patriotism, their global concern the sturdy child of vulnerability.

They are a challenge to the Campaign for Nuclear Disarmament, the Committee for a Sane Nuclear Policy, and the other conscientious protesters, some of whose aims they further. For their policies and attitudes are saying that one can have a safer world (though not a safe one), a better world, and a sane nuclear policy without a fundamental change in moral position. Theirs is the challenge that the reformer poses always to the revolutionary, offering improvements in the system as an alternative to its overthrow.

On counterforce, the Russians seem to have received the message from Washington and replied clearly in the negative. They rejected the strategy, with its implied city-sparing bargain, repeatedly and specifically. Marshal Vassily Sokolovsky, the highest-ranking Soviet writer on military affairs, set the tone for the Soviet response when he scoffed in an article in *Red Star*, the military newspaper, at McNamara's 'attempt to make "rules" for a nuclear war'. Khrushchev himself alluded to the policy in a speech, calling it an attempt to divert the weight of Soviet retaliation for aggression away from America's cities, and warned that it would fail.

This is not really surprising. Every strategy for employing nuclear weapons has its own paradox. Counterforce, which is intended to have a stabilizing effect, in fact encourages an arms race, by making superiority in numbers of weapons a substantial advantage, and it favours a first strike. It also brings on its own obsolescence by encouraging the hardening of strategic forces.

In the first years after the counterforce policy was announced, the trouble was the opposite one: the Russians had not hardened their missile sites, the missiles would have to be fired immediately in the event of war, and McNamara had to admit to the House Armed Services Committee in 1963 that 'Under today's circumstances, I personally believe that any nuclear attack by the Soviet Union on the United States will include an attack on the major urban areas.'

In Moscow, there was little inclination to see the world the way McNamara and his intellectuals saw it, and to act upon their precepts. This was partly because military strategy in Russia is promulgated largely by military men: there was and is no equivalent in Russia of the American defence intellectuals. The Schelling picture of a world of mixed motives, and blends of shared and conflicting interests, is contrary to the

military man's view of the world, as the McNamara intellectuals found.

The United States had more long-range bombers than
Russia, and, through most of the 1960s, a superiority in
missiles ranging from three-to-one to five-to-one, though the
Soviet warheads were bigger. It clearly made sense for America
to propose a strategy that would make this superiority decisive,
and to want Russia to adopt the same strategy. But it also
made sense for Russia to threaten the United States with total
destruction instead of the staged retaliation in which America
would have an advantage.

The Russians rejected the whole idea of controlled response,
both nuclear and non-nuclear. They insisted in most of their
rhetoric that, contrary to American hopes, not only would any
nuclear war be total, but any major war would be nuclear.
Khrushchev said, in a typical pronouncement on the subject,
that if war broke out in Europe between N A T O and the Communist bloc, 'neither side could be expected to concede defeat
before resorting to the use of all weapons, even the most devastating ones'. (American proponents of controlled response
would agree, but would argue that if the use of weapons was
limited, the degree of victory or defeat that could be conceded
or demanded would also be limited. There could be no question of conceding total defeat.) There have been hints recently
that this Soviet attitude is being modified, and that they can
allow for the possibility of a non-nuclear war between the blocs.

In the two nations' strategic postures so far, there is a reversal of characteristic national attitudes. Traditionally, the
United States has taken a moralistic view of war, and has seen
it as justifiable only if it is a crusade. A strategy of limited
war and controlled response, with its political character and its
compromise aims, is the opposite of this view. On the other
hand, the Soviet leadership, as good Marxist-Leninists, should
see war primarily as a political instrument, the armed-phase
struggle of class conflict. The most authoritative Soviet textbook of strategy, *Military Strategy,* confirms this view as doctrine in the nuclear age: 'The essential nature of war as a con-

tinuation of politics does not change with the changing technology of armament.' But it is the Russians who talk of war between the blocs in terms of a spasm war, unrelated logically to any political aims.

For a long time, the Soviet posture seemed to be something like a minimum deterrence. But, starting in 1966, Russia speeded up its production of I C B Ms. Some Americans asked whether their country should not keep the same distance ahead of Russia in the number of missiles, which raised the question of what was enough. McNamara's answer, and it has stuck, was 'assured destruction': the assured capability of inflicting near-total destruction on any enemy nation or nations whatever they do first, an invulnerable second-strike force. 'Assured destruction' became the key phrase in American defence planning, and it remained so.

Counterforce became less and less relevant as missiles were emplaced in hardened, concrete-protected silos. A prolonged, pure counterforce war is difficult to imagine in these circumstances. But counterforce remains a plausible though much more limited strategy for certain desperate contingencies, and a useful coin in the currency of strategic discussion. The claims made for this or any other limited nuclear war strategy are minimal. No one feels confident that they would succeed in limiting destruction; certainly no one feels sanguine about nuclear war because such plans are in existence. The attitude is that one *might* one day be an effective alternative to all-out nuclear war, and therefore it would be criminally negligent not to prepare for it. But the emphasis is placed more and more upon the non-nuclear option rather than any nuclear one.

Scenarists of conflict today distinguish between nuclear war and *the* nuclear war. They usually envisage a nuclear war, if any, that is limited and controlled, limited in part by the invulnerability of the most powerful forces, with two sides inflicting punitive or retaliatory damage on one another, until they negotiate a peace.

The Russians accepted in practice the most obvious precepts for a nuclear-armed world: the importance of the nuclear threshold, the need for communication, the need for hardened, second-strike forces, the advantage to both sides of some arms control measures. As we have seen, they rejected some of the more subtle points, for reasons that are not altogether illogical from their position. But in theory as opposed to practice, they rejected entirely the American view of the world.

The question of the anti-missile missile demonstrated this. When the McNamara men in the Pentagon were arguing that neither side should deploy these, the Russians could have argued against this within the framework of a nuclear consensus. But the dialogue showed that the two sides were not talking within the same framework.

When they first appeared, I C B Ms were thought to be unstoppable; that is, engineers and technicians in the missile field as well as laymen thought they were. But research and engineering produced missiles that could destroy them in flight. The principle was to track the I C B M with radar, have a computer plot a collision course for another missile with a nuclear warhead, and launch it to intercept the incoming I C B M. The I C B M would be put out of action by the blast or by its radiation. The engineering problems were vastly complicated, and new developments in radar were necessary before the first effective American anti-ballistic missile, or A B M, was possible. Furthermore, any A B M system could be countered by the use of decoys, chaff or electronic baffling equipment. It was found that the farther out the interception, the easier it was to deceive with decoys.

By the beginning of 1967, both America and Russia had developed A B M weapons with some degree of effectiveness, and Russia deployed some around Moscow. McNamara argued for a long time against deploying such weapons. He argued partly on his own cost-effectiveness terms: a dollar spent on an A B M defence can be nullified by the other side's spending much less on more rockets or penetration aids. But he opposed it also by the criteria that McNaughton laid down in his arms control speech; that there was no real defence in the nuclear age, and that A B M deployment would reduce stability and step up the arms race. The Joint Chiefs of Staff opposed this reasoning. It conflicted with two military reactions to the ABM situation that are almost instinctive: to defend the country by any means available; and to build any weapon system that the other side has, and do it better.

American strategists of the arms control school hoped that the Russians, as well as the U.S. Congress, would heed Mc-Namara's arguments and refrain from deploying the weapons. When they showed every sign of ignoring them, President Johnson suggested negotiations on a treaty banning ABMs.

The Russians' attitude at first was disappointing. They might have argued that ABM defences on both sides would narrow the American lead in offensive weapons. Instead, they took the line of the most brass-bound generals in the Pentagon. They could not see that defence of any kind is de-stabilizing, and, in any case, they did not feel like taking advice from the other side on how to defend their territory. General Nikolai Talensky, who virtually began Soviet discussion of strategy with his articles in *Military Thought*, put the Soviet attitude in an article in the Moscow magazine *International Affairs*.

Only the side which intends to use its means of attack for aggressive purposes can wish to slow down the creation and improvement of anti-missile defence systems [he wrote]. For the peace-loving states, anti-missile systems are really a means of building up their security. ... The creation of an effective anti-missile system enables the state to make its defences dependent chiefly upon its own capabilities, and not only mutual deterrence, that is, on the goodwill of the other side.

Nothing could illustrate more clearly the gulf between some Soviet and American views of the world. The statement contains invidious moral distinctions between 'aggressive' and 'peace-loving' states that are eschewed by American arms control men. And the last phrases show that General Talensky still sees the world within a traditional military man's framework: a strong country can rely for protection on its arms, 'its own capabilities', and does not need to care about 'the goodwill of the other side'. The men who make American military policy look on this as out of date. They can see that no country today is in this happy position, that no power can prevent another from destroying its cities and wiping out its population. Every one is dependent for its safety on deterrence, on the attitudes, if not the goodwill, of the other side. The peoples of the world today are all exposed, all vulnerable, all hostages to reason and restraint.

13. Tigers in the Tent

Through common caution more than common understanding, there seemed to be for a while the possibility of a mutually acceptable strategic stalemate between the Soviet Union and the United States, at just about the time when the concept became obsolete. Its obsolescence was brought on by the acquisition of nuclear weapons by other countries, which meant that there were more than two sides to be balanced. The idea of mutual self-restraint on anti-missile defence, for instance, took on a totally new aspect when there was another country to be defended against, and, in the end, this new aspect broke the opposition to an American A B M system.

Students of international affairs had long been studying this aspect of stability. The Nth country problem, as it was sometimes called in these circles, exercised a number of people in the research corporations; reports and papers were produced, and several books dealt with the spread of nuclear weapons to other countries. But government departments, however much they try to keep in touch with advanced and long-range thinking, and to tap leisured, academic minds, tend to get engrossed in short-term problems to the exclusion of others. Long-term problems get put away in the mind's pending tray. John McNaughton, the Assistant Secretary of Defense,* admitted in a conversation, 'When we took office with Kennedy, and for some time afterwards, we thought in terms of a bipolar world. Then China thrust its head into the tent like a tiger.'

The problem was seen first as an alliance problem. Con-

* McNaughton was later appointed Secretary of the Navy, but died in an airliner crash in July 1967 before taking up the post.

cerned as he was with the tight control of the strategic situation, McNamara was anxious that all the nuclear forces in the NATO alliance should be under central control. 'There must not be competing and conflicting strategies to meet the contingency of nuclear war,' he said in his key Ann Arbor speech He was appalled at the idea that the consequences of rational planning could be wrecked by unco-ordinated actions.

Nevertheless, some anxiety was expressed in Western Europe about America's commitment to Europe's defence now that Russia had the power to bombard the United States. This was felt particularly among the West Germans, who were in the front line, and were exposed to nibbling tactics in Berlin. 'Would an American President go to war for Frankfurt or Paris if it would mean sacrificing the lives of most of the American population?' was the question sometimes asked. Few of the people who asked it seemed to realize that it concealed yet another of the paradoxes of thermonuclear weapons. Clearly, it would be illogical for an American President to sacrifice the American people, not only for Frankfurt or Paris, but also for New York or Chicago.

Anxiety about American willingness to defend Western Europe could lead to a desire among European allies for their own nuclear weapons. As an alternative, some called for a share in the use of those nuclear weapons already existing. Many diplomatic man-hours have been spent in the capitals of the NATO countries devising forms for a NATO nuclear force. All would give the non-nuclear participating countries the shadow of nuclear power without the substance. In theory, they would share some of the nuclear powers' weapons, that would be assigned to this nuclear force. In practice, whatever the degree of participation, the nuclear powers would always retain a veto on these weapons' use. For a government to give up this veto would mean giving to others the power to initiate nuclear war on its behalf, the power of life and death over its population. The capacity for self-delusion in such matters can be seen in the fact that some such surrender of national control was being discussed by Western European nations as a possibility at a time when, in the Common Market, they took a year to agree on surrendering control over their cereal prices. Talk of joint NATO control was finally dropped, but there were similarly unrealistic proposals for an Anglo–French nuclear force to be held 'in trust' for Europe.

The U.S. Government increased its commitment to Europe by shipping over more and more tactical nuclear weapons and placing them in forward areas, so that any extensive ground fighting was bound to go nuclear. This violated their own policy of strengthening the non-nuclear option, but it was done to allay Allied anxieties.

Some people in Western Europe welcomed the controlled response policy because they saw it, as U.S. officials did, as a more credible deterrent than massive retaliation, and more likely to be used in their defence than a suicidal strategy. But others, and they were in a majority at first, feared that a graduated deterrent was less of a deterrent than the threat of instant and total devastation. The West Germans in particular felt that any major East–West war in Europe would be fatal to Germany, and that such a war would be less likely if it were fatal to other countries as well.

Others besides Germans feared that if nuclear war were restrained, the major powers only would benefit from the restraint, while Europe would be the battleground. The French General Pierre Gallois, the most extreme advocate of national nuclear independence, said once, 'In the Korean War, every town and village in Korea was razed to the ground. One and a half million people were killed, 85 per cent of them civilians. The Americans call it a limited war. Limited for who? Not for the Koreans!'

In fact, NATO has never put enough conventional forces into the field to match Warsaw Pact forces, so that the non-nuclear option was never much of an option for a major war in Europe. Discussion of war plans focused on how to handle the brief pause before it became necessary to escalate to nuclear weapons to avoid being overrun, and how to use tactical nuclear weapons in the first instance so that they constitute a warning as well as a blow, and have a chance of stopping the escalation. In part, the American tactical nuclear weapons in Western Europe, like the American troops, are hostages, signs of America's commitment to the continent's defence. Secretaries of State have said privately that the United States could never allow 7,000 tactical nuclear weapons to fall into enemy hands.

Washington's worries about unco-ordinated allied forces never extended to the British nuclear force, since it was and probably always will be co-ordinated with the American. The French *force de frappe*, or nuclear striking force, however, was created as an independent one with complete freedom of action. The British blurred the issue of the independent use of their nuclear force, but the French, with their intense concern for logical positions, delineated the issue sharply, in terms that were logical if not always relevant to actual circumstances. France practised the international nuclear anarchy that is implicit in every nation's sovereign right to arm herself as she chooses. That this choice might now threaten the whole globe was beside the point; other nations decided for themselves without consulting the whole globe, and she would too.

There is a widely held misconception that the French nuclear bomb was a product of General de Gaulle's national pride, a misconception that is beginning to fade only now that his passing from the presidency leaves the French nuclear weapons programme intact, apart from some budgetary problems. According to one picture, France was pigging along as a comic but contented second-rate country when de Gaulle arrived on the scene full of vainglory, and determined, like Mussolini in an earlier decade, to foist on his country the trappings of world power, however empty and inappropriate. Apart from gross errors about France contained in this view, it is a curious picture to hold of a man who spent his first years as a national leader fighting off revolt to end a war by accepting defeat. But then, de Gaulle has too often been judged by the style of his policies rather than their content; many people went on saying that he cared nothing about economic realities and only about military glory when he was putting his generals in jail and making the director of Rothschild's Bank his Prime Minister (and, as it turned out, his successor).

The French nuclear weapons programme came to fruition during de Gaulle's regime, and it fitted into his ideas of national independence. But it was carried out with remarkable consistency under every government before him since 1946. The progress of this programme continued independently of the changes of government, even under heads of government who were apparently opposed to French nuclear weapons, so that here again, one has the eerie impression that the development of a thermonuclear bomb is an organic process with a life of its own and a growth that is inevitable, and independent of the wills of individuals. More realistically, this seems to show, as did the British nuclear bomb programme after 1964, that it is not in the nature of politicians voluntarily to reduce their country's national military power, whatever form this power takes.

French scientists were very active in the field of atomic physics before the war, and several worked in Britain and Canada on the wartime atomic bomb. With some of these as a core, the Commissariat à l'Énergie Atomique was established within months of the war's end, and it proceeded slowly to build nuclear reactors for research and then for power. The first head of the C.E.A. was France's leading nuclear physicist, Frédéric Joliot-Curie, but he was replaced in the first year by Francis Perrin because of his pro-Communist leanings. Scientists are prominent in the ranks of the French left-wing intelligentsia who oppose the creation of nuclear weapons; the biologist Jean Rostand is a particularly eloquent advocate of the view that it is only at our peril that we tamper with the make-up of this planet. But there were many physicists who were willing to work on atomic power and atomic weapons. They were in something of the same position as Russian physicists. It was not given to them to decide whether the world should have hydrogen bombs; it already had many. They had only to decide whether they would refuse to allow France to acquire its own, leaving the Western monopoly to others, and this was a political issue on which there was less reason to take a firm stand.

Every new step in the French atomic energy programme contained the possibility of building nuclear bombs, though this was not always stated at the time. So much was published about the wartime development of the fission bomb in America that the course to be followed was well laid out. The hydrogen bomb presented additional problems when the time came to approach this, but, here too, a lot was published. The French scientists did not know how Teller worked his trick with the deuterium-tritium reaction, but they knew that it could be done.

Two big reactors began producing plutonium at Marcoule in the late 1950s, and then a third followed. In 1954, during the premiership of Pierre Mendès-France, the most liberal of postwar French leaders and later a strong opponent of the *force de frappe*, a military commission was attached to the C.E.A. In 1955, Edgar Faure, as Prime Minister, announced that there would be no research specifically directed to the development of nuclear explosives. But the next year his successor Guy Mollet, a Socialist who was also later to be a critic of the French independent deterrent, gave the go-ahead to the construction at Pierrelatte, a picturesque village just north of Avignon, of the expensive gaseous diffusion plant that would provide the uranium-235 for France's hydrogen bomb.

This was the first time that the issue of a French nuclear bomb was debated at length in the National Assembly. Several arguments in favour of it were heard. A few members cited the recent amendment to the U.S. Atomic Energy Act. This permitted the sharing of American information on some aspects of nuclear weapons with other countries that had already developed nuclear weapons themselves. Britain had benefited from this; when France built her own atomic bombs as Britain had, they said, then she too would benefit. Others said France would speak with a more powerful voice in the alliance if she had these weapons. Many saw it as a European bomb, representing European interests instead of American, and this in-

fluenced their decision. On this issue as on many others, the
nationalistic right touched a sympathetic chord in left-wingers.

The National Assembly voted the funds for Pierrelatte, on
the understanding that this would not necessarily imply construction of a nuclear weapon. This was in 1956. Late in 1959,
when de Gaulle had come to power, the Government announced that a test explosion of a French atomic bomb
would take place the following year in the Algerian Sahara.
When an argument ensued in the National Assembly, the
Foreign Minister, Couve de Murville, said with some surprise
that the decision had been taken five years before, and had
never been seriously contested.

France exploded several plutonium fission bombs in its
Sahara testing ground, ignoring U.N. resolutions and foreign
protests about fallout, for this was in the period of the test
moratorium. She then proceeded to the development of a
hydrogen bomb, using the enriched uranium that was being
produced at Pierrelatte. The Government established another
testing ground in some French-owned islands in the South
Central Pacific, with the base on Tahiti and the test site itself
on Mururoa. Once again, as in the Marshalls and on Christmas
Island, the military and the technicians moved in to create a
base camp for modern technology on an uninhabited coral
atoll, and exploded France's H-bomb there in 1968.

For the French, a greater technical difficulty was the construction of a force to carry the bombs, or, as the contemporary
terminology has it, a delivery system. In terms of technology if
not invention, it is probably a more difficult feat. After all, five
countries have produced nuclear bombs, while only four have
built jet airliners or bombers, and at this writing only two have
produced accurate intercontinental rockets.

The French Air Force, unlike the British and American, had
at this time no tradition of strategic bombing, and had never
possessed any heavy bombers. To create a nuclear bombing
plane, the Air Force enlarged and modified a fighter, the
Mirage 3, to make the Mirage 4. With a two-man crew, this
can fly at about 1,200 miles an hour, twice the speed of sound

and twice the speed of Britain's Vulcan bomber. It has a range of 1,000 miles or so, or more with refuelling, which puts most of the cities of European Russia within reach.

It is a stubby-looking plane with a needle nose, and it carries its nuclear weapon underneath its fuselage, so that the bomb, the thing itself, can be seen from the ground as the plane flies low overhead, a silvery object with a black-painted nose cone, in the shape of a conventional bomb with small tail fins. Many American aviation experts say the Mirage 4 is a better aircraft, though a less complicated one, than the nearest American equivalent, the medium-range, supersonic B-58 Hustler.

The French Air Force created a new command, the *Force Stratégique Aérienne*, or FAS. It built also the apparatus of a hair-trigger nuclear deterrent, so that there is yet another telephone line in existence over which the signal can be given to blast cities off the face of the earth, and yet another group of men pledged and trained to do it. It created a command post 125 feet underground at Taverny, just outside Paris, where rock-walled tunnels lead into functional, antiseptic-looking offices, operations rooms and communications centres; it created twelve bases with five bombers to each, with their barbed wire perimeters patrolled by dogs. It created also an alert system similar to the British and American ones, with one plane ready on the runway at each FAS base, and the two crew members living in their blue flying suits and red parachute packs, ready to run towards their planes at a klaxon sound and be off the ground in four minutes, heading towards the Iron Curtain and their pre-assigned targets. The fliers themselves are mostly men in their thirties, technically highly proficient, and trained out of the daredevilry that is a mark of the French Air Force even in the age of jet technology – most French Air Force pilots will cheerfully take off after a litre lunch, or crash through the sound barrier low over a beach to startle the sun bathers.

France, though a stage behind the two super-powers in weaponry, has travelled the same route. She too has built rockets to supersede bombers, and buried them underground and in submarines. Eighteen rockets with 150-kiloton warheads with a 2,000-mile range are being buried in silos in the Vosges Mountains in central France, trained on the main cities of Russia. France is developing a small fleet of submarines powered by nuclear engines built at Pierrelatte, each carrying sixteen missiles with warheads of about half a megaton. These are due to start carrying out their deterrent mission in 1971 when there will be three of them in operation, and a fourth under construction.

The commanders of France's nuclear submarines, unlike those of Britain's, know for certain that the targets of their missiles are Russian cities. One officer refused the command of one of the submarines because of his conscientious objection to the mission.

As in Britain and America, each boat has two crews, who take it to sea on alternate missions. Unlike the British Navy, the French did not learn the system from the Americans, but arrived at it independently. The requirements for operating a nuclear deterrent are so restrictive that there are not many different ways to do it. The first French missile-carrying submarine is the *Redoutable*. One of its commanders, Captain Bisson, a thoughtful man and a church-going Catholic, was interviewed about his mission by the Paris newspaper *Le Figaro* and he spoke in terms that are by now familiar: 'If, one day, I receive the order to fire, I'll fire. But then deterrence will have failed, and it can't fail. What would be left of the world after a nuclear cataclysm?' Just as there are not that many different ways to organize a nuclear deterrent fleet, so there are not that many different ways to think about the job of serving in one, if you are going to do it.

The French *force de frappe* will never be large enough to permit graduated and alternative strategic target lists; in any case, a wide selection of targets would be difficult without access to the information obtained from American reconnaissance satellites. It is a one-shot force, and that shot would be aimed at causing the maximum possible loss to an enemy country. Its targets are civilian and industrial centres, or – the French phrase translated into English sounds even more frightful – 'demographic targets'.

French officials believe that the independent *force de frappe* is an added deterrent to aggression against Western Europe, adding a new element of uncertainty. In a situation where the NATO area is threatened, they believe, it might also have a specific deterrent value with regard to France. For instance, an enemy threatening NATO, in an escalating conflict, might demonstrate its resolve by exploding one nuclear bomb on a Western European city. With the *force de frappe* in existence, this would not be a French city. They also believe that nuclear self-sufficiency and the political independence that this implies can give France more power to stay out of a war. Some officials have in mind specifically a war between the United States and China, in which, they believe, the United States might involve other NATO members.

A new orientation of French defence policy was explained by General Charles Ailleret, Chief of Staff of the French Armed Forces, in the semi-official *Revue de la défense nationale* in December 1967. He wrote that traditionally the French armed forces were orientated towards one potential opponent, a 'favoured enemy'. For much of the last century this was Britain, then it was Germany, then Russia. In the future, a threat could come from any part of the globe, and France must have a force with a global reach that could strike at any place in the world.

This was a zenith of the policy of nuclear self-sufficiency. More recently, the policy has been modified, and the aim has become more limited. Official articles have appeared that once again see the Soviet Union as the 'favoured enemy', and that link France's fate more closely with that of NATO forces. They have found a role for the tactical nuclear rockets that France is developing, and have predicted a kind of graduated response.

Critics of the *force de frappe*, and there are many in France as well as elsewhere, point often to its military weaknesses that come from the technological lag behind the super-powers. Even supersonic bombers are very vulnerable today to anti-aircraft missiles, they say, and most or even all of the French bombers could be destroyed before they reach their targets. The missiles might be stopped by a Soviet anti-ballistic missile force which, if the attacking force is small in number and unaided by decoys or electronic baffling devices, might have a 100-per-cent success. Most important, the entire force is vulnerable to first-strike attack on the ground. The bases and even the underground missile sites are few enough so that several H-bomb rockets could be trained on each, with a high probability of blasting out the silos and the command post for the submarines, along with most people living in France.

To ask questions in Paris about the *force de frappe* and its worth is to go right back to the days in America of pure deterrence, of 'If these weapons ever have to be used they've failed.' The interest is entirely in deterring a war. Indeed one man, and a senior Air Force officer at that, said 'I get worried when people talk about actually *fighting* a nuclear war, and dropping nuclear bombs. That's not what this force is for.' The answer to any questions about whether the force would be effective is that it *might* work, and therefore it *will* deter.

As President de Gaulle put it at a Press conference: 'The French atomic force will have the sombre and terrifying capability of destroying within a few moments millions and millions of people. This cannot help but exert at least some influence on the intentions of a potential aggressor.'

The French hold to the theory of proportional deterrence as expounded by Sir Dermot Boyle, that a smaller country needs a smaller force than a large one to serve as an adequate deterrent. Indeed, French officials see the hydrogen bomb as the great equalizer of international life, that makes it possible for a power like France to have the same degree of protection as the two greatest powers in the world. Theirs is the strategy of minimum deterrence, in its purest form. This means that the force is a defensive one, that can be used only to deter conquest. In a military sense this policy, far from making France a world power, has tended to make her an isolationist one.

For many people in France, particularly among the military, the main justification for the *force de frappe* is not strategic but psychological. They wanted the feeling of being able to defend their own country, at least by deterrence, with the most powerful weapons available, instead of having to rely on a larger country. Some senior French officers speak of the bad 'moral' effect of depending on another power for a deterrent force, and the superior sense of having their own. The hydrogen bomb enhances the national super-ego.

De Gaulle even talked in spiritual terms of military sovereignty. He told the École Militaire in a speech in November 1959: 'If a country like France has to go to war, it must be *her* war. The effort must be *her* effort. Otherwise, our country would be denying everything it has stood for from its beginnings, its role, its self-esteem, its soul.'

The place of French military power in the life of the country has shifted. The military budget has increased by 25 per cent since 1960 (though its share of the national budget has dropped) but the number of men under arms has been reduced, and the average length of national service has dropped from over two years to around sixteen months. The increased military spending has gone on machinery and equipment; the budget for research and development alone quadrupled between 1960 and 1965.

The idea of the citizen-army, which the French Revolution gave to the world along with the modern nation-state, is closely bound up with Frenchmen's concept of their republic, a republic created by a popular revolution and defended by the people in arms. France has had compulsory military service for longer than any other major democracy, and it always had a symbolic and civic role as well as a military one. But a recent pamphlet issued by the Ministry of the Armed Forces announces 'a new doctrine: the security of the nation rests in the first place on the power of weapons and their modernization'. Where does the citizen-soldier fit in now? In France too, weapons have become more important than people.

In so far as France's *force de frappe* has any effect internationally, it weakens stability rather than strengthens it. In a major East–West war, it could prevent the carrying out of a co-ordinated strategy designed to limit destruction. France is encouraging other countries to build nuclear weapons by her example. In the long run, if some kind of supra-national, perhaps federal, structure arises in Western Europe, the French nuclear weapon will be the joker in the pack. A surrender of nuclear sovereignty may be out of the question at the moment, but it could be a possibility at some time in the future, as a part of some fundamental political reorganization. Then France's bomb might pass into the hands of some new body; something would have to happen to it. If West Germany played a major role in this new body, this would be certain to produce a sharp reaction east of the Elbe.

The great powers resent France's disruptive effect with all the annoyance that is directed at the non-co-operator, the one who won't play the game, and fouls up the system. But the rules of the game were made by the great powers, and they were made for their own benefit and no one else's. Since de Gaulle's time the French have pointed this out constantly. They have had no interest in NATO nuclear sharing arrangements since the United States made it clear that it will not surrender ultimate control. They have dismissed the test ban as a conspiracy by the nuclear powers to maintain their monopoly. France has refused to take part in the non-proliferation agreement, presumably because its double standard for nuclear and non-nuclear countries offends the stark logic of her own position. This is impregnable to stratagems designed to soften the edges of the picture of thermonuclear anarchy, and make it seem a little less foreboding. Because the French position is a logical one, it will outlive de Gaulle just as the nuclear programme preceded him, and it will be argued in other accents besides French ones.

The French hydrogen bomb parodies those of the super-powers. Like theirs, it is an aspect of independence and national sovereignty. If the power contained in it makes one shudder, while those of the super-powers do not, this is a matter of habit; there is no reason for assurance that future governments in Washington and Moscow will be more intelligent and less bellicose than those in Paris. The French exploitation of the system of international anarchy is a challenge to the world's acceptance of it.

In retrospect, there can never have been any doubt in China that that country would have her own hydrogen bomb. The Communist Government set out to make China a great world power, and thermonuclear bombs seemed to be necessary equipment for the role.

Furthermore, the Chinese leaders had an even more urgent incentive than that ambition to build nuclear weapons. Like the Soviet leaders in the 1920s and 30s, they believe that Lenin's teaching that capitalist nations have an ineradicable hostility to a new socialist state has been borne out by their own experience: U.S. forces helped the Chiang Kai-Shek regime in the civil war; they protect the separation of Formosa, which is recognized by every government including the American as Chinese territory; they have established bases around China's perimeter; aircraft carriers and Polaris submarines cruise off her coast; and over the years, there have been harassing activities. Considering all this, China's early defiance of the Soviet Union, then a trustworthy ally pledged to come to her defence, seems an indication of the remarkable tenacity with which the Chinese leaders will defend their beliefs.

China began developing a capability in nuclear physics in 1950, with the help of the Soviet Union. An Institute of Atomic Energy was established in Peking, and China and Russia formed a joint corporation to mine uranium in Sinkiang, the vast, sparsely-populated central Asian province which borders on Siberia. With an initial staff of Chinese who had studied at American and European universities, the Chinese

Academy of Science rapidly enlarged its training facilities in physics. Russia trained more than 1,000 Chinese physicists at Soviet scientific institutes, and she helped in the setting-up of a chemical separation plant in Sinkiang to extract atomic fuels, though this was probably under some kind of Soviet control. In April 1955 the two governments signed an Atomic Energy Co-operation Treaty. Russia supplied the Chinese Institute of Atomic Energy with its first experimental reactor, and sent Soviet scientists and technologists to China to help with research facilities. All this was scientific and technological aid, and had no specific military significance.

In October 1957 the two governments signed a secret agreement in which Russia promised to give China help in developing military technology. The existence of this treaty was revealed four years after its breakdown in the bitter exchange of polemics in 1963, though its terms were still not published. The Chinese claimed that Russia had promised to give China a sample atomic bomb and details of its manufacture and had not done so. In 1959 and 1960, the Russians halted their technical aid and withdrew all their scientists and technologists. Whatever the consequences of to the Sino-Soviet alliance, they were evidently determined not to help China build her own atomic bombs. This decision was not known in the West, and, even if it had been, it is doubtful that anyone would have proposed Nikita Khrushchev for the Nobel Peace Prize. Nevertheless, he is seen in the episode as the most dedicated opponent in the world of the spread of nuclear weapons.

What angered the Chinese even more than this, and brought the argument out into the open, was the signing of the test-ban treaty in August 1963. It was bad enough that the Russians should refuse to help their allies to develop nuclear weapons. To co-operate with the Americans in trying to prevent anyone else developing them (since testing is regarded as an essential part of such development) was betrayal. If the French regarded the treaty as an attempt to maintain the nuclear monopoly, the Chinese spoke of it in stronger terms still. The Foreign Minister, Chen Yi, said 'We regard this treaty as a form of blackmail applied to us. It is merely a plot to prevent China from acquiring her own self-defence.'

A few days after the treaty was signed in Moscow, he announced that China was developing her own nuclear bomb. 'Without it, China will remain a second- or third-class power,' he said. The programme was, in fact, well advanced by that time, much further than anyone in the West or in Russia knew.

This announcement was followed by an argument between Russia and China, still allies and Communist comrades despite their differences, about whether China needed her own nuclear weapons. The argument was conducted with faultless logic on both sides, and is a paradigm of mutual mistrust between allies.

Russia said, through the Moscow *New Times*:

The Chinese People's Republic ... does not have to devote its resources and energies to producing nuclear weapons. It can rely on the defence potential which the Soviet people have created and which provides effective protection for all the countries of the socialist community.

China said, through the *Peking Review*:

True, if the Soviet leaders really practised proletarian internationalism, China might consider it unnecessary to manufacture its own nuclear weapons. But it is equally true that if the Soviet leaders really practised proletarian internationalism, they would have no reason whatever for obstructing China from manufacturing nuclear weapons.

In the first years, the progress of the development of Chinese nuclear weapons exceeded Western expectations at every single stage. China exploded her first atomic bomb on 16 October 1964, in the Takla Makan Desert in Sinkiang. Western analysts assumed unanimously that it was a plutonium bomb, since China now had several nuclear reactors, which together could produce enough plutonium for a bomb. The alternative fission material is uranium-235, a radioactive isotope, and its separation from ordinary uranium is very complicated, painstaking and expensive, a difficult undertaking for even an advanced industrial country. This was some comfort, since a plutonium bomb probably cannot be used as the trigger of a hydrogen bomb. A few days after the explosion, the U.S. Atomic Energy Commission analysed the radioactive particles from the upper atmosphere and concluded that the explosive was u-235. This meant that China had leapfrogged France, which had not yet produced at Pierrelatte enough u-235 for a bomb, a remarkable achievement.

It showed also considerable technological versatility in the development of the bomb itself. The simplest method of bringing together suddenly a critical mass of fissionable material, by firing one piece slightly smaller than critical size into another, works for plutonium but not for u-235. The technique for u-235 was developed at Los Alamos in 1945 and explained in published material, but is still a difficult technical feat. This is implosion, in which the fissile material is formed into a hollow sphere and surrounded by TNT, then pushed into a tight ball by the explosion of the TNT. The use of u-235 showed, also, that China was determined from the very beginning of her programme to go for a hydrogen bomb.

Satellite observations showed that the Chinese had produced the u-235 at a gaseous diffusion plant at Lanchow, a city in north central China on the ancient silk routes that was being developed as an industrial centre. It was an enormously expensive operation, even though the most expensive requirement, a huge electricity supply, was in surplus since, in the chaotic period of the manic 'great leap forward', China had produced more electricity plant than her industry needed. (During the Second World War the gaseous diffusion plant at Oak Ridge, Tennessee, at one time accounted for more than 10 per cent of the electricity consumption of the United States.)

Seven months after her first atomic bomb, in May 1965, the Chinese exploded a second bomb. This was dropped from an aeroplane, an old Russian-built TU-4. A year later, they exploded a third bomb, and it contained lithium-6; they were already working towards a hydrogen bomb. Western analysts estimated that it would be 1970 before they achieved this.

Furthermore, they said, China had no modern delivery system; the TU-4 was of Second World War vintage, and it would take the Chinese years to develop any kind of missile.

The next Chinese bomb, exploded in October 1966, was the warhead of a missile, which carried it 400 miles. Two months later, China exploded a 200-kiloton bomb in which thermo-nuclear reactions took place, something like the American Greenhouse test at Eniwetok in 1952.

In June 1967 she exploded a hydrogen bomb. 'This marks the entry of the development of China's nuclear weapons into an entirely new stage,' the Chinese Government announce-ment said. Western analysis showed that it was a remarkably sophisticated device, a clean bomb in which nearly all the explosive power came from fusion, the kind of device that American and Soviet scientists achieved only after years of improving and refining their original hydrogen bomb.

After this, the pace of development appeared slower. There is reason to believe that the programme suffered for a while from the cultural revolution, as did every other structured institution in the country. Several leading Chinese physicists were denounced by the Red Guards, and everyone educated abroad, as they all were, came under suspicion. There was a second H-bomb test in December 1968, and a third in September 1969. Then, in April 1970, China put an earth satellite into orbit; the rocket that did this was a potential ICBM. In creating a delivery system, China is reaping the benefits of being a late starter in modern weaponry. She is skipping the bomber phase of warfare, and building rockets from the start.

In early 1969, relations with the Soviet Union deteriorated dramatically with a series of armed clashes along the border. From then on, Chinese propaganda organs talked of the Russians as potential aggressors along with the United States, and warned the population and armed forces to be ready for war. There was a new need for urgency in building up military strength.

Urging upon the world the dangers of nuclear proliferation,

Lord Chalfont, as Britain's Minister of State for Disarmament, said often at the Geneva talks on non-proliferation that the world must be rid of the idea that these terrible weapons are a status symbol, and carry with them any form of prestige. No doubt Lord Chalfont is sincere in his message, but to a nation like China, it must have the unconvincing sound of a rich man telling a poor but ambitious one that money doesn't bring happiness.

The bomb seems to have brought the Communist Government prestige domestically. Foreign correspondents in Peking reported that at every announcement of a test, there were celebrations, fireworks, and genuine jubilation, and hotel porters would stop foreigners in the corridors to tell them proudly of the news. In much of the Afro-Asian world, the reaction to the Chinese bomb was respect and admiration, even in those countries that have reason to feel nervous about growing Chinese strength. Protests came from Japan and India, both temperamentally anti-nuclear for their different reasons. But Tunku Abdul Rahman, the Malaysian leader and a staunch anti-Communist, commented 'The detonation ... showed the world that such attainments are not the prerogative only of the West. Asians also are capable of doing it.' The Pakistan Press Association said it would be 'a source of strength to Asian countries'.

The United States was committed to a policy of trying to isolate China. But when the Chinese exploded their first bomb, and coupled it with a call for a world summit conference to discuss the abolition of nuclear weapons, a suggestion that the State Department dismissed out of hand, the *New York Times* commented 'Ultimately, a world summit conference on these matters such as the Chinese suggest may have merit.' Two days after the second Chinese test, a House Foreign Affairs Subcommittee said in a report that the time had come for increased contacts between American and Chinese scholars and journalists. After the third test, the *New York Times* said in an editorial that it was now 'urgent' that China be invited to join the Geneva disarmament talks, and recommended

China's inclusion in the United Nations and 'the comity of nations'. Senator Robert Kennedy said in the Senate that the United States should now invite China to a conference on controlling nuclear weapons, and two other senators backed him. If this is not status, it is something very much like it.

China reiterated the call for the abolition of nuclear weapons and for a world disarmament conference. This was her answer to a test-ban treaty, and to other arms control proposals which seemed to discriminate in favour of the nuclear powers. The Chinese Government said in several statements that it was building nuclear weapons in order to hasten the day when they will be abolished, something others have said as well.

On the day after the explosion of the first Chinese bomb, Chou En-lai, the Prime Minister, sent a letter to the heads of all the governments of the world containing a promise: 'At no time and under no circumstances will China be the first to use nuclear weapons.' No other country has ever said this. After the second test, China proposed to the U.S. Government in a secret communication a mutual promise that neither country would be the first to use nuclear weapons against the other, and the proposal was turned down. This exchange was only revealed a year later.

This Chinese promise not to use the bomb first has received little attention, probably because China now figures in most pictures of the world as the West's prime enemy, and therefore not to be trusted. But the Chinese Government was not asking for anything in exchange for this. In the circumstances, it can be seen, not merely as a promise, but as a policy statement. It would be rash to assume for purposes of military planning that this will always be the policy of any future Chinese Government but there is every reason to believe that it is the policy of the government that made it.

It is consistent with Chinese attitudes. They want to use their nuclear weapons primarily in order to defend themselves, to counter any threat by either America's or Russia's strategic bombing force. They are confident that they can defeat an invasion with conventional forces, if necessary by guerrilla tactics. They may even be over-confident, since their military doctrines as publicly stated rest partly on the absurd pretence that the Chinese Communist guerrilla armies not only fought courageously and effectively against the Japanese, but played the decisive role in defeating Japan. The Chinese leaders see a world of revolution, not of clashes between great powers, though they fear that the United States might react to revolution by making war as, in their view, she did in Vietnam.

China denied the supreme importance of nuclear weapons, not only before she acquired them, but afterwards as well. In its announcement of the first atom bomb test, the Chinese Government said,

'The atom bomb is a paper tiger.' This famous saying by Chairman Mao Tse-Tung is known to all. This was our view in the past, and this is still our view now. China is developing nuclear weapons, not because we believe in the omnipotence of nuclear weapons and plan to use nuclear weapons. ... China's aim is to break the nuclear monopoly of the nuclear powers and to eliminate nuclear weapons. The Chinese Government is loyal to Marxism-Leninism and proletarian internationalism. We believe in the people. It is the people who decide the outcome of a war, and not any weapon.

In the repeated Chinese statements that the will of the people, the strength of the masses, will decide the outcome of a future war rather than any weapons, there is an echo of the Stalinist argument that the 'permanently operating factors' in the Marxist-Leninist scheme are decisive.

In Sino-Soviet arguments on the subject, the Russians usually portray the Chinese as being reckless, and blind to the terrible consequences of nuclear war. The Chinese, on the other hand, say that to stress repeatedly the dangers of nuclear war is defeatist, and plays into the hands of the imperialists.

Mao Tse-Tung put the Chinese view several years before China had a nuclear bomb, in a private speech at a Moscow congress in November 1957, published by the Chinese in 1963. Mao said that nuclear war would not break out, and that even if it did, Communism would triumph.

If fighting breaks out now [he went on to say], China has got only hand grenades, and not atomic bombs, which the Soviet Union has, though. Out of the world's population of 2,700 million, one third – or, if more, half – may be lost. It is they and not we who want to fight. When a war starts, atomic and hydrogen bombs may be dropped. I debated this question with a foreign statesman. He believed that if an atomic war was fought, the whole of Mankind would be annihilated. I said that if the worst came to the worst and half of Mankind died, the other half would remain, while imperialism would be razed to the ground and the whole world would become socialist; in a number of years, there would be 2,700 million people again, and then more. ... If every day you are afraid of war and war comes, what will you do then? First, I have said that the East wind prevails over the West wind and war will not break out, and now I have added these explanations about the situation in case war should break out.

This attitude was reiterated later in an editorial in the *Peking People's Daily* (19 April 1960) about the possibility of nuclear war which concluded: 'On the debris of a dead imperialism, the victorious people would create with extreme rapidity a civilization thousands of times higher than the capitalist system, and a truly beautiful future for themselves.'

Statements like these, weighing the deaths of half of mankind in the balance against the fruits of victory, are almost as inexplicable as they are terrifying to most people in the West. They stem from the totalitarian nature of the Chinese Communist political philosophy. Politics, to the Maoist, dominates every aspect of human life, and not just a part of it. To him, the issue in a political battle is the nature of human beings. The global revolution is the struggle to inaugurate a new era of Man's history, and, in Karl Marx's phrase, to bring to a close the childhood of humanity.* The fight against the opponents of this revolution is something like Armageddon.

This totalitarian view of politics has been held by some others in the past, and they, or their successors, modified their views. It remains to be seen what will happen in China, but the

*The phrase occurs in the closing sentences of Marx's *Critique of the Gotha Programme*.

cultural revolution seems to have been an attempt to insure against such backsliding among the next generation of party cadres. In terms of nuclear war, a totalitarian view of the issues puts the notion of 'acceptable losses' into a different perspective, and a frightening one.

Compared with statements on nuclear war and its consequences coming from the Pentagon, Mao's pronouncement seems remarkably lacking in scientific realism. The prophecy that Communism would inherit the ruins of a postwar world can only be taken as a statement of faith. It seems to be supported by no serious calculations of how many people would survive thermonuclear war and where these people would be, nor the kind of environment in which they would live, and the social organization that is likely to take shape.

The British and French nuclear forces serve a defensive purpose. They cannot deter anything except the threat of a direct attack on the homeland. Britain and France do not plan to employ them in support of a role as a world power. Indeed, since they acquired nuclear weapons, both countries have cut their overseas commitments. China, on the other hand, does want to play a global role, and did not wait to acquire nuclear weapons to do so. She believes she has a mission to encourage and support revolution all over the underdeveloped world. This support is to be political and economic rather than military, but the Chinese accept that even this can bring them into conflict with other major powers. This indicates that China will want to build up a whole range of nuclear weapons and delivery systems, at whatever cost to her people's standard of living, so that she can match a threat by a super-power at any level. Her hydrogen bombs will not be put at the service of the revolution, but they may, in one circumstance or another, be made available for its defence.

The official Chinese attitude to nuclear weapons is cautious. In its announcement of the first atom bomb test, the Chinese Government said 'On the question of nuclear weapons, China will commit neither the error of adventurism nor the error of capitulationism. The Chinese people can be trusted.'

The Chinese have an interest in nuclear stability. The abolition of all nuclear weapons is, after all, a kind of nuclear stability. They believe that with the threat of nuclear weapons out of the way, the historic forces of the revolution, the revolution of the 'countryside' of the world against the industrialized nations, the 'cities', in Lin Piao's formulation, will proceed unhindered. For they do not have an interest in political or economic stability. On the contrary, they support violent change all over the world. Their object is to see this change brought about within a framework of nuclear stability, which means without a thermonuclear war, as a mutiny may occur on a ship without capsizing it.

In his book *On the Prevention of War*, published in 1962, the late John Strachey foresaw 'a war without fighting', with horrors to dwarf those of Passchendaele and Stalingrad. 'It would be waged by squads of technicians,' he wrote. 'In such a war, there would be little room for courage, comradeship, endurance – for those military virtues the flickering light of which has at least relieved the blood and filth of traditional warfare.'

Today the squads of technicians are there, sitting at instrument panels that control huge rockets, ready to wage the most terrible war that the world has ever known. They are at stations underground over much of the United States, and much of the Soviet Union. They are in Polaris submarines resting on the ocean bed, off Northern Europe and the Asian mainland. Soon, according to schedule, they will be sitting at underground control panels in Western France, and later on, presumably, in China.

Most of the American long-range rockets are Minutemen, although a number of the liquid-fuelled Titans are still in service. The rockets stand vertically in concrete-lined launching tubes, or silos, all over the northern half of the United States, with a few below the dividing line. Most of them are far from cities, so that an attack on them would be unlikely to hit a population centre. They are under the rolling hills of the

Dakotas, and under long, grey stretches of prairie in Wyoming and Montana, and the deserts of the Southwest.

Above ground, there is little to see. From a hundred yards away, you could pass by the spot without noticing anything. There is a twelve-foot high wire mesh fence about 120 feet in diameter, an ordinary sort of fence that might be erected to keep out cattle, or chicken thieves. Inside this, there are three things that look like the ventilators on a ship's deck pointing inwards, to form a much smaller triangle. These set up an electronic field, and if anyone or anything crosses it, an alarm signal sounds in an Air Force Police shack some miles away. If you get very close, you might just notice the top of the silo, a dull, silvery-coloured slab about twelve feet across, almost flush with the ground, like the hubcap of a car. Actually, it is three feet thick and made of concrete.

This will be a lonely spot, although a good road leads to it. This silo is one of ten arranged in a circle that may be anything up to sixty miles in circumference. At the centre of this circle is the underground control capsule where the two men sit who control all ten rockets. (If they are Titans, there are five men in the capsule.) This circle of ten missiles make up one flight. There are four other flights like it in the immediate area, and these make up a squadron. Nearby, there are two other squadrons, each with its five circles of ten rockets each, and these three squadrons make up a wing.

The wing, with its 150 rockets, is commanded from the SAC base, which has the offices, the administrative buildings and post exchange, the living quarters, and the whole Air Force infrastructure. It may be more than 100 miles away for some of the silos under its command.

The Minuteman F is a three-stage rocket fifty-five feet long, the height of a three-storey building, that can carry a small hydrogen bomb 5,000 miles in twenty-eight minutes and land it near the target a high percentage of the time. It is painted white, and has the U.S. Air Force insignia on it.

Each of the three stages, which is a separate rocket, burns for exactly one minute, and the path of the missile is determined during these three minutes. An autopilot, like the autopilot on an airliner, senses the altitude of the rocket, its movement on its axes, and its speed. A guidance system with its own computer makes 200 computations per second with the autopilot's information, and controls the flight of the missile by regulating the ducts and thrust termination. It must be more complicated than a jet plane because it has no human pilot. It is constructed with such intricacy and such precision, its thousands of separate mechanisms working together so smoothly, that it seems a sin that such a beautiful instrument should be built only to destroy itself, let alone destroy other things as well.

The hydrogen bomb warhead is not just a deadly cargo. It is closely linked to the rocket, and is set to explode only in the target area, and nowhere else. Seventeen electrical circuits must be completed before the firing mechanism can work. The sixteenth is completed when the rocket's guidance system sends a 'message' to the warhead that it is descending over the target area, and the seventeenth when it pulls 17Gs, which means that the deceleration creates a pull seventeen times that of normal gravity, and it is therefore on the last stage of its descent. Only then can the bomb's firing mechanism work.

When a Minuteman is launched, the silo cap slides back quickly and smoothly, and the rocket motors start to work down below. The first thing visible above ground is the white smoke from the motors; first it streams out in two jets, then this pattern dissolves into a high-pressure cloud. Then the long white rocket rises slowly through the billowing white smoke, the flame from its motor glowing faintly like a headlamp in a fog, a sight that stirs faintly images of some Greek god rising out of the sea or the earth. The missile turns slightly from the vertical as it soars faster into the sky, gathering speed, smoke billowing out behind, giving out with the throaty roar of a racing car. It is loud enough to be heard three miles away. It is not loud enough to be heard by the men who fired it in their control capsule, since they are seven to ten miles away and sixty feet underground. A light signal tells them that the rocket has been launched, their mission accomplished. Even then, they do not know its target. Not even the base commander knows that. The separation of an action from its consequences, which has been increasingly a characteristic of modern warfare with the advance of technology, is here complete.

The missile's guidance system is programmed to take it on a certain trajectory by a targeting kit, a metal box some four feet long, with two dials on the outside. The targeting kits are made up at Offutt by technicians who belong to a special unit, the 544th Aerospace Reconnaissance Technical Wing (Motto: *Hic Et Ubique, Here and Everywhere*). In the First World War, men in the trenches used to speak of 'the bullet with your name on it'. The men of the 544th Wing put the names on the long-range rockets, only they are not the names of people but of places. The kit goes to the base with the missile, and it is inserted when the missile goes on alert status.

Men who join the Air Force to fly aeroplanes, in a spirit of adventure and combativeness, do not welcome their four-year tour of duty on missiles – silo-sitting, they call it. They prefer a tour of flying duty. But the ambitious young officer knows that missiles are now the most important part of SAC, and that experience in missilery is a very useful qualification for higher command. Furthermore, the Air Force is now getting – it might even be accurate to say 'breeding' – a new kind of officer, less narrowly militaristic than the traditional mould, and more worldly and sophisticated. One now meets in the Air Force young officers who find the service intellectually challenging, and who feel it to be an interesting and useful career in peacetime, not merely a long interlude of waiting until they can get on with the job they were trained for. Some of these men are not unhappy to be on missile duty, though its challenges are technical rather than intellectual, because they find the higher-level problems of missile deterrence interesting, and see this as a path to contact with them.

The senior man in a two-man missile crew is a captain or a major, the other a lieutenant. They live on the base, usually in spacious, ranch-type houses set in a landscaped officer's housing area. They drive together to their silo to begin their shift, or, if it is more than thirty miles away, they may be flown there in a helicopter. At the top of the silo there is a small shack where two armed Air Force policemen are posted. The policemen do not let them down the shaft. The crew on duty below do this, after the incoming senior officer speaks a code word into a speaker tube, by pressing a button that opens a door. They go down in the elevator, which, like all the other machinery in the silo, is coloured pea-green. At the bottom, they face the door of what looks like the biggest safe in the world. It is a four-ton blast door, which swings back lightly on its hinges when the handle is turned, deceptively lightly for it could easily smash a man's bones and must be handled gently.

The outgoing senior officer briefs the incoming pair on the state of missiles, using a technical slang. Then there is a moment of uncharacteristic formality as the two outgoing officers hand over the keys that hang around their necks on chains, their ·38 revolvers, and a small plastic card containing the current firing code, and the four men exchange stiff salutes.

The capsule has two chambers, each about twenty-five feet by twelve feet, connected by a narrow corridor a few feet long that is not so high as the chambers and narrower, so that together they form a dumb-bell shape. One chamber is filled entirely with a huge diesel engine that supplies electric power for the control lines to the missiles, and refrigeration and air conditioning. The other is the control room, in which they spend their time. Each chamber is on huge shock absorbers, and you feel the spring very slightly as you walk across the metal floor; it can be knocked by a blast eighteen inches to one side or the other without shattering the framework.

There are two duplicate consoles in the control room a few yards from each other, each with a comfortable red leather armchair in front of it, the only touch of softness in this metal world. At least one officer is sitting in his armchair at all times. They spend their time monitoring the conditions of the rocket's systems, going through maintenance checks where ordered, and spotting and usually correcting by remote control faults in the circuits or systems. Each control panel has ten rows of eleven lights each with a lock at the end. Each row represents one missile, each light a different part of the missile's workings. If a light shows that there is a fault in a system, the officer presses a switch and a tape-recorded voice speaks the nature of the fault: 'Hydraulic pressure low', or 'Warhead alarm'.

This underground chamber is a part of the same SAC communications network as the bomber bases. It is linked to the other fourteen capsules in the wing, to the command base, and to SAC headquarters at Offutt, in Nebraska. Messages come in code over a loudspeaker, with a warble preceding each one, and over a teleprinter that is clattering away much of the time. The crew see all the messages that go from SAC h.q. to any missile base.

They have meal packs, and there is a stove down there on which they can warm them up. There is a bed that folds into the wall, and the crew members are entitled to four hours' sleep each on a shift if they can get it, but few of them do. The atmosphere is not conducive to sleep; there is a background whine, the clicking and voices of the monitoring, the frequent warbles of the loudspeaker.

When they lean back from the consoles in their armchairs, the men usually spend a lot of time studying technical information on missiles, techdata, as they call it. Many study for a master's degree in science or engineering (everyone must have a bachelor's degree already) through an Air Force programme. Or they read novels, drink coffee and talk, about their philosophies of life, politics, marriage, women, the Air Force. Somehow, the job they are doing, the warheads on the end of the missiles they control, do not come up. Ask why and you get the expected answers. 'Well, there's nothing to say about it,' says one. 'We all know why we're here,' says another. 'It's because the other side has got people manning other missiles. We're ready to do the job if we get the order. And we don't expect to get it.'

If the President ever decides to press down fingers on keys to play a nuclear war chord, he will give the order to SAC in specific terms. He will tell SAC what kind of nuclear strike he wants, and what kind of targets he wants to destroy, perhaps what specific targets. SAC will translate this into the relevant firing orders, and these will go out to the missile bases. SAC will tell them what missiles to fire, at what targets, whether in salvo or, if in sequence, in what order. The men in each silo know the code names for each of the targets for which a Minuteman is assigned, and by pressing switches they can adjust the guidance system for each one.

There are far more ways to prevent a missile from being launched than there are to launch one. It is easier to lock the weapon than to unlock it, even without the permissive action link. On the ground, as when the rocket is in flight, everything is done to make certain that if there is an error, it will mean that an H-bomb does not explode that should, rather than the other way around.

Every officer in a squadron has a veto over every other officer's missiles. The 'fire' message comes over the loudspeaker, and is repeated on the teleprinter, and both officers must agree that it is an order to fire before they act on it. Then the commander presses the 'enabling switch', which is the first step towards launching the rocket; the other four capsules in the squadron all get a signal that he has done this. They have seen the order to fire that has gone to him. If someone in another capsule has *not* seen it, and therefore presumes that the order was not sent, then he must press the 'inhibiting switch' on his own control panel, and this prevents the missiles from being launched.

The launching mechanism is locked anyway for a very short while after the enabling switch has been pressed, to give time for anyone to stop it. Then it is released, and the two officers begin pressing switches that set the firing mechansim going and start the countdown. As they do, they read out conditions from the console: 'Fuel pressure rising', 'Hydraulic pressure amber'. As the last step, both officers take the keys from around their necks and insert them simultaneously in locks on the consoles, then turn them. The firing mechansim only works if the keys are inserted simultaneously. An electromagnetic device ensures

349

that there can be no second try; once a key is inserted in the lock, it cannot be taken out again.

A few SAC missile crews have gone through this procedure. They have gone to Vandenberg Air Force Base, some 150 miles up the California coastline from Los Angeles, and launched a rocket out over the Pacific test range. As they are turning switches, only the lights on the console tell the two officers that the firing mechanism has started. There is also a slight change of tone in the background humming as the electricity power supply is increased, but it has no dramatic quality like a crescendo. Finally, a light goes on next to the sign saying 'Missiles away'. Less than five minutes have elapsed since the enabling switch was pressed. Down there in the capsule, there is no difference between a test and a war. The men do not even know what is happening in the land above their heads, though there are detectors in the capsule which will register the amount of radioactivity outside. Most assume that if they have pressed all their switches, H-bombs will have exploded up there as well.

At the beginning of 1970, the United States had 1,054 ICBMs in underground silos, forty-one submarines carrying 656 Polaris and Poseidon missiles, and some 450 intercontinental bombers carrying nuclear bombs. The figures have remained constant for three years, apart from a slight drop in the number of bombers. This is because of a decision made by the Johnson Administration, and continued under Nixon, to allow the Soviet Union to catch up with the United States in numbers of missiles, once she had clearly set out to do so, and not increase its own numbers and remain ahead. Russia moved away from what seemed like a finite deterrent posture in 1966–7, and stepped up her production of long-range missiles. By early 1970, according to the Institute for Strategic Studies in London, she probably had slightly more ICBMs than the United States, and with more powerful warheads. But she lagged behind in other areas, with only 160 submarine-launched missiles and 200 long-range bombers. The Soviet submarine force is much less sophisticated than the American. There are fifty submarines equipped to launch three missiles each as a secondary function, though Russia is building a fleet of submarines that carry missiles comparable to the Polaris.

America could allow Russia to catch up since by 1967 both sides had a substantial assured-destructive capability. In that year, the Department of Defense made public some calculations of casualties in an all-out Soviet-American war, and they have not bothered to amend them since then. These showed that if the Russians struck first, 120 million Americans would be killed and 120 million-plus Russians. If the United States struck first, 120 million Americans would die and 70 million Russians. (It may seem curious that more Russians would be killed if America struck second than if she struck first. This appears to be because the calculations assume that an American second strike would be retaliatory, and aimed at cities, while a first strike would be counterforce.) Actually, the precision of these figures is more an attribute of the Pentagon style than of realistic predictions about nuclear war. There are far more uncertainties than this kind of talk would indicate, about the success of the missile strike, the state of the population, the long-term effects of radiation upon people and upon environment.

This last could be more important than the immediate effect of a nuclear attack, according to a United Nations report issued by U Thant. This report indicates also that the most numerous victims of a limited nuclear war might be the children of future generations. 'In general,' it said, 'the long-term genetic effects of nuclear radiation on living organisms are cumulative ... it is reasonably certain that a population which had been irradiated at an intensity sufficient to kill even a few per cent of its members would suffer important long-term consequences.'

The report also contained a few examples of the application of Pentagon-type calculations of bomb effects to other, more crowded lands. One diagram showed that if a 15-megaton bomb were exploded on London, the fallout could kill most of the population of Calais and bring sickness and death to Paris.

When the age of the ICBM arrived, it was widely thought that a kind of awful stability had been reached, that the balance of terror was a plateau of military power. But human ingenuity pushed the super-powers away from this plateau, with the development of means to make weapons more powerful still. And the action-reaction process, by which each super-power reacts to its expectation of what weapons the other side will build, propelled them onwards.

The development of new weapons has been widely reported. What is less often realized is the remarkable improvement in the accuracy of long-range rockets, that has probably done just as much to change the calculus of nuclear exchange. Precise figures are a closely-guarded secret, but missile men are now talking in terms of a CEP of less than half a mile over a range of 5,000 miles. An improvement in accuracy increases the chances of destroying a target just as increasing the number of missiles does, only more so. That is, increasing accuracy by a certain factor has the same effect as increasing the number of missiles by the square of the same factor. Halving the CEP of a missive force (which means doubling the accuracy) is equivalent in destructive power to multiplying the number of missiles by four. The improvement in accuracy of the American missile force over the years has the same effect as multiplying the number many times would have. This brings concepts like invulnerability into a new perspective. It becomes possible to envisage a missile putting another one out of action even in a hardened silo.

There have also been changes in the weapons. The United States has developed a multiple-warhead missile, and the Soviet Union has followed suit. The most advanced American model is the Multiple Independent Re-entry Vehicle, or MIRV. A MIRV is an ICBM equipped with up to ten nuclear warheads. As the third stage of a MIRV rocket re-enters the atmosphere, it goes through a series of gyrations that propels each warhead towards a different target. The Soviet multiple-warhead rocket, the S S-9, is less sophisticated. It releases three warheads as it re-enters the atmosphere, so that they travel in together and land a few miles apart. But this makes it an effective weapon against missiles in hardened silos grouped in a squadron.

The Soviet Union has developed missiles that challenge a defensive radar screen by travelling in a low path rather than plummeting in from space, where they are more easily detected (over a 5,000-mile range, a rocket has an apogee of about 800 miles). These are called Depressed Trajectory Missiles. They are particularly useful against manned bombers, which, in a high alert state, can take off when an incoming missile is detected on a radar screen and be out of range by the time it lands. One of these is called the Fractional Orbital Bombardment Missile. It is fired at a speed that will put it into an orbit around the earth about 100 miles up. It brakes after only a part of the global orbit is completed, so that it drops down on the target. There are possibilities of other depressed trajectory missiles, perhaps fired from a submarine offshore.

The manned bomber, once written off as obsolete in the face of heat-seeking anti-aircraft rockets, has been given a new lease of life, in America at any rate, by the development of fast and accurate new air-launched missiles with nuclear warheads, with ranges of 800 miles and more. These can be launched on the comfortable side of an enemy's rocket defences.

Attention has focused most of all on defensive missiles, the ABMs. The long argument in the United States about whether or not to deploy ABMs was the most prolonged, widely reported and best-informed public debate about nuclear weapons that has ever taken place, a public counterpart to that secret debate in Washington about whether or not to build an H-bomb in the first place.

Originally, the strongest argument against the ABM was a cost-effectiveness one. Every dollar spent on an anti-missile system could be nullified by spending fifty cents or less on penetration aids, as they are called, to defeat the system, or simply on more offensive missiles. But this argument was eroded as the cost-effectiveness of the anti-missile missiles was improved. Others said there were so many unreliabilities intrinsic to an ABM system, which could not be properly tested, that it would be dangerous to base any strategy on its effectiveness. It was said also that an ABM system would be provocative, and would cause an escalation of the arms race, and that it would give a false sense of security.

Some of those who argued for an ABM system wanted the United States to have any weapon Russia had; others emphasized the dangers in Russia's early ABM missiles and SS-9 development of a first-strike disabling capability, that is, the capability of destroying the American nation, and the bombers and missiles before they can be used. Some stressed the need to provide defence against the kind of light missile force that China would have in the 1970s. Some strategists argued that the balance of terror would be just as stable if the level of assured destruction on both sides is lowered, providing it is still high enough to deter.

For a while, the argument divided the strategic and scientific communities in America along familiar lines: on one side, the liberals, the worriers about the big bomb, like Wiesner, Bethe, York, opposing ABM; on the other, the conservatives who worry more about the need for national defence, like Teller, Wohlstetter, Kahn. But as the arguments become more complex and more morally ambiguous, the lines were crossed.

Donald Brennan, a qualified supporter of the ABM, once characterized his opponents' determined opposition by saying 'The credo "We cannot defend so we must deter" seems to have become "We can deter so we must not defend." ' And indeed, in some people's opposition to an ABM system one can see lurking behind their arguments an unspoken attitude that is often seen when nuclear weapons are discussed. This is a fear, not that an ABM system would not work, but that it might in fact provide some defence, that the total vulnerability of all the peoples of the world, which would make all-out nuclear war an insane policy in any circumstances, might be qualified, and that, with some protection, it might become again a thinkable policy. This was expressed with rare candour in conversation by one junior American official who said: 'I don't want an ABM system, and I don't want fallout shelters, because I don't want any American president to even *think* that he can get away with using nuclear weapons.'

The decision to deploy a limited ABM system was taken first under the Johnson Administration, and revised by President Nixon. The Sentinel System, as the Nixon Administration termed it, concentrates on defending a number of Minuteman silos, bomber bases and command centres, and, as a secondary function, provides some continental defence against a light nuclear attack, such as could be mounted by China in the 1970s. Thus, it preserves America's retaliatory power, without trying to deny the American people to Russia as hostages, even though it sets out to deny them to the Chinese.

President Nixon made this clear in his statement announcing the Sentinel programme, in a paragraph directed at the Soviet leaders as much as at the American public. This showed that the guidelines on arming for defence as laid down in the McNamara era, about judging the potential effect of each new weapon on the arms race and on the adversary, have stuck.

The programme is not provocative [Mr Nixon said]. The Soviet retaliatory capability is not affected by our decision. The capability for a surprise attack against our retaliatory force is reduced. In other words, our program provides an incentive for a responsible Soviet weapons policy, and for the avoidance of spiraling U.S. and Soviet strategic arms budgets.

The U.S. Administration went to some lengths to avoid a provocative posture. One suggestion that was put to it was to mount ABMs on ships stationed within easy reach of the Soviet Union, or else on the sea-bed, where they would be launched and guided via the computer and radar system in the United States. These would be able to intercept a Soviet missile before the last stage of its trajectory, and, in the case of multiple warhead missiles, before the warheads split off, which could be vitally important. One reason why this was rejected was that the ABM missiles would be indistinguishable from medium-range offensive missiles, and could appear to the Russians to be part of an offensive build-up.

Much of the anxiety about a new imbalance is a fear that one side or the other might acquire a first-strike disabling capability. This would mean an offensive force of accurate, multiple-warhead rockets that could destroy on the ground almost all of an enemy's rockets and bombers, and, ideally, some still-to-be-devised anti-submarine weapon that would destroy the Polaris submarines while they are under the sea. If nearly all of an enemy's force had been destroyed, an ABM system could ward off the remaining missiles. The calculations are being done all the time: the percentage probability of destroying 90 per cent, or 95 per cent of an enemy's missiles on the ground, and the probability of an ABM force destroying 100 per cent of the remainder in flight.

The worrying scenarios about a first-strike capability do not involve anyone actually using it to annihilate an enemy's population, meanwhile polluting the world's atmosphere with dangerous radioactivity. This is almost beyond imagining. Usually, the possibility of a first strike decides the outcome of political conflict. It is like the capture of the king in chess. The king is not actually captured; once this is imminent, the side about to lose its king capitulates and the game is over.

One scenario has a situation in which an American president, in a brink-of-war situation, perhaps after some kind of war has actually broken out, anticipates an all-out nuclear attack, and is under pressure to pre-empt. Another has him seeing signals on his radar screen that *seem* to indicate a full-scale missile attack, which would give twenty minutes' warning, oppressed by the thought that if he waits it will be too late to retaliate because the retaliatory force will be destroyed. (A more rational view might be that there is nothing to be lost by waiting, since, if the American people is to be wiped out, the American national interest is not advanced if it has wiped out the Russian nation posthumously.) More commonly, the scenario depicts a confrontation such as the Cuba missiles crisis in which one side has to retreat because the other has a first-strike capability in the background.

This makes it a subjective concept. Like deterrence, it works if one power responds to the threat; it doesn't work if the same power refuses to be frightened. And it seems likely that a super-power can refuse to believe in a first-strike threat. It is difficult to imagine a government contemplating seriously a calculated first strike, even in the most extreme circumstances. Whatever the figures show, there is always an area of uncertainty, and the consequences of failure would be terrible.

In January 1968, after the year in which the U.S. Government first decided to go ahead with an ABM programme, and the MIRV and the Depressed Trajectory Missile made their appearance, the *Bulletin of the Atomic Scientists* moved the hands of the clock on the cover forward five minutes, from the twelve minutes to midnight position where it had been moved back after the test-ban treaty in 1963. The editors said this was 'in sad recognition that the past six years have brought mankind farther down the road to nuclear disaster'.

From the beginning, American officials hoped for an agreement with Russia not to deploy these new weapons. For one thing, the nuclear non-proliferation treaty, in which most non-nuclear countries pledged themselves not to acquire nuclear weapons, obliged the two super-powers to take steps to reduce their stockpiles of nuclear weapons. For another, they wanted to save money.

At first, it was hoped that there might be a tacit agreement not to deploy ABMs. When McNamara was arguing with the American military that an ABM system made little sense, he hoped that the arguments would be heeded by the Soviet military, to whom they were just as applicable. When this clearly was not happening, President Johnson proposed talks between the two countries to limit strategic missiles. The Soviet Government at first said defensive missiles should be left out of the talks, still clinging to the view that defence is a country's own business and does not threaten anyone else. Then, in August 1968, it agreed to the talks. But when the two governments were about to announce this, Russia invaded Czechoslovakia, and the United States withdrew its agreement. The talks finally opened in Helsinki in November 1969, to be resumed in Vienna and then in Helsinki again. The delay may have been crucial; it may have killed any chance of barring in effect multiple-warhead missiles. An agreement to ban the deployment of these missiles cannot be verified without close inspection, which Russia will not allow. The number of missiles can be counted from a reconnaissance satellite, but it is impossible to tell whether each missile has one or several warheads without taking it apart. A ban on *testing* multiple-warhead missiles would have put a brake on their development. This might have been possible in 1968, but by the time the talks were finally under way, testing was very advanced. Nor was there much chance of banning ABMs. Whatever the position of the Soviet–American balance, Russia would insist on keeping the right to erect a thin shield against a Chinese nuclear attack (though her first ABM deployment was directed against a possible attack from the West).

There are other possibilities, however, for a limited, detailed arms control agreement. These, in turn, might pave the way for others that are more far-reaching, which would provide a framework of agreement covering the balance of terror.

Continued talks might lead to a better understanding between the two super-powers. Already, they have drawn closer together. The Russians have come to accept the Americans' view that security is achieved more by stability than by self-defence, that both sides have an interest in easing each other's fears about a first strike, and that even defences can be threatening. A wider understanding between the two super-powers of each other's anxieties and intentions may do more to slow down the arms race than signed treaties; this holds out some hope for a safer world, however limited.

14. A Permanent Aspect of Human Culture

The knowledge of how to produce the weapons will remain with us always, and . . . mankind is therefore less secure than it was before it had this knowledge. Thus, the full force of our situation must be emphasized. We now possess the actual weapons, and we shall always possess the knowledge of how to produce them. They have become a permanent aspect of human culture.

From *Christians and the Prevention of War*,
a World Council of Churches document

We now have the answers to most of the questions that loomed over the first years of the super. The hydrogen bomb was developed as a weapon; it is here to stay; it has spread to other countries, though not as rapidly as many people thought it would; it has not produced so far any change in the international system of competing sovereign states, nor has it ever been used in war. The dilemmas of those first years, however, have not been resolved; in fact, now that their novelty has worn off, they are being forgotten. Mankind has neither united nor perished; it remains, disunited and in peril. We are still living with the bomb. As W. H. Auden wrote in his poem *Leap Before You Look*,

> It is not the convention but the fear
> That has a tendency to disappear.

The building of the first hydrogen bombs were moves in the Soviet–American Cold War. 'Will there be a war?' meant, in those days, 'Will there be a nuclear war between the West and Russia?' The H-bomb will never again be seen in so narrow a context. The H-bomb question from now on is not what men in the Kremlin or the White House may do, but what men of any government with H-bombs may do at any time, anywhere. People have this power. Will anyone use it?

We are living in an interim period. The Soviet–American conflict has abated, partly under the threat of the bomb. Other thermonuclear cold wars are not yet fully grown.

No new thermonuclear power is likely to arise in the next few years. If any other country does build nuclear weapons soon, it will probably build fission bombs rather than hydrogen bombs, intended to deal with some local situation, like the threat of another Israel–Arab war. The bombs will not be a means of exercising global power, nor will they be acquired for that purpose.

Co-existence with the hydrogen bomb has imposed a number of special characteristics on the international scene.

The conduct of international relations is cautious. The major nations are restrained in their actions towards one another, however hostile their words. The U.S. Government, when it escalated its war against North Vietnam, did not promise more and greater violence unless its wishes were complied with, but a limit to the violence; it assured the North Vietnamese that it has no plans to conquer their country or overthrow their government. In an earlier age of diplomacy, an American administration might have seen an advantage to itself in a war between its two principal enemies, Russia and China. But now the United States is alarmed at any such prospect. A war between any two major powers makes the world a more dangerous place for everyone.

Political hostility in most of the great powers is inhibited. In the presence of the H-bomb, intense hostility can be dangerous, and even one's own violence must be repressed. Dean Rusk gave testimony to this necessity in a speech on 2 May 1967: 'Our military power ... is so vast that the effects of its use are beyond the comprehension of the mind of man. It is so vast that we dare not allow ourselves to become infuriated.'

The nuclear threshold is universally recognized, and care is taken to stay well on the right side of it. When President Eisenhower took office, he sent a private warning to China that if the Korean truce talks at Panmunjom broke down, he would feel free to use nuclear weapons. But the hydrogen bomb has come since then, and attitudes to nuclear weapons have changed, so that there was never any question of such a warning on Vietnam.

The phenomenon of nuclear incredulity persists. This can be seen even in people who are devoting their energies and intelligence to the problems of waging nuclear war; these assume on the rational level that it could happen and therefore must be prepared for, while at another level many act as if it is out of the realm of the possible. It may be that some people can plan for nuclear war only *because*, at a deeper level, they feel that it cannot really happen. This fundamental disbelief can be seen in the extraordinary fact that no major country has built shelters to protect its public in the event of nuclear war. Sweden has built multi-purpose shelters, for nuclear bomb protection among other things. The United States and Russia have both earmarked and stocked existing buildings as fallout shelters; other countries have not even done that. Yet all calculations show that many millions of lives at the least could be saved by even a modest shelter-building programme. The Defense Department wanted to build shelters, but Congress refused the funds.

In our time, the safety margin of the super-powers is enormous. They have so many long-range missiles so well hardened that it would be almost impossible for this force to be destroyed, or even a large part of it. A super-power today can afford to take risks in strategic rearrangements or in an arms control agreement, because it can lose a great deal of advantage and still not endanger its safety.

Thermonuclear weapons today are the ring within which conflict must be contained. If they were not in existence, it is likely that Chinese troops would have poured into South Vietnam long before now to fight beside the Vietcong, and that American forces would have helped the Hungarian uprising. There may be room for a dangerous error of judgement about where the lines of the ring are drawn, but the outer limits, at least, are clear. The vital national interests of the super-powers may not be threatened.

This seems to limit the kinds of change that can take place. The world may alter in all sorts of ways. There can be wars, and great nations can lose their power. But, if they possess a powerful second-strike H-bomb force, these nations cannot be conquered from without. Most historical processes take place more rapidly today than ever before, but some may be in stasis. A thermonuclear power can freeze its sovereign status for as long as her people want it. With a second-strike thermo-nuclear force, Rome could have been corrupted but never sacked, Byzantium might have lost her empire but would have held her walls.

All this makes up a nuclear consensus, a set of agreed rules about what can and cannot be done, agreed in the sense that they are obvious to everyone. But the consensus has not yet been severely tested. It is like a craft that has been out only in a calm sea. The world during the years of the super has been stable.

There is a lot of talk about the present era being one of revolutionary change. But in international affairs, we live in a time of only gradual and marginal change. The world looks much the same as it did ten years ago. Most of the global changes since 1945 took place in the first five postwar years: the advent of the Cold War, the break-up of the colonial empires, and the growing disparity in national wealth. After 1950, most events were a continuation of these, and nothing really new and unexpected happened. Things happened, and they seemed important at the time. But no major nation changed its form of government or its frontiers. We can see how relatively stable the last ten years have been when we compare it with a decade of profound international change, say, 1914–23, or 1932–41. Furthermore, all the expectations are that this relative stability will continue.

Nevertheless, the future may not be so stable. Just beyond the immediate horizon, there are international conflicts that could come to the boil, and, given a certain amount of rashness and unreason, no more than we have seen often in recent times, any one of these could threaten the thermonuclear consensus. To suggest a few: a Chinese Government might press its claim to Formosa or parts of Siberia, perhaps press them militarily with conventional forces under a thermonuclear umbrella; there may be German irredentism over East Prussia, a land where so much of Germany's national origins lie; uprisings and civil war in Eastern Europe could draw in West Germany; Southeast Asian countries, with their vast, overcrowded, underfed masses, might lay claim to some of the huge, rich, empty country to the South, Australia; or – and this possibility, unlike the others, which are collisions of national interest in classical form, has a peculiarly contemporary flavour to it – revolutionary upheaval in the underdeveloped world could draw in China and the United States.

This does not look far into the future, only to conflicts arising out of current international situations. It is likely that all the conflicts of this century will pass without hydrogen bombs being used. The margin of safety is considerable, the danger signs obvious for all to see. So far, in the risk-consequence equation, we have got it both ways. The awful dangers of thermonuclear war have reduced its likelihood, while the powerful and varied armouries and strategies have made it possible that even if it does occur, the disaster will be less than total.

As the possible paths of the future fan out, the risks multiply. The idea has been mooted that once a nation has reached the state of scientific and technological development necessary to produce a hydrogen bomb, then it will have attained a level of safely rational behaviour. This idea might have afforded some comfort if the years between 1933 and 1945 had not shown what can happen to a scientifically and industrially advanced country.

There are technical possibilities that no one has so far had reason to exploit. There might be smaller atomic bombs, much more easily manufactured than those today, perhaps even smaller fusion bombs, that could be used by guerrillas or even gangsters. Some government might build cobalt bombs (this is a nuclear bomb packed in the metal cobalt, which would disintegrate into highly radioactive and long-lasting fallout) to fill the target continent with radioactivity with a good deal left over for the rest of the world. A thermonuclear power today is a country that has the bombs, protected long-range delivery systems, and the military technology to go with all this. But any government with only a hydrogen bomb can exploit it for certain purposes. It is not necessary to have an ICBM to deliver one. It could be delivered in an airliner, or a fishing boat, or, depending on the geography, a lorry. Imagine a guerrilla force or even a whole nation that feels its very existence threatened by Soviet actions, and that has a few H-bombs. It could put one of the bombs and a dedicated suicide squad on to a small boat, sail this into Leningrad harbour or Vladivostok, whichever is closer, and then announce that the crew is ready to detonate the bomb if Russia does not desist. This kind of possibility will always be present as long as the H-bomb is.

A doomsday machine might be built by a government that feels threatened by destruction and has a Messianic sense of mission. One day, in a world no further removed from ours culturally than, say, the Middle Ages, a device might be built that is designed, not, like the doomsday machine, to threaten the whole human race, but to destroy it, by some religious group that goes beyond Manicheism in its dislike of the flesh, and is dedicated to ridding the universe once and for all of this corruption of the Holy Spirit.

The hydrogen bomb's power to destroy in an instant all that man has created, and, perhaps, all that man is, has contributed to one of the general characteristics of our time: a preoccupation with the ephemeral. This is not a frivolous lack of concern with lasting values, but a conscious rejection of them. It is seen in the growing interest in package more than content, in techniques more than ideas. It is seen in some of the ideal types of our time: the swinger, the cool cat, and, in popular literature and films, the chameleon-like professional spy. It has produced the phenomenon of pop art. It emerges often in the ideas of young people of the post-Bikini generation practising the arts, particularly the secondary arts like films, photography and architecture. These often show a disregard of any aspiration to lasting value veering towards hostility. At an exhibition illustrating radical new ideas in architecture, like throwaway homes and a plug-in city, one architect in his twenties remarked 'The bomb has exploded a lot of myths. Like the myth that there are some things that can't be destroyed. People used to believe that.'

The knowledge of what the bomb can do has made people afraid. Just as it inhibits people's political emotions, so it mars their optimism. No one can feel today the exultation at man's future that some people have felt at certain times in the past; any vision of a new dawn arising must always be qualified with 'unless'. This fear is not a localized one, but a general fear of what can be done, the kind of fear that men once had of God. It is not something people talk about often, and indeed there is little to say about it, except 'Watch out', 'Be careful', for the rest of our lives and our children's lives, or we might blow up the world on which we are all standing.

William Faulkner observed this phenomenon, and gave voice to his concern, in his address accepting the Nobel Prize for Literature. He said:

Our tragedy today is a general and universal fear so long sustained by now that we can even bear it. There are no longer problems of the spirit. There is only the question: When will I be blown up? Because of this, the young man or woman writing today has forgotten the problems of the human heart in conflict with itself. He must learn them again.

It may well be that people in some future era, looking back on a global agony from which the cries will still be echoing through the centuries, peering past this in time, will regard those who were involved in the production and development of hydrogen bombs with incomprehension. If thermonuclear war happens, it will seem afterwards to be so obviously and inescapably the end to which these people are now devoting themselves that it will seem incredible that they could have worked so assiduously on the details of such a monstrous event, as scientist, engineer, military planner, submarine commander or economic analyst. Their motives will appear unbelievably trivial compared with their results. They may be classed with those German chemists who devoted their working hours to finding a more efficient way of synthesizing the gas zyclon b, without hating or even taking note of the millions of people it was intended to murder; or a circus technician in Nero's day using his imagination and ingenuity to devise new entertainments, as a part of which men and women were torn to pieces by wild animals or coated with pitch and burned alive.

This may be. But in our time, most people can see the hydrogen bomb only from one necessarily limited point of view. We are all trapped in the situation of our time and place, and must make some concessions to its demands. To the politician, the bomb is a form of power, and therefore an instrument of government. To the scientist, it is a series of problems to be solved, something to be created at the bidding of the community of which he is a member. Many scientists have sought some other way of looking at it, some way that recognized usefully its transcendent importance, but few have found a satisfying one. The military men see it as a weapon; there is a nation to be defended, a national interest to pursue, also at the bidding of the community. The moral protester finds his conscience outraged, but cannot make his voice of protest heard often through the clash of interests in the world. The strategic analyst can see no alternative to teaching governments to use the bomb intelligently other than watching them use it stupidly. So politicians ordered the bombs, scientists and engineers built them, military men aimed them, stategists devised plans for them, and here we all are.

But the bomb cannot be encompassed in any one of the traditional roles that people play, with their limited perspectives. The situation it has created cannot be grasped solely in political terms, in military terms, or in moral terms. And in fact, in the face of the bomb, the limits of traditional roles are breaking down, and people's concerns are spilling over beyond them.

Alastair Buchan, a leading authority on strategic problems, Commandant of the Imperial Defence College, has become interested in non-violent resistance, and has helped to edit a book about it. He wrote an introduction to an earlier pamphlet on this subject, *Civilian Defence*, published by *Peace News*, the pacifist weekly. In this, he said:

It is ... essential that as the classic direct strategies for preserving the integrity of nations, the threat of attack or retaliation, lose their reality with the development of weapons, which can destroy civilizations, and as the older defensive strategies have become totally outmoded by technical innovations, we should pay increasing attention to the indirect strategies for preserving our societies from domination or external rule. For it may be that in concepts like the non-violent defence of countries lies the key to the preservation of society in a world order that contains so many explosive new forms of power, physical, psychological and economic, that firearms will become too dangerous to use.

Lord Chalfont, as Britain's Minister of State for Disarmament, wrote an illuminating essay on disarmament in *Encounter* (October 1966) and had to go beyond professional considerations of disarmament techniques in his conclusion:

The development of new political philosophies and new insights into individual and group psychology, international systems of education, and the perfection of supra-national organizations are essential elements in the pursuit of peace; but the safety of mankind is too precariously balanced to allow us the luxury of long-term thinking and planning without the need for urgent action. The political revolution must begin soon if, as Pandit Nehru believed, the human spirit is to prevail over the nuclear weapon. The first signs that the revolution has begun will be the acceptance by the great powers of the risks – political and military – without which the most modest steps in arms control and disarmament are impossible.

Adam Yarmolinsky, when he was Robert McNamara's Special Assistant in the Defense Department, burst the usual bounds of official discussion in addressing a meeting of the American Orthopsychiatric Association on social science today:

Social scientists particularly have to deal with questions in situations in which any sensible person would throw up his hands and go home. We can't afford to throw up our hands and go home, because there isn't any place to go! We have to face up to the problems of civil defense, we have to face up to the problems of arms control and disarmament. We have to build weapons which are fearful to think about while we negotiate with people whom we really do not understand, about issues which involve the continuation of the world as we know it.*

These are all men of power, reaching out beyond the normal assumptions of the power game. There is a reaching out from the other direction also. Pacifists today are not recoiling from power and violence with distaste, as a teetotaller recoils from liquor, but are learning their structure.

It seems likely that this mingling of concerns and values must continue if thermonuclear war is to be avoided – these are now merely a few personal impressions. The situation requires the strategist's dedication to reason, the politician's acceptance of the world as it is, the moralist's crying awareness of the world as it ought to be, even the military man's sense of interests to be defended.

There are attitudes found among people who deal with nuclear weapons that militate against this reaching out, that bar the door to imagination and hold reins on reason. One, for instance, is a curious attitude to what is and is not 'realistic'. Discussion in terms of power politics, blocs, and diplomatic or strategic gains and losses is regarded as realistic; while talk about burning flesh and the screams of a mutilated child are often dismissed as emotional, sentimental and unrealistic. As it happens, such talk very often is sentimental. Every political choice is a choice between evils, and this kind of talk often dwells on the evil involved in one alternative only, disregarding

* Quoted in *Strategy and Conscience* by Anatol Rapaport.

the others. But it is *not* unrealistic. It concerns the most substantial realities of all. Power conflicts, diplomatic gains, blocs, nations even, are abstractions, meaningful abstractions it is true, but meaningful only in so far as they refer back to the hard matter of individual human beings' flesh and feelings. In the end, the well-being or suffering of individuals, their relations with one another, whether children are healthy, sick or dying in agony, is what power politics is about. These are the *realities* of the situation.

Another attitude is seen in the language of nuclear conflict, which enables people to talk about it without thinking about it. This has two different forms. In one, the language is desensitized. The terminology is technical, neutral and abstract: the weapon, megatons, countervalue. In the other form, the language is invested with totally inappropriate connotations which suggest a virile, personal combat that is the very opposite of nuclear war, in which the perpetrator of a blow is a technician and the victim a bystander and his family: the 'nuclear Sunday punch' (U.S. Navy) and the 'devastating blow at the aggressor' (Soviet Government). There is a point at which a metaphor becomes a lie.

Thermonuclear war may be a horror without parallel, but it is still a kind of war, and a product of the same political processes as other wars. It is being widely appreciated today that war is not simply a natural manifestation of the violence inherent in human beings, but a sophisticated and highly organized social phenomenon. (When a missionary to the Canadian Eskimos in 1916 was trying to explain the war in Europe, an Eskimo said in surprise 'You mean you kill people you don't even know?') As such, war could conceivably be abolished, as other long-lived and once-ubiquitous social institutions have been abolished, without waiting for some Millennium when violence will have vanished from the hearts of men.

As thermonuclear war is a kind of war, anything that reduces international tensions reduces the chances of its occurring, anything that heightens it increases the chances. The H-bomb may be much more than a weapon, it may create rules for its employment that do not apply to other weapons, but it is still a weapon, and in time of danger a government reaches for one by instinct. If there is more danger to nations in the world, more nations will want nuclear weapons. North Vietnamese probably believe that if they had nuclear weapons, they would be treated with more respect, and the United States would not have rained down bombs upon their country; other small countries probably feel the same way.

Arms control and disarmament are not themselves enough, but they are probably necessary steps towards the long-term prevention of thermonuclear war. At some point, the superpowers will probably have to agree to reduce their forces to a minimum-deterrence level, which is what some people in the arms control field want to see right now. This would mean that nuclear weapons could only be used for defence, and it would make it very unlikely that a clash of arms in peripheral areas would escalate to nuclear war. This reduction in force levels would involve risks for some countries' strategic and foreign policies, for a government could no longer seriously protect its allies with a nuclear deterrent. This in turn might mean pressures on some countries to acquire their own nuclear weapons for their defence, perhaps West Germany, perhaps Japan. On the other hand, such an arms control agreement would have to come in a *détente* atmosphere, so that these pressures might not be as urgent as in a period of intense Cold War. Some strategists have said that a minimum deterrent would be dangerous because it would leave only enough nuclear weapons to destroy populations, and not enough to fight any more limited, controlled nuclear war. It is hard to see that the world situation would be any more dangerous because of this; it would mean only that those high rungs of the escalation ladder that cover limited nuclear war would be replaced by non-nuclear conflict; the central war rungs would be just as high as they are now.

Ultimately, the prevention of thermonuclear war will probably require some new international system, to replace the present one of competing sovereign nation-states. As the object of its creation would be to avoid massacre rather than to express the brotherhood of man, its form may well disappoint some of the aspirations of those who look forward today to world unity. Some people's rights and independence might be trampled on, some ugly *status quos* accepted, in the formation of a war-negating system that is acceptable and that works. The prevention of nuclear war is the avoidance of the worst, not the attainment of the best.

A change in the international system will require that people first reduce their commitment to the separate parts of the present one, that there be some change in loyalties, albeit, perhaps, subtle, undramatic and limited. The motive force for a change of this dimension cannot come only from an extension of intelligence and analysis, though these are certainly necessary. It would seem to require also some change in moral outlook, some shift in values; some greater sense of charity towards all people who are caught in this new and sharper version of the dilemma of means and ends that is a part of the human condition; some greater consciousness of the violence of nuclear explosives and its effects upon people's bodies and minds; and some reduction in the many impediments to the sense that we are all a part of one another.

A Note on Source Material

As I said in the introduction, I cannot usefully name all the many people who contributed with their time and knowledge to the material for this book, and to whom I have reason to be grateful. However, among the scientists, Professors Otto Frisch and Josef Rotblat and Dr Ralph Lapp all read over sections of the book for accuracy, and provided helpful comments. None of these is responsible in any way for the quality of the passages dealing with science.

Among the people about whom I have written here at length, Mrs O'Connell and her family put up with a great deal of intensive questioning over what turned out to be a period of years, without making in return any stipulations about what I did with the answers. So did Herman Kahn, who also invited me to a seminar at the Hudson Institute, which, apart from its specific relevance to the subject matter of this book, was a very stimulating experience.

Published material on the subjects of this book has supplemented my own researches.

Two specialized periodicals that have been particularly valuable are the *Bulletin of the Atomic Scientists*, and *Survival*, published by the Institute for Strategic Studies.

The most fruitful single source of published material on the events recounted in the first two chapters is the transcript of the hearings on the suspension of Dr Oppenheimer's security clearance, published by the A.E.C. under the title *In the Matter of J. Robert Oppenheimer*. Other books on which I drew occasionally are Volume 2 of David E. Lilienthal's diaries, *The Atomic Energy Years*; *Men and Decisions*, Lewis Strauss's memoirs; and the memoirs of Harry S. Truman.

I refurbished my sparse picture of the world of atomic physics, acquired years ago during a brief period of adolescent fascination with the subject, with the help of several books written for laymen. I found particularly useful *Explaining the Atom* by Eugene Rabinowitch and Selig Hecht, and, on atomic weapons, *Survival*, a collection of articles edited by John Fowler. The hearings of the Joint Senate-House Atomic Energy Committee's Radiation Subcommittee also provided some interesting material on weapons and their effects. *The Voyage of the Lucky Dragon* by Ralph Lapp is the most complete account there is of the fate suffered by the Japanese fishermen at Bikini.

Brighter Than a Thousand Suns by Robert Jungk is the fullest book that I know on the roles played by the leading atomic scientists up to the middle 1950s, though in a few instances the author's findings or interpretations do not accord with my own. *American Scientists and Nuclear Weapons Policy* by Robert Gilpin is a scholarly account of their roles on some specific issues. A number of other books tell parts of the story from one or another partisan viewpoints.

All the material on Soviet weapons and policy comes from published Soviet material or else from Western sources, public and private. The quotations from Soviet publications that illustrate the arguments over the significance of nuclear weapons are taken from two books by American authors, *Soviet Strategy in the Nuclear Age* by Raymond Garthoff and *Soviet Strategy at the Crossroads* by Thomas W. Wolfe, and also from some papers printed privately by the Rand Corporation.

There is a sizeable literature on nuclear strategy. Many of the new ideas were published, if at all, as articles in specialized journals. The most pertinent books to the general field are mostly cited in the text, Herman Kahn's books, and two by Thomas Schelling, *Strategy and Conflict* and the more recent *Arms and Influence*. A few others are: *Strategy in the Missile Age* by Bernard Brodie and *Limited War* by Robert Osgood, both still interesting, though concerned with the arguments of the massive retaliation era; *The Great Debate* by

Robert Aron, an excellent account of the major debates of the early 1960s, particularly as they affected Europe. *The Troubled Partnership* by Henry Kissinger also contains an interesting N A T O-orientated view of the strategic debate. *The McNamara Strategy* by William Kaufmann is a useful, though early account of the changes in strategy in the early 1960s by one of the men who participated in making them. *The Economics of Defense in the Nuclear Age* by Roland McKean and Charles Hitch is surprisingly readable, and shows the influence of the economist's mentality in the formulation of strategic problems.

The only book I know devoted specifically to the British bomb is *British Defence Policy and Nuclear War*, by Emanuel J. de Kadt of the London School of Economics, a didactic work which contains useful references and ideas. H. A. de Weerd of the Rand Corporation has written several interesting papers on the subject. For a while, the Campaign for Nuclear Disarmament published a very sophisticated and informative newsletter called *The Month*. Christopher Driver's book *The Disarmers* is a perceptive history of the C.N.D.

The material on the Chinese bomb comes from official Chinese statements and from Western sources, public and private. On the general subject of the acquisition of nuclear weapons by countries other than the two super-powers, *The Spread of Nuclear Weapons* by Leonard Beaton and John Maddox is a valuable work.

Index

Index

Index

Index

Index